CONSCIENCE
AND CALLING

CONSCIENCE AND CALLING

Ethical reflections on Catholic
women's church vocations

BY
ANNE E. PATRICK

B L O O M S B U R Y

LONDON · NEW DELHI · NEW YORK · SYDNEY

Bloomsbury T&T Clark
An imprint of Bloomsbury Publishing Plc

50 Bedford Square	175 Fifth Avenue
London	New York
WC1B 3DP	NY 10010
UK	USA

www.bloomsbury.com

First published 2013

British Library Cataloguing-in-Publication Data
A catalogue record for this book is available from the British Library.

ISBN: PB: 978-1-441-14452-2
ePub: 978-1-441-17594-6
ePDF: 978-1-441-10059-7

Library of Congress Cataloging-in-Publication Data
Patrick, Anne E.
Conscience and Calling/Anne E. Patrick p.cm
Includes bibliographic references and index.
978-1-441-14452-2 (pbk.)
2012045678

Typeset by Deanta Global Publishing Services, Chennai, India
Printed and bound in Great Britain

To my sisters and brothers-in-law

Helen P. and Jerry Varner

Maureen Patrick and Robert Selig

Peggy P. (1947–1984) and Gene Miles

Susan P. and Nick Inzeo

Mary Patrick and John Garate

And to Mary Petr Miles

And all their cherished children and grandchildren

CONTENTS

ACRONYMS

CARA   Center for Applied Research in the Apostolate.

CCUM   Catholic Committee on Urban Ministry.

CFFC   Catholics for a Free Choice.

CDF   Congregation for the Doctrine of the Faith (Vatican).

CICLSAL   Congregation for Institutes of Consecrated Life and Societies of Apostolic Life (Vatican).

CRIS   Congregation for Religious and Secular Institutes (Vatican).

CTSA   Catholic Theological Society of America.

CMSW   Conference of Major Superiors of Women (after 1971, LCWR).

CMSWR   Council of Major Superiors of Women Religious.

IPJC   Intercommunity Peace and Justice Center.

LCWR   Leadership Conference of Women Religious (before 1971, CMSW).

NAWR   National Assembly of Women Religious (after 1982, NARW).

NARW   National Assembly of Religious Women (before 1982, NAWR).

NBSC   National Black Sisters' Conference.

NCAN   National Coalition of American Nuns.

NCCB   National Conference of Catholic Bishops (after 2001, USCCB).

RCWP   Roman Catholic Womenpriests.

USCCB   United States Conference of Catholic Bishops (before 2001, NCCB).

WFF   Women for Faith and Family.

WOC   Women's Ordination Conference.

WOW   Women's Ordination Worldwide.

PREFACE

Vocation is a powerful religious symbol that warrants new analysis in every era of Christian history. I believe it should be examined today from many perspectives, and I find myself especially prepared to do so from the vantage of Catholic women, and particularly of women who have been influenced by feminism to pose new questions about their relationship to the church. Are twenty-first century Catholic women called, like St Catherine of Siena, to seek reforms in the church? Are some of them called to the Sacrament of Orders, whether diaconal, priestly, or episcopal? Are calls to the Sacrament of Orders compatible with calls to marriage and parenting? How can women designated as "lay ecclesial ministers" obtain just working conditions for themselves in a system based on clerical authority? How should religious communities of women celebrate the mysteries of the faith? Such questions have gained new urgency today as Catholic women face decisions about whether to belong to a church community, and if so which one, in a social context very different from that of their great-grandmothers.

To help focus a potentially wide-ranging discussion, I will concentrate on Catholic women's church vocations, especially those involving permanent and publicly recognized life-commitments. Some of these chapters deal with the experiences of Catholic women religious, and others with Catholic women more generally. What unifies the work is an interest in Catholic women's moral agency and in their vocations to church ministry. Although I am aware that there have sometimes been tensions between those we call "sisters" and "laywomen," both groups share the status of "lay" as opposed to "clergy" in official Roman Catholicism, and both are canonically excluded from sacred orders, sacramental leadership, and decision-making power in the church. For simplicity's sake I will usually retain the ordinary distinction between "sisters" and "laywomen" in this work, although in some contexts I may speak of "sisters and other laywomen."

Besides this fact of sharing the status of "lay" in an important canonical sense, Catholic women of various vocational commitments have come together in new ways since the Second Vatican Council. Many former sisters have rejoined the ranks of the laity, many laywomen hold positions comparable to those dominated by sisters in the past, many laywomen now work as supervisors or colleagues of sisters in different ministerial contexts, and many laywomen have affiliated with religious congregations as associates or oblates. Although there remain important theological and canonical distinctions between women consecrated to God by vows in religious communities and other Catholic women (whose commitments may or may not include marriage, membership in secular institutes, or private vows of consecration), all Catholic women share the same baptism and the same call to holiness of life. This common gift of grace involves a summons to proclaim the Good News of God's saving love and to advance the Reign of God in history. In the past, Catholic women who have felt this summons with a special urgency have found ways to organize themselves that sometimes lasted beyond their lifetimes. Their creativity has led to convents and women's monasticism, to active religious congregations dedicated to missionary and charitable works, to foundations of hospitals and colleges, and to lay movements such as the Beguines in Europe, the Grail in Europe and North America, and many others.

I believe that the self-chosen narrowing of options that comes with acceptance of a calling or mission provides a context for conscience that can promote the development of particular strengths of character. I also think that shared vocations can foster long-term collaborative efforts resulting in significant work, and this sometimes changes the course of history. One example involves the Mayo Clinic, which originated from the "call" that a nun extended to a country doctor. After a tornado had devastated the frontier town of Rochester, Minnesota in 1883, Mother Alfred Moes, OSF, persuaded Dr William W. Mayo to staff a hospital if she would build it. With the support of her religious community she delivered on this promise, and raised enough funds to open St Mary's Hospital in 1889. A more recent example is the founding of the Tutwiler Clinic in an economically depressed Mississippi Delta town in 1983 by four Sisters of the Holy Names of Jesus and Mary. Vocation, virtue, and history were connected from the first, when Medical Director Sister Anne E. Brooks, D.O., made the decision that only *one* of the two waiting rooms in the empty clinic building that she would bring back into service should be used. Black and white patients would wait together to see Dr Brooks, a small but revolutionary change for Tallahatchie County as recently as 1983. A question that intrigues me now is how to nurture a new generation of Catholics who will go to other places of unmet needs in the future, carrying on the tradition of founding new gospel-inspired institutions that will serve as effective frameworks for labor suffused with love.

What new organizations, strategies, and movements are needed today? It will fall to the creative moral agency of contemporary women to answer this question. The chapters that follow are intended to contribute to their discernment process by providing historical examples and theological and ethical insights designed to inform the thinking of Catholics who seek to fulfill their unique vocations and make a positive difference in this world. I believe we do well to recognize our responsibility for maintaining and developing the ideological and institutional frameworks that will prove intelligible, inspiring, and supportive to women of tomorrow who will experience the grace of vocation in new circumstances. These conditions will be as ambiguous as they ever were, with the salvation of the world— our world of AIDS and addiction, of violence and hunger, of climate change and environmental degradation, of beauty and kindness— at stake.

The perspective I take on the question of Catholic women's church vocations is that of a feminist, by which I mean someone who believes in the equal dignity and worth of women and men, and who seeks to reform structures and thought systems so that this equality is fully respected. My perspective is of course limited by circumstances of race, class, age, experience, and other factors. Whether or not my feminism deserves the adjective "radical" I will leave to the reader's judgment.

* * * * *

As this book was nearing publication Pope Benedict XVI surprised the world by announcing his retirement from the Petrine office, effective 28 February 2013. The College of Cardinals also made history by electing the church's first pope from the southern hemisphere. On 13 March Cardinal Jorge Bergoglio of Buenos Aires assumed the papal ministry and took the name "Pope Francis," thereby showing his desire to emulate the saint who had been called by God to "repair my church." One hopes now that the reforms he seeks to achieve and the evangelical Catholicism he is inclined to promote will mean truly good news for women, especially those who are poor and marginalized.

This book has been written with much support and assistance from others. I am especially grateful to my extended family and to my religious community, the Sisters of the Holy Names of Jesus and Mary, for supporting me in so many ways over the years. All those friends and family members who helped me make the move from Minnesota to my native Washington, DC area, in 2009 (and deal with the endless packing, unpacking, and settling in) have earned very special and enduring gratitude. Carleton College has provided faculty development grants and generous leaves and course reductions, along with intellectual stimulation and regular encouragement from colleagues. When I needed to begin cancer treatment in 2002, colleagues Richard Crouter, Louis Newman, and Roger Jackson cheerfully took on some of my departmental chairing duties, and the late Dean Shelby Boardman authorized a light teaching load for the year. When medical advice in 2008 indicated that I needed to decide whether to continue teaching or make the move back east to write and retire near my community and family, then Dean H. Scott Bierman and President Rob Oden authorized a medical leave prior to my official retirement in 2009. This made a difficult transition much easier, and allowed me to continue working on these chapters while transferring my "medical career" to the Washington, DC area. In both locations I have had access to excellent libraries, and I thank the librarians of Carleton College and Woodstock Theological Center at Georgetown University for their assistance.

Over these ten years of continual treatment for cancer I have been abundantly grateful to nurses, doctors, lab and medical technology specialists, physical therapists, pharmacists, and others too numerous to mention, for the excellent care I have received. As I write these words I remember specific persons whose impact for good is incalculable. Illness continues to teach me many things, especially gratitude, and it has deepened my conviction that all persons should have the sort of access to quality health care that I have known.

Especially in a book on this topic I want to thank the communities of women religious who helped support and inspire me during my thirty years of living at a distance from my own congregation, for the sake of my teaching ministry. These include the School Sisters of Notre Dame, who welcomed me for years of Minnesota snowstorms to their convent in St Dominic's parish in Northfield; the Sisters of St Joseph of Carondelet, who were likewise welcoming in St Paul; the Sisters of Charity of Halifax in Queens, New York; and the Sisters of St Benedict's Monastery in St Joseph, Minnesota. I especially benefited from belonging to a small group of sister-writers that Dolores Super, OSB, helped initiate in 1995, when she was director of the monastery's Studium. The late Nancy Hynes, OSB, read early versions of some of these chapters and provided wise suggestions, and Mara Faulkner, OSB, has read everything and offered most helpful advice down to the present.

I am also most grateful to Susan A. Ross and Susan Van Baalen, OP, for reading the entire manuscript with care and offering many insightful suggestions. I thank as well the other friends and colleagues who have read portions of the book at various times, especially the late Anne E. Carr, BVM, Joan Cook, SC, Mary Jeremy Daigler, RSM, Karen Kennelly, CSJ, Mary Aquin O'Neill, RSM, Anita M. Pampusch, Patricia A. Parachini, SNJM, Sandra M. Schneiders, IHM, and Carol A. Tauer. The encouragement of other friends and relatives has been immensely helpful as I worked on this project, and I am particularly grateful to Avis Allmaras, CSJ, Anne E. Brooks, SNJM, Kate Casper, OSB, Heather Dubrow, Jacqueline Farrell, OSF, Clare and Mike Foley, Mary Haskins, SNJM, Mary Ellen Holohan, SNJM, Patrick J. Lynch, SJ, Francis Rothluebber, Janet Walton, SNJM, and Lorean Whiteman, SNJM. When I first designed this project I worked with editor Frank Oveis, then Publishing Director of Continuum International, and since his retirement he has generously offered advice on occasion. Frank was the very model of a perfect theological editor when he helped me publish *Liberating Conscience* in 1996, and I remain most grateful for all he has done. Since Continuum was acquired by Bloomsburry, I have enjoyed working with a number of publishing advisors and editors, and I am especially grateful for the assistance of Anna Turton, Ken Bruce, Subitha Nair, and Kara Zavada.

Some of the chapters were first developed for special occasions, and ideas for portions of the book were occasioned by invitations to lecture at different places. I am grateful to all those who invited me to reflect and share on various topics concerning women and Catholicism, and I thank here the publishers Sheed & Ward (now an imprint of the Rowman & Littlefield Publishing Group), Indiana University Press, and University of Notre Dame Press for permission to develop and revise earlier versions of some chapters.

CONSCIENCE AND CALLING: ETHICAL REFLECTIONS ON CATHOLIC WOMEN'S CHURCH VOCATIONS— INTRODUCTION

The Easter Alleluias were still sounding on 18 April 2012, when the Vatican's Congregation for the Doctrine of the Faith (CDF) made public its displeasure with an important group of U.S. sisters, the Leadership Conference of Women Religious (LCWR). Tensions had been simmering for decades between Rome and this organization of some 1500 elected leaders of communities comprising 80 percent of the 54,000 sisters in this country, but the official reprimand stunned the group's officers and much of the American public. The CDF's "doctrinal assessment" judged LCWR as deficient in both doctrine and practice, and said that its operations should be reformed within five years, under the supervision of Archbishop Peter Sartain of Seattle. This action was based on reports provided by Bishop Leonard Blair of Toledo, who had investigated LCWR during 2008–10. The assessment accused LCWR of fostering dissent on women's ordination and ministry to homosexuals, failing to speak out against abortion and euthanasia, and promoting "radical feminist" distortions of doctrine.[1]

This assessment of LCWR had coincided with a much larger investigation of nearly 400 noncloistered U.S. women's communities during 2009–11, by a committee appointed by Cardinal Franc Rodé, head of the Vatican's Congregation for Institutes of Consecrated Life and Societies of Apostolic Life (CICLSAL). Canonically known as an "apostolic visitation," the investigation was unprecedented in size and scope. The process involved communication with major superiors, an extensive questionnaire, and on-site visits to a representative sample of communities. Its stated purpose was to "look into the quality of life of apostolic Congregations of women religious" in this country, although the very launching of such a visitation presumes that the findings will turn up problems.[2] Mother Mary Clare Millea, Superior General of the Apostles of the Sacred Heart of Jesus, was the official Apostolic Visitor, and she announced on 9 January 2011 that she had completed the investigation and submitted an overall, confidential report to Rome, noting that "[a]lthough there are concerns in religious life that warrant support and attention, the enduring reality is one of fidelity, joy, and hope." She also stated that all reports for individual communities would be completed by spring 2011.[3] The fact that these communities had heard nothing about what the investigators thought of their quality of life made the Vatican's public announcement against LCWR in April 2012 all the more stunning. LCWR officers immediately expressed surprise, and waited until their board could meet to discuss the matter before issuing a preliminary response.

Meanwhile, the CDF action was widely noted in the media, and this led many U.S. Catholics to rally in defense of the sisters. The lay-edited magazine *Commonweal* declared on 1 May 2012 that the Vatican's action amounted to placing LCWR under "receivership" and was "certain to be a pastoral disaster." Noting that the CDF provided no evidence for its claim that LCWR was "unduly influenced by 'radical' feminism," the editors observed that the group is diverse, and might be described as having "faced the same challenge as the bishops and met it better—namely, maintaining community and solidarity, dialogue and conversation, and encouraging innovation, creativity, and risk-taking in service to the gospel."[4] On 1 June, LCWR released its preliminary response, stating that "the assessment was based on unsubstantiated accusations and the result of a flawed process that lacked transparency," and the sanctions were "disproportionate to the concerns raised" and put the organization's mission at some risk.[5] The group's officers also expressed their concerns to Cardinal William Levada, then Prefect of the CDF, and Archbishop Sartain, and said that a full response would be given after LCWR members had discussed the matter in regional meetings and at the national assembly in St Louis, 7–10 August . After much prayer and discussion, LCWR announced on 10 August that their officers would meet with Archbishop Sartain in the expectation that "open and honest dialogue may lead not only to increasing understanding between the church leadership and women religious, but also to creating more possibilities for the laity and, particularly for women, to have a voice in the church." Their investment in this process would continue "as long as possible," but would be reconsidered "if LCWR is forced to compromise the integrity of its mission."[6]

Archbishop Sartain had been more sanguine about the possible results of the assessment than were *Commonweal*'s editors. On 18 June 2012 he contributed an article for the online edition of the Jesuit magazine *America* that praised the historic contributions of sisters, noted that conflicts between religious communities and bishops are not new, summarized the CDF's concerns, and voiced the hope that the post-assessment process will deepen communion and collaboration. "No one expects that such a sensitive task will be accomplished quickly or effortlessly," he declared, "but by God's grace and with mutual respect, patience and prayer it can indeed be accomplished for the good of all."[7] In that same online issue of *America* Fordham University ethicist Christine Firer Hinze responded to Sartain's article, and noted that if there is to be a good outcome it will be necessary to recognize that there are presently "two distinct visions for radical discipleship" among U.S. sisters today, one represented by LCWR and another by a smaller group of leaders of women's communities, the Council of Major Superiors of Women Religious (CMSWR). She also indicated that if communion between the Vatican and LCWR is to be enhanced, "what John Paul II calls 'the dialogue that leads to repentance' must work in both directions." Such an atmosphere of mutual openness to change is essential for dealing with matters about which there presently seems to be an impasse, including "gender and power in church and society," "authority and freedom in the church," and the role of religious communities in discerning "their charism and missional priorities."[8]

Until 1971 there was only one organization of leaders of women's communities in the United States, the Conference of Major Superiors of Women (CMSW), which had been established in 1956 at a meeting initiated by the Vatican's Congregation for Religious. After the Second Vatican Council (1962–65), these leaders and their communities energetically undertook the renewal that had been mandated by the council's "Decree on the Appropriate Renewal of the Religious Life" (*Perfectae Caritatis*). Congregations varied widely in the extent and speed of changes made to implement the renewal, and in the theological understandings they brought to this work. Inevitably, differences and tensions emerged as they interpreted the mandate to "return to the sources of all Christian life and to the original inspiration behind a given community" and make "an adjustment of the community to the changed conditions of the times," both in its "manner of living, praying, and working," and in its constitutions and mode of governance.[9] Several years after the council most major superiors were ready to express the insights gained from the renewal process by making changes to their leadership organization, but a number of them objected to this and formed a separate group.

As journalist Monica Clark has noted, "When the conference [CMSW] met in 1971 to adopt new bylaws and change its name to Leadership Conference of Women Religious, a division emerged. A small group, calling itself Consortium Perfectae Caritatis, expressed concern that LCWR was deviating from what it believed was authentic church teaching." By 1992 this "splinter group" became the Conference of Major Superiors of Women Religious (CMSWR), and in 1995 it was officially recognized by the Vatican.[10] Since then the United States has been in the unique situation of having two canonically recognized organizations for the officers of women's religious communities: LCWR, representing about 400 congregations, and CMSWR, with 108 congregations. Officers of a few communities belong to both groups.

As Hinze stresses, although their visions for "radical discipleship" differ, both types of sisters have much in common:

[B]oth LCWR and CMSWR communities serve the gospel at contemporary frontiers, living lives of passionate love in and from the heart of the church. Both articulate and practice the basic elements of consecrated life (vows of poverty, chastity and obedience; life in community; and mission) in light of prayerful discernment of the needs of the church and signs of the times.[11]

Differences between the organizations are evident in their websites, which fifty years after the opening of Vatican II suggest that LCWR communities have been especially influenced by the "Pastoral Constitution on the Church in the Modern World" (*Gaudium et Spes*), with its emphasis on mission to eradicate injustice, while CMSWR communities have undertaken their renewal with greater concern for preserving certain monastic aspects of religious life and following an agenda set by the hierarchy.[12]

Hinze notes that the CMSWR communities tend to understand gender, sexual difference, and men and women's vocations in a way that is much closer to Pope John Paul II's emphasis on gender complementarity than do LCWR communities.[13] She and others observe that different theological emphases and interpretations of the council have contributed to these very distinctive understandings of what active religious life can and should mean for women. In all likelihood, both approaches are valid, and each has something to contribute to the church and the world. From my perspective as a vowed member of an LCWR community who still appreciates many aspects of "monastic" religious life, it is more useful to ask who gains from efforts to imply that one group is right and the other is wrong than it is to debate the merits of one approach over the other.

It is also worth noting that Catholicism has long afforded males more options for public religious life and service than it has for females.[14] Whereas in the past a devout man might have felt called to serve as a diocesan priest, or as a priest or brother in a religious congregation, for public dedication a woman has had only the option of religious sisterhood, whether cloistered or active. Diocesan priests promise celibacy and pledge to obey their bishop, but retain ownership of property and have the freedom to own cars and vacation houses, and considerable discretion over how to spend their time and money. Religious communities of men usually profess vows of poverty, as well as chastity and obedience. While some male congregations are more monastic than others, their life is governed by a rule that reflects the spiritual wisdom of the founder, often a well-known male saint, such as Augustine, Benedict, Francis of Assisi, Dominic, or Ignatius of Loyola.

For similarly devout women in the past, nothing like the diocesan priesthood has been available, and the religious vocation has generally meant some variation on the monastic option, whether cloistered or active. In the latter case, this often has involved congregations founded in modern times for specific apostolic works. Rules of some women's congregations were based on those of their male counterparts (Benedictine, Franciscan, Vincentian, etc.), but no rules to my knowledge were the work of female saints, and all were affected by the Vatican's increasing supervision of active women religious since 1900. As historian Mary Ewens has noted, this began with the papal bull *Conditae a Christo* in 1900 and its follow-up *Normae* in 1901, which both recognized and regulated the active congregations of sisters in simple vows (as distinct from the solemn vows of cloistered nuns). The *Normae* imposed some limits on apostolic activities, for example forbidding "the care of babies, the nursing of maternity cases, the management of clerical seminaries, and the staffing of co-educational schools," though these Jansenistic strictures were not always observed.[15]

The 1917 Code of Canon Law increased papal authority over all religious and greatly influenced the rules of active women's communities, which were revised to reflect its provisions. Vatican II's invitation to renewal in *Perfectae Caritatis* (1965) led to new rules and constitutions, all of which have needed approval from Rome. Dramatic advances in transportation and communications technology in these last fifty years have increased cooperation among women's communities and also facilitated Rome's awareness of developments among U.S. women religious. This has led to increasing efforts to control those the Vatican does not approve, culminating in the apostolic visitation of U.S. communities and the doctrinal assessment of LCWR mentioned above.

One topic that is often raised when today's sisters are discussed is the religious habit, or distinctive garb that made all sisters so easily identifiable in the past. Today, most U.S. sisters have chosen to wear secular clothes, although some retain a traditional long habit and others wear a simple dress or suit with a short veil. In the decades that I have observed sisters discussing these questions and moving through various stages of "modernization" and "secularization" of dress, I am aware that rarely does anyone remark that again, the options here have been very different for men and for women. Long before Vatican II, men in religious communities had several options for dress: the traditional habit, worn over pants and shirt, the clerical suit, sports clothes for golf or gardening, and most importantly, liturgical vestments for service at the altar. After the council their options increased, insofar as many male religious have chosen secular dress for professional work, while retaining clerical suits and religious habits for various occasions. By contrast, sisters have been much more limited in their options for dress.

Before Vatican II, sisters wore traditional long habits, headdresses, and veils for virtually all occasions and activities. Special dresses of lightweight fabric might have been available for cleaning or vacation, but even then heads were covered and veiled and the goal was to retain the appearance of distinctive religious garb. Often standard robes, gowns, and caps were required for nightwear in the convent. Generations of sisters were content with this situation because dress was a minor aspect of their lives of dedication to God's service. "The habit does not make the monk" was a saying they knew well. When Vatican II invited all communities to adapt to modern times in light of reflection on the unique spiritual gifts (charisms) of their founders, and sisters discovered that their "holy habits" were based on the simple garb of ordinary women from centuries when long dresses and head coverings were the cultural norm, it was not long before many began to experiment with garb more typical of modern society, for the sake of enhancing their ministries.

Many communities progressed from "modified habits" (sometimes sewn from the fabric of their long dresses) to secular dress, worn with or without a veil, and perhaps with a distinctive cross or pin signifying community membership. In some cases, the ring received at profession of vows is the only vestige of traditional religious symbolism worn by sisters today. On balance these developments may have been good, but it is worth noting that although there are now many options for *secular* clothing for members of these progressive women's communities, their options for recognizably *religious* clothing have been reduced. Such has not been the case for men in religious congregations. Among the reasons for the discrepancy is of course the fact that women are excluded from the roles of liturgical leadership and church governance.

More conservative communities have retained distinctive religious dress through their renewal process, though often in modified ways and with some flexibility in application. Their appreciation for symbolic dress tends to be accompanied by an acceptance of the ideas on gender and women emphasized in the writings of Pope John Paul II, which are also reflected in certain words of Pope Benedict XVI and the CDF. In his 1995 letter to women, Pope John Paul II emphasized the "'iconic' complementarity of male and female roles."[16] Assuming that gender is naturally correlated with sex, and not socially constructed, recent papal teaching asserts that women's rights should be respected, but certain roles, especially the priesthood, are incompatible with feminine nature. As theologian Ivy A. Helman remarks in *Women and the Vatican*, John Paul II advocated a form of feminism that emphasizes special "feminine" characteristics:

> Women are naturally nurturers, caregivers, concerned with relationships, and faithful, honest, and loving. A feminism that makes the most of these feminine ideals will make the world a better place, a more humane one tuned to a culture of life rather than death.[17]

To disagree with this understanding of women's nature may seem "radical" to those who espouse it, but nevertheless it is possible to retain a strong appreciation for human embodiment, sacramental symbolism, motherhood, marriage, and the value of life without holding that women are essentially destined for some ecclesiastical roles and men for others, and most observers would characterize the feminist leanings of progressive nuns as "liberal" rather than "radical." Much the same can be said of the many laywomen who question the gender-stereotyping of recent Vatican literature on philosophical and moral grounds.

In the chapters of this book, I shall deal more fully with some of the topics touched upon here, but for now I would simply highlight the fact that where church vocations are concerned, options for men have historically been more diverse than they have been for women. Whether that situation should continue is something I question, for in our times it seems better for the church to have the talents of women available for all ministries. However, the powers of religious definition and legislation are still exclusively in the hands of ordained men, as becomes clear whenever there is an important gathering of Catholic leaders, such as an ecumenical council, a synod of bishops, or a papal transition.

Pink smoke and Roman Catholic womenpriests

The death of Pope John Paul II and the election of Cardinal Joseph Ratzinger as his successor dominated the media for much of April 2005. The pageantry of ancient ceremonies in splendid buildings captured the attention of millions, and during this respite from news of war in Iraq much of the world seemed caught up in the power and beauty of Catholicism. Whether or not many television viewers noticed it, however, the Vatican ceremonies were a vivid reminder of how far women had *not* come in the Roman Catholic Church.

Although women reporters interpreted events on television, all the voices heard praying, singing, and preaching during the papal transition were male. The broadcasts from Vatican City celebrated the vocations and authority of men. They conveyed the message that women are called to follow rather than lead, listen rather than preach. One man's calling was central to the pageantry, the vocation to the ministry of Peter, and this calling would be discerned through the heavily ritualized process of election by the 115 cardinals eligible to vote, most of whom had been appointed by the recently deceased Pope John Paul II. The new pope's vocation would then be affirmed by his formal acceptance of office and announcement of his name. Eventually white smoke would appear over the Vatican, the bells would toll, and the words "*habemus Papam*" would resound over the airwaves, as indeed happened on 19 April 2005 when Cardinal Joseph Ratzinger was elected on the fourth ballot and chose to be called Pope Benedict XVI.

During the papal transition neither the secular media nor the traditionalist Catholic Eternal Word Television Network (EWTN) did much to raise questions about whether any reforms of the Catholic system of church authority were warranted, though the mainstream and liberal Catholic press picked up some indications that not everyone in the pews was content with the celebration of male religious authority. The *National Catholic Reporter*, for example, carried a brief report from Catholic News Service in its 29 April 2005 issue concerning a group that had assembled on 18 April outside Chicago's Holy Name Cathedral to protest the absence of women from the conclave and call for the full inclusion of women in church leadership and sacramental life. Their prayers and statements were accompanied by billows of pink smoke. Some fifty men and women took part in the Chicago protest, which had been organized by Donna Quinn, OP, and the idea was emulated by pink smoke activists in Cleveland, Denver, Lexington (KY), and Washington, DC, resulting in local television coverage as well as some coverage on the Cable News Network.[18]

The seriousness of these small instances of public protest was reinforced two months later when nine Roman Catholic women were ordained priests or deacons in a noncanonical ceremony on the St Lawrence River near Ottawa on 22 June 2005. The first such ceremony of the Roman Catholic Womenpriests (RCWP) movement had taken place 29 June 2002 on the Danube River, when seven women were ordained by two bishops from a schismatic Catholic group, Romulo Braschi and Ferdinand Regelsberger. Although the "Danube 7" were soon formally excommunicated, the movement has continued to grow since then.[19] Three of the original seven womenpriests have subsequently been ordained bishops (Gisela Forster, Christine Mayr-Lumetzberger, and Ida Raming), and a fourth bishop, Patricia Fresen, was soon chosen to coordinate the Program of Preparation for Roman Catholic Womenpriests, which in 2005 involved some 120 candidates internationally. Fresen, a South African who had taught theology and homiletics at the national seminary in Pretoria for seven years, was ordained a priest in 2003 and later asked by an unnamed European bishop in good standing with Rome to consider episcopal ordination. Theologian Marjorie Reilly Maguire describes the 2005 ceremony that ensued thus:

Tears streamed down his face, as well as hers, when he laid hands on her head and said he was ordaining her in full apostolic succession. He gave her documents naming his predecessor bishops in apostolic succession back to the early centuries of the Church. The name Patricia Fresen is printed after his in this long ecclesiastical genealogy. Those documents are in a bank vault, only to be made public after the male bishop dies. To follow all the rules of canon law, the male bishop who ordained her was joined by two other legitimate male bishops.[20]

In the summer of 2006, Fresen, Forster, and Raming presided at the ordinations of several women priests and deacons on Lake Constance in Switzerland, and Fresen also traveled to North America to ordain women near Pittsburgh (twelve priests and four deacons) as well as one woman priest at an undisclosed Canadian location. The last ceremony, termed a "catacomb ordination" by movement leaders, was designed to celebrate the ministry of a woman whose livelihood would be threatened by public disclosure of her ordination. Fresen herself had been required to seek a dispensation from her vows after 45 years as a Dominican sister following her 2003 ordination to the priesthood.[21]

By 2012 RCWP had grown from a small symbolic movement into a fledgling organization, with more than 130 priests, bishops, deacons, and candidates for ordination internationally, three-fourths of them in the United States. In some locations Catholics now participate in weekly liturgies at which womenpriests preside, undaunted by the Vatican's description of the "attempted ordination of women" as a serious crime against the sacraments.[22]

Interpreting the standoff

How are Catholics to understand these developments in a church whose leader forbade even discussing the question of women's ordination as recently as 1994? Pope John Paul II declared in *Ordinatio Sacerdotalis* #13 "that the Church has no authority whatsoever to confer priestly ordination on women and that this judgment is to be definitively held by all the Church's faithful."[23] Then in 1995 he approved a document stating that this teaching "is to be understood as belonging to the deposit of the faith," and as having been "set forth infallibly by the ordinary and universal magisterium."[24] Infallibility, however, is a technical term with a more limited meaning than is popularly understood. Only the dogmas of the Immaculate Conception and the Assumption have been generally accepted as infallibly taught in the years since papal infallibility was explicitly affirmed by the First Vatican Council in 1870. Reputable Catholic scholars have for various reasons questioned the application of the term "infallible" to teachings about the ordination of women.

When a task force of eminent Catholic theologians studied these Vatican texts from 1994 and 1995, they concluded that "There are serious doubts regarding the nature of the authority of this teaching [namely, the teaching that the Church's lack of authority to ordain women to the priesthood is a truth that has been infallibly taught and requires the definitive assent of the faithful] and its grounds in Tradition." They argued their case in a report whose conclusion was affirmed by 216 of the 248 members voting at the 1997 convention of the Catholic Theological Society of America (CTSA).[25]

Arguably Pope John Paull II's efforts to stem debate by papal edict were not successful. Although most bishops have not publicly challenged his teaching on this matter, the cooperation of even one of them in the womenpriests movement and the occasional questions raised by others testify to the practical limits of papal authority in ways that have significance beyond the immediate question of women's ordination. In a 1994 article for *America,* interpreting the significance of *Ordinatio Sacerdotalis,* Michael H. Kenny, then bishop of Juneau, observed that this papal letter "is much more about authority than it is about ordination," and goes on to pose questions about its wisdom and effectiveness.[26] And in 2008 Bishop Geoffrey Robinson, a retired auxiliary bishop of Sydney, Australia, declared in *Confronting Power and Sex in the Catholic Church*:

> I have not been impressed by the arguments put forward to claim that women cannot be ordained to the priesthood, so whenever I mention bishops or priests in this book, I do not assume that they will be exclusively male forever, and I hope that the language I use reflects this.[27]

Catholics will tend to interpret these differences and tensions according to their basic philosophical stance toward the tradition, which Canadian theologian Bernard Lonergan (1904–84) has characterized broadly as either classicist or historically conscious.[28] While the former perspective emphasizes the stability of truth and tradition, the latter stresses the modern recognition that all formulations of truth are culturally conditioned and limited by the social and historical circumstances in which they were developed. Ethicist Richard Gula has drawn out the implications of these two approaches for moral theology, and noted that the classicist vantage emphasizes conformity to authority and established norms while the historically conscious perspective emphasizes "responsibility and actions fitting to changing times."[29] Thus from the classicist perspective, those who persist in raising the question of women's ordination are seen as disobedient and in need of stern discipline. From the historically conscious perspective, however, they may be viewed as contributing to a normal process whereby a religious system contends with developments in the surrounding culture, in this case democracy and feminism.

My belief is that both the RCWP movement participants and their supporters are operating from a historically conscious mindset. They have also taken to heart the postconciliar theme of coresponsibility for the systems, including the ecclesiastical systems, in which they participate. The womenpriests and their supporters have chosen to act in ways that call the Catholic tradition to reform its structures and modes of operating. Their actions are part of a much larger struggle on the part of many Catholics—bishops, clergy, religious, and laity—to realize the unfinished agenda of the Second Vatican Council. In particular they would like to see the dignity of women and laymen more meaningfully affirmed and the collegiality of bishops more effectively respected. In place of authoritarian edicts and punitive measures they hope to see a form of religious authority that inspires by the authenticity of its witness and convinces by the cogency of the reasons given for its positions.[30] The tears streaming down the faces of the unnamed bishop and Patricia Fresen during her 2005 episcopal ordination ceremony testify to the depth of feeling and religious conviction involved in their actions. They suggest that both agents felt God was calling them to transgress rules they considered unjust. Both have lived long enough to know that history sometimes turns on such deeds.

Fresen in particular brings knowledge from her experience as a white South African who struggled against apartheid, and with support from Archbishop Denis E. Hurley, OMI, of Durban, integrated the school of which she was principal years before such action was legal. She found it had been essential to violate the rules of apartheid in order for political reforms to become possible. She has since developed a theology of "prophetic obedience" to articulate how this experience in the secular arena is applicable to injustices she perceives in the church.[31]

I shall deal more fully with the RCWP movement in the final chapter of this volume, but for now I would note that, in addition to her experience of recent history and social change, Fresen, along with others in the movement, is aware of textual and archeological evidence for women's ministries in ancient Christianity. This evidence challenges assumptions that the current limitations on women's ecclesial roles have been firmly in place since the beginning. She is also well aware that the chief arguments against ordaining women in the medieval period, which supported the original canon against the practice, were based on clear teachings about the supposed ontological, intellectual, and moral inferiority of females. Such teachings have been explicitly rejected by modern popes. As the CTSA task force report from 1997 makes clear, the grounds for denying women the sacrament of orders have shifted dramatically in recent decades. There is no longer mention of women's lack of requisite dignity for the sacrament; instead there are historical and theological assertions by the magisterium that are not convincing to many Catholics.

The 1997 CTSA task force report deals explicitly with several claims it finds problematic, including one about the significance of Jesus' intentions in designating men as "the Twelve," another about the practice of the early churches, and a third about the "infallible" status of a teaching that has not been shown to have been held by all the bishops nor commonly adhered to by the faithful. On the first point, concerning the magisterial claim that Christ called only men as apostles and subsequently limited priestly roles to men, the report declares that "reputable Catholic biblical scholars" are not convinced that the words, "Do this in remembrance of me" (1 Cor. 11:24) were meant to refer to an ordination of the Twelve to priesthood or to limit the Church to decisions about ordaining only men in the future. Instead the report stresses that most exegetes regard the fact that Jesus chose men for the Twelve as having to do with "the nature of their symbolic role as 'patriarchs' of restored Israel," and not as a paradigm for the future of priestly ministry.

The report also notes that scholars question whether "'the apostles' were coextensive with 'the Twelve,'" and believe that there was considerable "fluidity of ministries" in the first years of Christianity.

Furthermore, a number of women were coworkers of St Paul, and although their ministries were curtailed later on, as texts such as 1 Timothy 2:12 demonstrate ("I do not permit a woman to act as a teacher, or in any way have authority over a man"), the reasons for imposing these limitations "had nothing to do with an example given by Jesus." Rather they depended on misogynist interpretations of the story of the Fall, and on general assumptions about the inferiority of women, which have been the basis for subsequent teachings against ordaining women until recent times.[32]

Finally, the report discusses some technical matters regarding infallibility, and points out that the criterion of Canon 749.3 of the Code of Canon Law ("No doctrine is understood to be infallibly defined unless this fact is clearly established") has not been satisfied by the teachings of *Ordinatio Sacerdotalis* (1994) or by the Sacred Congregation for the Doctrine of the Faith's 1995 "Response" concerning this document. Thus the CTSA report concludes: "In support of its assertion that the doctrine excluding women from the priesthood has been taught infallibly by the ordinary, universal magisterium, the Congregation did not, and indeed could not, appeal either to a consultation of all the bishops or to the common adherence of the Catholic faithful."[33]

Historical consciousness and change

Such knowledge about the complexity of the Christian past is what makes historical consciousness a potential force for change. When men and women of faith appreciate that things have not always been the way they are, and realize that choices by finite human beings like themselves have shaped the inherited teachings and practices, they ask themselves how God may be calling *them* to take a hand in shaping the future. The response of Catholics to the scandal about clergy sexual misconduct (and episcopal mismanagement of the problem) that came to wide attention in January 2002 is interesting in this regard. Within months of the *Boston Globe's* first reports of the scandal, a group of laity had organized the Voice of the Faithful, using the internet to mobilize tens of thousands of Catholics in an immediate effort to support survivors of abuse as well as priests of integrity, and in the long-range project of reforming church governance, with particular concern for pastoral and financial accountability. Moreover, conferences held at Boston College and Yale University in the wake of the scandal have resulted in books emphasizing what Catholics today should learn from events and changes during various stages of the tradition's history.[34]

In describing the Yale conference, Francis Oakley and Bruce Russett observe that there was considerable agreement among participants that the sex-abuse crisis was due to "long-established pathologies in the clerical culture, in our modern structures of ecclesiastical governance, and in the well-entrenched and almost instinctive mode of ecclesiological thinking prevalent among so many of our church leaders."[35] The clear implication is that Catholics must somehow reform the clerical culture and mode of church governance, which will require replacing the now dominant classicist ecclesiology with one informed by historical consciousness. Several of the speakers at Yale raised this point, including Donald Cozzens, a priest from Cleveland with expertise in psychology and experience as rector of a seminary. He declared:

> We are presented here with two very different understandings of church—one which is static, radically hierarchical, and ahistorical; the other, organic, communal, and respectful of history. The first fosters a culture of silence and denial. The second a culture of conversation, consultation, and collaboration. . . . We now understand that a static, ahistorical church structure overemphasizing the distinction between shepherds and flock does indeed do harm: it fosters a clerical culture that in turn fosters clericalism with its penchant for privilege, status, preferment, exemption, and secrecy.[36]

At the same conference historical theologian Francine Cardman criticized the common tendency to imagine the church as "an unchanging, divinely willed institution that has always looked the way it looks now." In her view, "ahistorical ecclesiologies" cover up the ways in which the church behaves like secular institutions, and fail to respect the historical fact that "from the beginning the 'church' was a dynamic, evolving, diverse movement—not a fully formed, monolithic institution."[37] As she observes, "Recognizing the mythic narrative of ecclesial origins for what it is allows us to engage the historical complexity and diversity of the Catholic Church. If its past is far more various than default ecclesiology imagines, its future may also be."[38]

For historically informed Catholics there is no denying that God's Spirit has been with those who shaped things in the past. They are unwilling to assume, however, that the process has a fixed stopping point, or that only the highest officials have a role to play in continuing it. Such Catholics feel a sense of responsibility for their institutions and practices, and they are discerning whether and how to intervene in the historical processes they experience in the church. The prudent among them will affirm some key values of classicism— stability, order, and respect for scripture, tradition, and legitimate authority—while differing from rigid classicists (or ecclesiastical fundamentalists) in that they refuse to award an absolute status to traditional understandings and practices.[39] In theological terms, they distinguish God from what has been divinely established, respecting God's freedom to call for new ways in new times.

Purpose and contents of this work

In light of this theological reality, the present volume seeks to assist the efforts of historically conscious Catholics to contribute to the renewal of patterns of ministry and governance in the church by mapping some options before us and asking what we can learn from recent history, all with attention to the changed status of women in the twenty-first century. I am building here on my earlier work on conscience by examining the relationship between the exercise of personal moral agency and the historical and vocational contexts of a believer's life. In *Liberating Conscience* (1996) I develop a social theory of conscience that takes account of the paradox that although conscience is an individual religious experience, one's personal sense of obligation before God is reached and held in the presence of a community of accountability. I argue against absolutizing the autonomy of conscience, and I also critique metaphors implying that conscience is some sort of "thing," like a piece of moral radar equipment that allows one to home in on the right deed like a plane landing in a fog. Instead, conscience is an aspect of the self, perhaps on a par with intelligence. We all have some of it, but degrees vary greatly, and even a lot of it is no guarantee we'll always be right. I define conscience as personal moral awareness, experienced in the course of anticipating future situations and making moral decisions, as well as in the process of reflecting on one's past decisions and the quality of one's character. This leads me to affirm the value of the church's teaching authority, the legitimacy of dissent in certain circumstances, the importance of personal responsibility, and the urgent need for persons in locations of social privilege to attend to voices from the margins.[40] More recently, in *Women, Conscience, and the Creative Process* (2011), I suggest that we can avoid the tendency to reify and depersonalize conscience by thinking of it as "the creatively responsible self."[41]

My 1996 study took inspiration from the Second Vatican Council's "Decree on Priestly Formation," which states that "Special attention needs to be given to the development of moral theology. Its scientific exposition should be more thoroughly nourished by scriptural teaching. It should show the nobility of the Christian vocation of the faithful, and their obligation to bring forth fruit in charity for the life of the world."[42] *Liberating Conscience* pays particular attention to the criterion of fruitfulness "for the life of the world," concluding with chapters about ways of integrating a spirituality of social justice and ecological concern with the process of moral discernment. *Conscience and Calling: Ethical Reflections on Catholic Women's Church Vocations* takes inspiration especially from an earlier phrase of the same mandate, namely that moral theology should show "the nobility of the Christian vocation of the faithful."

Chapter 1, "'His Dogs More Than Us': Virtue in Situations of Conflict Between Women Religious and Their Ecclesiastical Employers," sets the stage for our considerations by comparing two cases of conflict between sisters and churchmen, one from the Diocese of Brooklyn in the 1930s and another from Key West, Florida, in 1989–90.[43] My analysis shows how in the earlier context the sisters' consciences were governed by a patriarchal understanding of virtue, while in the more recent context the sisters made decisions in light of an egalitarian-feminist view of what goodness required. The title was chosen to honor the experiences of all who have endured injustice of the sort known by an eighty-nine-year-old sister interviewed in 1998 about her experiences sixty years earlier. Without bitterness, she summed up her years in an abusive employment situation by saying quite simply, "Father cared more about his dogs than about us."

Chapter 2, "Women and Church Authority: A Map of Responses to Injustice," names the institutional sexism responsible for much of the suffering women experience in the church, and focuses on the question of what God seems to be asking of Catholic women in relation to the church at this juncture of history, which may be likened to the ending of a sexist ice age. Drawing on Protestant theologian H. Richard Niebuhr's (1894–1962) insight that the first ethical task for the responsible moral agent is to interpret what is going on, I adapt the typology from his 1951 study, *Christ and Culture*, to describe the various stances that women today take toward the church.[44] My map of women's responses to ecclesiastical injustice includes Women Against the Church, Women Content with the Church, Women Above the Church, Women and the Church in Paradox, and Women Transforming Church. I argue for the last position as generally more adequate, and I conclude with some recommendations for transformationist women and men, emphasizing the need for those attempting to achieve transformative ideals to be self-critical.

Chapter 3, "A Ministry of Justice: The 25-Year Pilgrimage of the National Assembly of Religious Women (NAWR/NARW)," analyzes the history of an organization that epitomized the ideals of transforming both church and secular society in the direction of justice.[45] Founded in 1970 by U.S. Catholic sisters, the National Assembly of Women Religious (NAWR) sought to implement a particular post-Vatican II vision of Christian life, one profoundly affected by a sense of prophetic vocation to work for social justice and liberation from all forms of oppression. The ideal of inclusivity was especially strong, and this led the organization to change its name to National Assembly of Religious Women (NARW) in 1982 in order to welcome laywomen (including those of other religious faiths) to what had been a Catholic sisters' organization. Before closing its office for lack of funds in 1995, NAWR/NARW had considerable influence through publications, educational programs, and projects, and it helped to establish groups that continue to carry out its ideals, including the

Women's Ordination Conference and Network, the Catholic social justice lobby in Washington, DC.

Chapter 4, "'Framework for Love': Toward a Renewed Understanding of Christian Vocation," deepens the analysis by probing the theological meaning of vocation. Here I show how vocation involves both a religious myth of tremendous power and a mystery that eludes attempts at full certainty about what one should be doing with one's life. That having been said, an individual's vocation can be analyzed as a composite involving three sorts of callings: the basic summons to holiness through fulfilling the biblical command to love God and neighbor; the sense of being invited to focus love, creativity, and sexual energy in a particular life-context; and, the invitation to productive activity through work and devotion of time and energy to various persons, projects, and causes. In developing this analysis I draw especially on the writings of moral theologian Margaret A. Farley concerning commitment and justice.[46] Farley, who taught Christian ethics at Yale Divinity School for nearly forty years, is also a Sister of Mercy, and my discussion pays particular attention to certain struggles that were going on in the 1980s between the Vatican and her religious congregation.

Finally, Chapter 5, "Vocation in a Transformed Social Context," probes the situation in which Catholic women will make decisions about church vocations in the future. After analyzing the tensions between the Vatican and U.S. women religious that came to wide attention in 2012, I describe a number of changes that make today's vocational situation for women so different from that of the mid-twentieth century, when vocations to the sisterhoods peaked in this country. I also discuss the burgeoning of lay ministries, some suggestions for new roles for women, and the efforts of reformers eager to implement changes that are not yet authorized. Finally, I suggest that we who seek to overcome ecclesiastical sexism can learn from earlier women and men of faith, and especially from African Americans, who have dealt heroically with injustice and impasse in the past. In a world church it is a constant task for North American women, especially those privileged by race, class, and education, to keep the injustice we suffer in perspective, and to choose our deeds with prayerful attentiveness to God who is coming to us from the future.

Notes

1 Congregatio Pro Doctrina Fidei, "Doctrinal Assessment of
   the Leadership Conference of Women Religious," 18 April
   2012, http://www.usccb.org/loader.cfm?csModule=security/
   getfile&pageid=55544. (accessed 27 April 2012). This matter is
   discussed more fully in Chapter 5. Most literature on the controversy
   cites the figure 57,000 for U.S. women religious, but the Center for
   Applied Research in the Apostolate (CARA) counted 54,018 sisters
   in October 2012. See http://cara.georgetown.edu/caraservices/
   requestedchurchstats.html (accessed 17 October 2012). Because
   many of the sisters are elderly, deaths over recent months may largely
   account for the discrepancy.

2 Cardinal Franc Rodé, CM, letter to Superiors General, 2 February 2009,
   quoted in Colleen Mary Mallon, OP, "Gracious Resistance: Religious
   Women Charting an Ecclesial Path," in Richard R. Gaillardetz, ed.
   *When the Magisterium Intervenes: The Magisterium and Theologians in
   Today's Church* (Collegeville, MN: Liturgical Press, 2012), p. 65. Sandra
   M. Schneiders emphasizes the "implied accusation and presumed
   guilt" associated with this visitation in *Prophets in Their Own Country:
   Women Religious Bearing Witness to the Gospel in a Troubled Church*
   (Maryknoll, NY: Orbis Books, 2011), p. 9.

3 "Apostolic Visitation closes with final report submission," 9 January
   2012, press release from the Apostolic Visitation website: http://www.
   apostolicvisitation.org/en/materials/close.pdf (accessed 12 July
   2012).

4 "Rome & Women Religious," *Commonweal* (18 May 2012), p. 5.

5 "Statement of the Leadership Conference of Women Religious
   Regarding CDF Report," 1 June 2012. Press release available at:
   https://lcwr.org/media/news/lcwr-board-meets-review-cdf-report
   (accessed 22 July 2012).

6 LCWR Press Release, "Leadership Conference of Women Religious
   Decides Next Steps in Responding to CDF Report." http://www.lcwr.
   org/sites/default/files/media/files/lcwr_2012_assembly_press_
   releases_-_8-10-12.pdf (accessed 13 August 2012).

7 Peter Sartain, "Deepening Communion: The Vatican's assessment of
   the L.C.W.R. offers an opportunity for discernment and collaboration,"
   18 June 2012: http://www.americamagazine.org/content/article.
   cjm?article_id=13456 (accessed 23 June 2012).

8 Christine Firer Hinze, "At Cross Currents? The Vatican, U.S. sisters and
   the L.C.W.R," 18 June 2012: http://www.americamagazine.org/content/
   article.cjm?article_id=134567 (accessed 23 June 2012).

9   "Decree on the Appropriate Renewal of the Religious Life" (*Perfectae Caritatis*) #2-3, in Walter M. Abbott, SJ, ed. *The Documents of Vatican II* (New York: America Press, 1966), pp. 466–82.

10   Monica Clark, "Two groups, two paths for US women religious," 26 May 2012, *National Catholic Reporter*, http://ncronline.org/news/women/two-groups-two-paths-us-women-religious (accessed 19 September 2012).

11   Christine Firer Hinze, op. cit.

12   See http://lcwr.org/social-justice/resolutions-to-action (accessed 12 July 2012) and http://www.cmswr.org/ (accessed 17 September 2012).

13   Christine Firer Hinze, op. cit.

14   I focus here on the popular, publicly recognized forms of dedicated service, while acknowledging the importance of less well-known forms of dedication, including private vows, secular institutes, and the recently recognized vocations to "lay consecration" as virgins or widows. Also, the permanent diaconate, available in recent decades to married men, is not my focus here, though it does further increase the vocational options for Catholic men.

15   Mary Ewens, OP, *The Role of the Nun in Nineteenth-Century America* (New York: Arno Press, 1971), p. 256.

16   Quoted here from Ivy A. Helman, *Women and the Vatican: An Exploration of Official Documents* (Maryknoll, NY: Orbis Books, 2012), p. 204. The full text is available at: http://www.vatican.va/holy_father/john_paul_ii/letters/documents/hf_jp-ii_let_29061995_women_en.html.

17   Helman, p. 174.

18   "Pink smoke declares 'priestly people come in both sexes,'" *National Catholic Reporter* (29 April 2005), p. 3. See also Aisha Taylor, "Pink Smoke Rising," *New Women New Church* 28(1) (Spring 2005): 4.

19   Only Braschi is named, together with the seven women, in the official Vatican "Decree of Excommunication Regarding the Attempted Priestly Ordination of Some Catholic Women" issued by the Congregation for the Doctrine of the Faith on 5 August 2002, which notes that "as a schismatic, he has already incurred excommunication reserved to the Apostolic See." This document (as will be the case with related Vatican texts subsequently) is cited here from Deborah Halter's *The Papal "No": A Comprehensive Guide to the Vatican's Rejection of Women's Ordination* (New York: Crossroad, 2004), p. 236.

20   Marjorie Reiley Maguire, "The Lady Is a Bishop." In *The Rebound 2003, 2004, 2005, 2006, 2007* (c. 2006 by Dorothy Irvin, 1360 University Ave., #463, St Paul, MN 55104), Dorothy Irvin, ed. p. 64. Irvin's publication compiles several calendars featuring archeological evidence of women's traditional ministries and includes essays and photographs concerning the contemporary women's ordination movement.

21 See Fresen, "Weiheämter für Frauen: Ordination for Women." *New Women New Church* 27 (Fall 2004): 3, and "Prophetic Obedience: The Experience and Vision of R.C. Womenpriests," a presentation given in March 2005 in Pennsylvania, and available online at http://www.romancatholicwomenpriests.org/history.htm (accessed 19 August 2006). Pressure from church officials caused Fresen's religious superiors to impose the sanction of leaving the congregation in view of her unwillingness to renounce her ordination, whose validity is officially denied but whose symbolic power is enhanced by her willingness to sacrifice for its sake and by her stated intention of remaining in union with her Catholic tradition, in other words, of avoiding schism.

22 The RCWP movement will be discussed more fully in Chapter 5. The Vatican document revising the norms concerning *gravioribus delictis* against morals and the sacraments (Norms AAS 102 [2010] 419–430) is available at http://www.vatican.va/resources/resources_norme_en.html. See John L. Allen, Jr., *National Catholic Reporter,* "Vatican revises church law on sex abuse," 15 July 2010, available at http://ncronline.org/news/vatican/vatican-revises-church-law-sex-abuse, which provides a link to the official norms (accessed 16 July 2010).

23 "On Reserving Priestly Ordination to Men Alone," 30 May 1994. Cited here from Halter, *The Papal "No,"* p. 213. Halter provides in an appendix to her study the texts of 12 Roman documents important to the discussion, and unless otherwise noted my citations to official texts are from this source. Official texts are also available online at www.vatican.va and www.womenpriests.org, as well as in *Origins,* the documentary publication of the U.S. Conference of Catholic Bishops.

24 Sacred Congregation for the Doctrine of the Faith, "Response to a Question Regarding *Ordinatio Sacerdotalis,*" 28 October 1995, in Halter, p. 225.

25 *CTSA Proceedings* 52 (1997), p. 194. The full report, "Tradition and the Ordination of Women," is found on pp. 197–204. Authors of the report are Margaret A. Farley, RSM; Mary Catherine Hilkert, OP; Jon M. Nilson; David N. Power, OP; Francis A. Sullivan, SJ; and John H. Wright, SJ.

26 Michael H. Kenny, "Women's Ordination—Uneasy Questions." *America* 171 (30 July–6 August 1994): 16.

27 Bishop Geoffrey Robinson, *Confronting Power and Sex in the Catholic Church: Reclaiming the Spirit of Jesus* (Collegeville, MN: Liturgical Press, 2008), p. 253.

28 See Bernard J. F. Lonergan, SJ, "The Transition from a Classicist World-View to Historical-Mindedness," in *A Second Collection,* ed. William F. J. Ryan, SJ, and Bernard J. Tyrrell, SJ (Philadelphia: The Westminster Press, 1974), pp. 1–9.

29 Richard M. Gula, SS, *Reason Informed by Faith: Foundations of Catholic Morality* (New York: Paulist, 1999), p. 33. I have treated the post-World War II trend in Christian ethics to emphasize responsibility over obedience in *Liberating Conscience: Feminist Explorations in Catholic Moral Theology* (New York: Continuum, 1996), pp. 112–15. Classicism taken to an extreme lends itself to Catholic fundamentalism, some implications of which I discuss on pp. 25–34 of the same volume.

30 Lay activism for reform has been evident in such movements as Call to Action, FutureChurch, Voice of the Faithful, and most recently, the American Catholic Council. See Jerry Filteau, "American Catholic Council: 2000 Meet to Call for Reform in Detroit," *National Catholic Reporter* (24 June 2011), pp. 5–6. For a theological perspective on these concerns, see Paul Lakeland, *Catholicism at the Crossroads: How the Laity Can Save the Church* (New York: Continuum, 2007).

31 Fresen, "Prophetic Obedience: The Experience and Vision of R.C. Womenpriests" (2005), mentioned in note #21 above, and "Prophetic Obedience: From Anti-Apartheid Struggles to the Womenpriests Movement," unpublished address, Carleton College, 26 October 2006.

32 *CTSA Proceedings* 52 (1997): 198–9. The report also argues that recent emphasis on gender symbolism as requiring an exclusively male priesthood is morally problematic: "Certain Roman texts justify the restriction of ordained ministry by appeals to iconic appropriateness and/or to beliefs in a natural gender complementarity. The use of these appeals in support of gender role differentiation has been contested in Catholic moral as well as systematic theology by those who argue that the 'effective history' of the practices supported by these appeals can be shown to involve consistent patterns of superiority and inferiority, domination and subordination, rather than of equality" (p. 202).

33 Ibid., p. 203.

34 See Michael J. Himes, ed., *The Catholic Church in the 21st Century* (Liguori, MO: Catholic Community Foundation, 2004), and Francis Oakley and Bruce Russett, eds., *Governance, Accountability, and the Future of the Catholic Church* (New York: Continuum, 2004).

35 Francis Oakley and Bruce Russett, "Introduction: How Did We Get Here and Where Do We Go?" op. cit., p. 9.

36 Donald Cozzens, "Standing in the Fire," in Oakley and Russett, pp. 191–2.

37 Francine Cardman, "Myth, History, and the Beginnings of the Church," in Oakley and Russett, p. 33 and p. 47.

38 Ibid., p. 47.

39 Richard P. McBrien suggests that Catholic moral theology should preserve a "dialectical tension" between the methodologies of classicism and historical consciousness, retaining values that are consistent with intellectual advances establishing that "the perception of all truth is historically conditioned." See McBrien, *Catholicism* (Minneapolis: Winston Press, 1980), pp. 942–3.

40 Anne E. Patrick, *Liberating Conscience*, pp. 35–9 and 198–99.

41 Anne E. Patrick, *Women, Conscience, and the Creative Process: 2009 Madeleva Lecture in Spirituality* (New York, Paulist, 2011), pp. 55–72.

42 *Optatam Totius* (#16), "Decree on Priestly Formation," quoted here from Walter M. Abbott, ed. *The Documents of Vatican II* (New York: America Press, 1966), p. 452.

43 This chapter has been expanded and revised on the basis of Anne E. Patrick, "'His Dogs More Than Us': Virtue in Situations of Conflict Between Women Religious and Their Ecclesiastical Employers," in *Practice What You Preach: Virtues, Ethics, and Power in the Lives of Pastoral Ministers and Their Congregations,* eds. James F. Keenan, SJ, and Joseph Kotva, Jr (Franklin, WI: Sheed & Ward, 1999), pp. 293–314.

44 H. Richard Niebuhr, *Christ and Culture* (New York: Harper & Row, 1951), and *The Responsible Self.* New York: Harper & Row, 1963.

45 This chapter expands an essay originally prepared for a study of liberal Catholicism funded by the Lilly Endowment and led by Mary Jo Weaver and R. Scott Appleby. See Anne E. Patrick, "A Ministry of Justice: The 25-Year Pilgrimage of the National Assembly of Religious Women," in *What's Left? Liberal American Catholics,* ed. Mary Jo Weaver (Bloomington: Indiana University Press, 1999), pp. 176–87.

46 This chapter draws on Anne E. Patrick, "'Framework for Love': Toward a Renewed Understanding of Christian Vocation," in *A Just & True Love: Feminism at the Frontiers of Theological Ethics: Essays in Honor of Margaret A. Farley,* eds. Maura A. Ryan and Brian F. Linnane, SJ (Notre Dame, IN: University of Notre Dame Press, 2007), pp. 303–37. In June 2012 Farley's prize-winning volume *Just Love: A Framework for Christian Sexual Ethics* (New York: Continuum, 2006) was censured by the CDF for taking several positions on specific sexual questions it found objectionable. Many colleagues and former students leapt to her defense, including the board of the Catholic Theological Society of America. See the U.S. bishops' 4 June 2012 news release, which includes a link to official CDF documents, "Vatican Critiques Book by Mercy Sister Margaret Farley" at http://www.usccb.org/news/2012/12-097.cfm and Joshua J. McElwee, "Theological society backs Vatican-criticized nun," *National Catholic Reporter,* 7 June 2012, http://ncronline.org/news/faith-parish/theological-society-backs-vatican-criticized-nun (accessed 27 June 2012). In a 4 June 2012 press release, Farley explained that her work is of a "different genre" than the official critics had taken it for, and indicated that her ultimate purpose had been to offer "a framework for sexual ethics that uses criteria of justice in evaluating true and faithful sexual relationships and activities." She added, "Although my responses to some particular sexual ethical questions do depart from some traditional Christian responses, I have tried to show that they nonetheless reflect a deep coherence with the central aims and insights of these theological and moral traditions." "Statement by Mercy Sister Margaret A. Farley," 4 June 2012, *National Catholic Reporter, http://ncronline.org/news/ vatican/statement-mercy-sister-margaret-farley* (accessed 27 June 2012). Farley has since resumed work on other writing projects and on promoting efforts against HIV-AIDs in Africa.

1

"HIS DOGS MORE THAN US": VIRTUE IN SITUATIONS OF CONFLICT BETWEEN WOMEN RELIGIOUS AND THEIR ECCLESIASTICAL EMPLOYERS

Your Holiness, the women of this country have been inspired by your spirit of courage. . . . Our contemplation leads us to state that the Church, in its struggle to be faithful to its call for reverence and dignity for all persons, must respond by providing the possibility of women as persons being included in all ministries of our Church. I urge you, Your Holiness, to be open to and respond to the voices coming from the women of this country who are desirous of serving in and through the church as fully participating members.

– TERESA KANE, RSM, WELCOMING
POPE JOHN PAUL II TO THE UNITED STATES[1]

When the president of the Leadership Conference of Women Religious (LCWR) spoke these words at a Washington, DC, prayer service on Sunday morning, 7 October 1979, she unleashed a storm of controversy. How could a "good sister" break with protocol and add a substantive request for change to her welcome to the pope during his first visit to this country? Those who objected to her greeting had a very different understanding of what it means to be a good woman religious than did those who applauded Kane.

Instead of reflecting the qualities associated with a patriarchal understanding of virtue, such as docility and unthinking obedience, Kane exemplified the creative responsibility more characteristic of an egalitarian-feminist view of what goodness entails. Whereas the former emphasizes control of the physical body by reason and of subordinates by those in authority, the latter emphasizes commitment to the well-being of oneself and others, which has both spiritual and material elements and involves building social relations of equality, respect, and mutuality. In my earlier work, *Liberating Conscience,* I indicate that the egalitarian-feminist paradigm of virtue is capturing the imaginations of many Christians today.[2] The patriarchal paradigm, however, is not entirely eclipsed, and this is why Kane's greeting has been so controversial. Her words and demeanor were respectful, but Kane, for reasons of conscience, had transcended the role choreographed by those who planned the papal visit.

As President of the Sisters of Mercy of the Union as well as head of LCWR, Kane had earlier sought an opportunity to discuss with Pope John Paul II the concerns of the thousands of sisters she represented. When such requests were repeatedly denied, she then felt obliged to mention these concerns during the one brief opportunity she had to address him. In my judgment, her statement succeeded in balancing some apparently conflicting obligations in an admirable way. There was the duty to offer a gracious welcome and also the duty to represent the concerns of sisters who experienced injustice within the church. Besides fulfilling both obligations, Kane widened her scope of concern beyond sisters to include all Catholic women called to ministries unattainable because of the laws of churchmen.

In the years since 1979, Kane's welcome has been seen as a turning point in the history of American sisters and Catholic women more generally, a prophetic moment that inspired hope in many women even as it evoked a backlash of anger among others. She herself has continued to minister in various capacities as a Sister of Mercy, and she has spoken about her experiences with journalists and audiences in many places. In 1994, she told historian Carole Garibaldi Rogers that the favorable responses from women to her famous greeting had meant much to her, "worth any anxiety I went through," and she would surely "do it again" under the circumstances.[3] In a 2009 talk to the National Coalition of American Nuns she spoke even more forthrightly: "In the Church today, we are experiencing a dictatorial mindset and spiritual violence. . . . I have one chance, one life, and therefore I have a responsibility to criticize."[4]

Is Kane's sense of urgency justified? How should Catholic women deal with tensions and conflicts between themselves and churchmen? To help address these questions this chapter will offer an illustration of the ecclesiastical injustice sometimes experienced by twentieth-century women religious, and will also demonstrate the difference made in recent years by the shift from a patriarchal to an egalitarian-feminist understanding of virtue. I do this by analyzing two cases of conflict between women religious and the churchmen who employed them, one from the Diocese of Brooklyn in the 1930s and another from Key West, Florida, in 1989–90. The first instance shows women of strong character who made difficult choices that were essentially guided by the patriarchal understanding of what good sisters should do. The second case shows women of equal dedication to the church's mission, whose egalitarian-feminist understanding of moral ideals and obligations led to a dramatically different series of responses. And because the experiences of women religious bear on the situation of women more generally, the chapter concludes by suggesting some virtues that all women considering church employment would do well to cultivate.

It is important to note three things at the outset of this comparative case study. First, although these cases focus on the women religious and their differing ways of practicing virtue when treated unjustly, clearly sisters share in the sinfulness of humanity. There are indeed instances of their own unjust behavior that warrant ethical scrutiny, although this is not my focus here. Second, the categories of patriarchal and egalitarian-feminist paradigms of virtue are abstracted from the complexities of life. I employ this typology for its heuristic value without intending to oversimplify the human experiences involved or to deny that middle positions exist between the two extremes. Finally, I have weighed the question of whether justice would be better served by fictionalizing these accounts, since they are told from the churchwomen's point of view, and the churchmen involved in the conflicts might tell things quite differently. The decision to present the actual details as found in the convent archives and through interviews with sisters was reached for two reasons. First, the value of honesty between ministers and laity is central to my ethical analysis, and seems well served by providing historical facts. As the sexual abuse scandals have shown, silence about truths that are scandalous tends to perpetuate injustice, whereas bringing facts to light offers hope of addressing systemic problems. And second, I believe it is important to give voice to the sisters who suffered from lack of information and from strictures against telling others what they did know in the 1930s. Moreover, the details of the 1989–90 case were well known to the public at the time they occurred, because the dispute received considerable attention in the Florida press, and national mention on the Cable News Network.

The chapter's title, "His Dogs More Than Us," was chosen to honor the experience of all Catholic sisters who have endured something like the injustice known by an eighty-nine-year-old nun I interviewed in July 1998, who did not want her name used for fear of giving scandal. Without bitterness, she summed up her years in an abusive employment situation by saying quite simply, "Father cared more about his dogs than about us."[5]

"His dogs more than us"—a case from the Brooklyn diocese, 1939

This sister was one of five Sisters of the Holy Names of Jesus and Mary withdrawn by her provincial superior from the Catholic parish in St James, Long Island, when the school year ended in 1939: the superior and principal of the school, three young teachers, and a sister who cooked for the convent and did sacristy work in the church.

The last received no pay; the four nuns involved in the school each received a stipend of $33 per month. The dogs were three—a Spitz and two shepherds—and Sister Joan Teresa remembered them as being "kind of nasty." One had ripped the veil of Sister Margaret of Jesus, and most of the women religious were afraid of the pastor's well-kept animals. They also lived in some fear of Father Clarence E. Murphy's power over their lives, for he controlled the heat and hot water, and forbade them to talk with parishioners or to accept rides from them, although the sisters had no car.

The sisters interviewed in 1998 recalled their assignment to St James as a "hardship post" because of the overly controlling pastor, although they loved the people and found their teaching work rewarding. A young sister's friendly conversation with a parishioner would be noticed by Father Murphy, and a complaint made to the superior. The 1930s were the Depression years, and there was no furnace until the sisters put on a school play to raise money for one. Even after heat became a possibility, however, the pastor kept the thermostat turned down and locked. The pupils wore coats in the classrooms, and each winter one or another of the sisters would be hospitalized for an illness such as pneumonia. On those occasions when Sister Casimira, the superior, felt impelled to beg Father Murphy for more heat, she would ask the other sisters for special prayers. Her situation was similar to that of the fictional superior in J. F. Powers' short story from the 1940s, "The Lord's Day." In that story, the need was for a stove that worked, and the pastor's response was not to replace the stove but rather to chop down the last trees remaining in the parish schoolyard, on the feeble premise that the trees were preventing the stove from drawing air properly.[6]

The nuns in the real case fared no better. In their convent home, the sisters could have hot water for bathing only on Wednesdays and Saturdays. They recalled with gratitude the times when members of their religious community came by train from Coney Island, where they staffed a thriving school and enjoyed a very positive relationship with the pastor of Our Lady of Solace Church, Father Francis Froelich. On these rare visits, the superior from Coney Island would bring cookies and candy to St James, for she knew that the sisters there were getting by on a very slim food budget, supplemented by donations from the vegetable gardens of parishioners.

Finally, after years of unsuccessful efforts to improve things, and in the wake of Sister Casimira's hospitalization for pneumonia, Mother Mary of Lourdes, the provincial superior, concluded she could no longer leave her sisters in this situation. When she informed the bishop of Brooklyn, Most Rev Thomas E. Molloy, of her decision he countered by saying that if the sisters left St James they would also have to leave their other mission in his diocese, the much-loved school on Coney Island. Nearly sixty years later, Sister Joan Teresa recalled her provincial superior's response: "Very well, your excellency, we will withdraw from the diocese."

Whether Molloy actually hoped the provincial superior would reconsider keeping sisters at St James in order to hold on to the excellent situation at Coney Island is not known, but what is clear is that Mother Mary of Lourdes had reached a point where she judged it wrong to ask sisters to endure the situation in St James any longer. Although the practice of religious obedience was very strict at that time, community members knew that the provincial superior had difficulty appointing new sisters to this mission. And what the sisters remembered above all is that when Mother Mary of Lourdes told them they were leaving both parishes, she instructed them not to discuss this with anyone.

The chronicles (official records) of the two convents are studies in the sort of restraint exercised by women who were striving for the ideals held up to them under the patriarchal paradigm of virtue. An entry for 28 May 1939 comments on the final May procession at Sts Philip and James parish in St James, Long Island: "Our pastor speaks at great length about the devotion to Our Blessed Mother and the imitation of her virtues," and one for 25 June remarks on the school graduation ceremony: After Father Murphy had presented prizes for scholastic achievement, "Benediction of the Blessed Sacrament brings to a close the simple yet impressive graduation, the last to be held under the direction of the Sisters of the Holy Names." There is no word critical of the priest or bishop in the chronicles, and indeed, the superior who had been hospitalized with pneumonia, Sister Casimira, was never known to have complained about Father Murphy's unreasonable control and stinginess. "I don't want to have to account to God for being irreverent to priests," Sister Joan Teresa remembered her saying. The final entry for St James, dated

1 July 1939, notes simply that the superior and the cook departed for Maryland, and "This marks the final departure of the Sisters of the Holy Names, who have labored so zealously during the past seventeen years for the glory of the Holy Names of Jesus and Mary." The statistics at the closing of the mission at St James showed there had been five sisters and 96 pupils.[7]

The Coney Island mission sacrificed at the bishop's insistence had been a much stronger operation; there were 500 pupils in Our Lady of Solace School when the thirteen Sisters of the Holy Names withdrew. One can infer that leaving this parish was much more difficult for the sisters, and that they enjoyed a much better relationship with their pastor, on the basis of things that are included in the chronicles for that mission, which contrast starkly with things left unsaid in the chronicles for the problem parish. According to Sister Charles Raymond, a teacher at Coney Island, their local superior had broken the news of the provincial's decision to remove them sooner than she was supposed to reveal it, after nuns who were shipping boxes of books to another school had been asked by postal clerks if they were moving. The official word came only one week before graduation, as the chronicles for 18 June 1939 state: "Mother Mary of Lourdes, Provincial Superior, pays us a visit and officially announces the news of our withdrawal from the diocese of Brooklyn because of lack of teachers. We accept the decision of Authority and beg graces from the Holy Ghost for those upon whom fall such painful duties."

Although the sisters' chronicles for St James give no indication of the pastor's opinions, and indeed imply that he uttered no words of gratitude about their seventeen years of labor in the parish, the entries for 25 June 1939 at Coney Island convey an altogether different tone. This pastor did not tell the full story to his parishioners, but he did his best, within the model of virtue reigning at the time, to show his appreciation for the nuns and to invite the people to accept the loss of their services without resentment. The final pages of convent records include these entries:

OFFICIAL ANNOUNCEMENT—This morning at the various Masses, Rev. Francis Froelich, Pastor, explains to the parishioners the reason for the Sisters' withdrawal. His words of appreciation for the work accomplished by the Sisters of the Holy Names, and the assurance of his sincere regret at our departure, tend to make his people understand and help to remove any ill feeling which might exist among them because of the present circumstances.

GRADUATION—Thirty-eight of our eighth grade boys and girls receive graduation honors this afternoon. Rev. Francis Froelich, Pastor, reminds them of their duties as Catholics and as American citizens, and again emphasizes the loyalty they should prove to their school and to their Sisters. Father seized this last opportunity to express once more his gratitude to the Sisters.

The wording of these chronicle entries is governed by a concern not to question the judgments of religious authorities, whether those of bishop or provincial superior. But it is clear that their author is worried that the laity may be hurt by the sudden departure of the sisters from their children's school because of "lack of teachers" elsewhere. The last entry for Coney Island, dated 3 July 1939, observes that "Since June 28 the sisters have gradually left, to take up their work [summer study] at the various universities and today the remaining three bid a final farewell to the work which has been ours for twenty-one years. God wills it thus and we humbly submit to his designs in our regard."

"Save the nuns"—a case from the archdiocese of Miami, 1989–90

Silence and humble submission were notably absent in the more recent case of conflict between Sisters of the Holy Names and their ecclesiastical employers, which showed women operating under dramatically different ideals of what it means to be a good sister than were exhibited in the pre-Vatican II era. Instead of emphasizing obedience, denial of conflict, and institutional loyalty, the paradigm of virtue inspiring their responses to difficulties laid stress on justice, honesty, and personal responsibility. No longer was God's will assumed to be contained within the directives of ecclesiastical authority; the presumption was rather that women and men in ministry ought to dialogue together in an effort to discern what God might want for the people. And if dialogue proves impossible, then the people who will lose the women's ministries have a right to know what has been going on. Sisters are no longer willing to "cover" for the clergy or to absorb the blame for decisions beyond their control.

In August 1989, at the invitation of the pastor of St Mary, Star of the Sea Church, the same religious community that had reluctantly withdrawn from the Brooklyn diocese fifty years earlier, sent four women to reestablish their mission in Key West, Florida. The returning Sisters of the Holy Names were warmly welcomed by islanders and church officials, including the pastor, Father Eugene M. Quinlan, and the Archbishop of Miami, Most Rev Edward A. McCarthy. This community of women religious had previously ministered in Key West, primarily in schools, from 1868 until 1983, and had played a vital role in the island's history. Their voluntary departure because of a significant decline in their numbers after the Second Vatican Council had left a void in Key West, and in 1988 Father Quinlan, who came as pastor in 1986, contacted the community.

Initially the pastor's purpose was to make arrangements for relocating the graves of sisters buried on land they originally owned, but which had been turned over to the archdiocese in the 1960s when the religious community could not otherwise meet debt payments for building projects that had been necessary for its work on the island. This contact in 1988 soon led to discussions of the sisters returning to minister in Key West, and on 20 January 1989 Father Quinlan wrote to Sister Kathleen Griffin, the Provincial Director, describing four possible positions and expressing "my fondest desire that the Sisters will return to St Mary's."[8]

After prayer and planning among several sisters with their provincial leaders, four were chosen to re-found the mission. Sister Dolores Wehle, who had previously worked for eighteen years in Key West (nine years teaching in the parish school, and nine serving as its principal), would come as Director of Religious Education, and Sister Eileen Kelleher as Associate Director of Religious Education; Sister Mary Patricia Vandercar would do historical research on the parish and convent, and Sister Audrey Rowe, who had taught in Key West during the 1950s, would focus on visiting the island's many AIDS patients and others suffering from illness. In August 1989 there was a joyful celebration when these women religious came to Key

West, reestablishing a long-valued connection between the sisters and the islanders.

Within a few months, however, the seemingly fine second foundation had fallen apart. At a parish staff meeting on 5 December 1989, a long-simmering misunderstanding between the pastor and the sisters over whether the two women with expertise in religious education should be expected to teach classes in the parish school erupted into an emotional exchange that led to the pastor declaring that the sisters' contracts would not be renewed for the following year. In a 7 December letter to Sister Kathleen Griffin, Father Quinlan expressed his understanding of the problems and stated his decision, indicating that salaries would be paid through 15 August but the four sisters would have to leave their leased residence by 1 July 1990. Griffin responded on 22 December that "the nature and content of your letter came as a great surprise," and said she needed to pray and reflect on the matter and would visit Key West again in February. On 8 January 1990 Quinlan wrote to Griffin that his decision was final, though he regretted that "the aspirations I visualized over the founding Sisters returning to Key West have not been met."

According to Sister Rose Gallagher, then Apostolic Director for the women's community, on 15 January 1990 there was a meeting of Griffin and herself with the Vicar for Religious in Miami, Sister Denise Marie Callaghan, for the sake of exploring "approaches to solutions," but this proved fruitless. Essentially the archdiocese viewed the problem as a local matter and did not question the pastor's decision. Gallagher sums up the community officers' failure to gain a hearing beyond the vicar's office thus: "Neither the Vicar for Religious nor the provincial were able to obtain any appointments, with the archbishop or archdiocesan officials, or even acknowledgement that correspondence or phone calls were received between mid-January and May."[9]

On 28 February 1990, Sister Eileen Kelleher wrote to Father Quinlan and to Archbishop McCarthy to tender her resignation as "Minister of Adult Education" and explain her reasons for leaving before the contract expired. To Quinlan she pointed out that he had objected to several initiatives she had proposed after listening to parish members, which ranged from planning a parish retreat day to forming a group for separated and divorced Catholics. She lamented the lack of a functioning parish council or liturgy committee and expressed dismay at the discovery that she was being paid from parish school funds, when she understood her position to be concerned with adult religious formation. To the archbishop she mentioned that she had uprooted herself from a thriving parish ministry in Schenectady, New York, in order to address "the greater need" in Key West, but that her efforts on behalf of adult education and sacramental preparation had been blocked at every turn by the pastor. She concluded by voicing a prayer that "someone will be attentive" to the people's great needs. Quinlan tersely acknowledged her resignation and asked her to turn in all parish materials by its effective date, 8 March; the archbishop did not respond.

Meanwhile the provincial superior agreed to meet with a group of parishioners who had requested this in order to "gain some understanding of why the sisters were leaving so that they, too, could seek solutions," as Gallagher recalled. Shortly thereafter, Griffin and the other three members of the sisters' provincial council prepared a letter that was addressed to the archbishop and the members of St Mary Star of the Sea Parish. This letter of 29 March 1990 was also shared with all the New York Province Sisters of the Holy Names. This public letter is a step that would have been unthinkable in the days of Mother Mary of Lourdes' conflict with the bishop of Brooklyn, and the fact that it was sent illustrates not only the great changes in sisters' ideals of virtue since the 1930s, but also the enhanced position of the laity in the post-Vatican II church. The letter opens by explaining the reason it was prepared:

> Since we believe that only Father Eugene Quinlan's story will be shared at the Archdiocesan and perhaps local level, we wish to lay out for you the sequence of events surrounding the return and dismissal of our sisters in Key West as we Sisters of the Holy Names experienced them. Our community's great joy, enthusiasm and sense of celebration at the return of four sisters to Key West in August 1989 have changed, in a few short months, to deep sorrow at the news that we are being asked to give up our mission among you and leave after less than a year.

There follow several pages of narrative, based on provincial administration records of events from 1989, which describe the way plans had been made to return to Key West after the community's reduced numbers had led to their voluntary withdrawal in 1983. The letter includes a powerful statement of the historical connection between the sisters and Key West:

> The people of Key West hold a unique place in the hearts and in the history of the Sisters of the Holy Names. One hundred twenty-two years ago, in 1868, before bridges, railroad or air travel, we came to Key West, bought and cleared our land and began our ministry of education in the faith. During periods when there were no priests on the island we were present with you to gather people for worship, to baptize, to teach. During severe epidemics we were present to nurse the sick, comfort the dying and conduct burial services. During the Spanish-American War we converted the school into a hospital and nursed the wounded. During calm and hurricanes, in periods of great economic growth and severe depression, we were present with you, in good times and bad. The return of four sisters to Key West was prompted by our desire to resume a long ministerial history of response to your needs.

The letter concludes with the sisters' clear statement of the message they most wanted to leave with the people, something that their predecessors at Coney Island had not been able to express in 1939:

> It is not our choice to leave.
> While Father Quinlan may choose to exercise his authority to dismiss these four sisters who freely and lovingly chose to return to Key West, his choice can never erode or dismiss the affection and the bonds we sisters have with you.

Scrutiny of the women's narrative reveals that the seeds of the misunderstanding over classroom responsibilities were sown in the early stages of the negotiations for the return of the sisters, because the provincial officers had not known that "the salaries of at least two of the sisters are paid by the school even though they do not work for the school."[10] The women had presumed that job descriptions would be refined cooperatively after some on-site experience and dialogue, and apparently Quinlan had not told them he was funding the religious education positions from the school budget. Meanwhile school administrators were counting on having nuns in their classrooms, but Sister Dolores Wehle (who had been principal of that school for nine years) understood her role to be one of working with teachers, not pupils, and Sister Eileen Kelleher expected to be doing adult faith formation.

On 21 March, the provincial superior had come to Key West, where she spoke with the pastor and deacon, the sisters, and the laity in separate meetings. The provincial council's 29 March letter states that "Father reiterated the finality of his decision that the sisters must leave," while parishioners were still "seeking a compromise, believing that Father Quinlan has left an 'open door,' in their view." It further observes that "The parishioners and Sister Kathleen [Griffin] noted that the sisters' names and positions are still not on the parish bulletin although they were assigned last June and arrived in Key West in August."

After their meeting with Griffin, a group of concerned parishioners undertook a public campaign to "save the nuns." Their response exhibited both their postconciliar optimism about having a voice in matters concerning their parish life and also their trust that church officials would respond favorably to the pressure tactics often employed by interest groups in the United States. Thus on 22 April they published a full-page ad in the *Key West Citizen*, featuring a picture of the foundress of the community, Blessed Marie-Rose Durocher, above the banner headline "Save the Nuns." The ad also included historical material from the council's open letter of 29 March, and declared in bold type, "It is not their choice to leave." Readers were encouraged to write to the archbishop and other churchmen and to post the ad in their windows. Two more display ads appeared in subsequent weeks, one with the entire text of the 29 March letter from the provincial council. Other activities organized by the laity included distributing hundreds of "Save the Nuns" buttons and having nightly gatherings to recite the rosary at the grotto of Our Lady of Lourdes near the church. This campaign resulted in frequent coverage in the Miami and Key West newspapers, and even mention on the television Cable News Network. According to Sister Rose

Gallagher, the campaign finally led to the archbishop's contacting the sisters:

> A biplane flew over the island after all the masses one weekend in April trailing the message, "Father, please keep the nuns." It was this event that prompted the first contact from the archdiocese. The archbishop phoned the provincial to tell her to remove the sisters as soon as possible. The provincial met with her council, talked with the sisters in Key West and then finalized their departure in May, three months ahead of time.[11]

Some sixteen months after the sisters' departure the *Miami Herald* reported in a 5 September 1991 article that Father Quinlan would be leaving Key West to become pastor in Marathon, Florida. The story noted that "Quinlan, 57, spent thousands of hours working on behalf of the sick and helped secure a property for . . . a group that supports people with AIDS. But it was his decision to force the nuns out of Key West that brought him the most publicity."[12]

Quinlan's successor was then appointed by the Archdiocese of Miami. Some sisters have since visited Key West on occasion, but the community has no plans to resume ministry there. And, the archdiocese holds title on land where sisters labored for over a century, which has appreciated considerably in value since the women gave it up in the 1960s to avoid bankruptcy over a loan incurred for the sake of continuing their ministry in Key West. In 1996 the parish published a sesquicentennial booklet, in which the Sisters of the Holy Names figure prominently for 115 years, from their arrival in 1868 until their voluntary withdrawal in 1983. In the entry for 1989, no mention was made of the return and rejection of four living sisters, although Father Quinlan's reburial of eighteen deceased sisters "next to the grotto which they had built in the early twenties" was noted. The pastor's subsequent transfers and eventual medical retirement are also mentioned under 1989, although he left the parish only in 1991. The year 1990, with its divisions over the unsuccessful "save the nuns" campaign, is omitted from the parish's historical record.[13] Likewise, in May 2012, when the parish church of St Mary Star of the Sea was elevated to the status of a basilica, coverage of the ceremony in the archdiocesan newspaper made no mention of the unhappy events of 1989–90, although the sisters were praised for their historic ministry:

> The Sisters of the Holy Names ministered in the archdiocese's oldest parish 115 years, from 1868 to 1983. They opened a school for girls, known as the Convent of Mary Immaculate; a school for boys, known as St Joseph; and a school for black children, known as St Francis Xavier. When the battleship Maine exploded in Havana Harbor and the Spanish-American war broke out in 1898, they turned the convent school into a hospital for the wounded. "Their presence here raised the bar for this parish," said Father John Baker, pastor since 2007 . . . . "As the needs grew, they responded constantly and adapted. They really did set the tone as to what ministry is." "They planted the seeds. Everybody talks about the sisters," said Sister Mary Silvestry Mushi, one of the three Sisters of the Holy Spirit from Tanzania who now work at the parish school.[14]

Implications of these cases

Although an idealized picture of the early church declares "The community of believers were of one heart and one mind" (Acts 4:32), there is evidence that disputes and conflict have been part of Christian life from the very beginning. The examples of conflict between women religious and their ecclesiastical employers described above are hardly unique in the church's history, and indeed, sisters are by no means the only Catholics who have felt powerless when they were in dispute with church authorities. But the cases under consideration here are interesting from the standpoint of virtue ethics because they illustrate a clear development in the ideals of virtue held by women who occupy an important role in Catholicism. This development is arguably an instance of a larger paradigm shift where virtue is concerned, which has been in progress among Christians ever since the experiences of World War II and the trials at Nuremburg put in question the great emphasis on submission and obedience that had held sway in the past. When it began, the paradigm shift placed responsibility instead of obedience at the center of Christian ethics, and among Catholics there followed an emphasis on "coresponsibility in the church," which took hold at the time of the Second Vatican Council, largely through the influence of the Belgian cardinal, Léon-Joseph Suenens.[15] Subsequent developments have led me to characterize the shift as a change from a patriarchal to an egalitarian-feminist understanding of virtue, which I will describe more fully below.[16]

The patriarchal paradigm of virtue is based on a now-discredited view of women's alleged ontological inferiority to men, which although rejected at the conscious level by most persons today, nevertheless continues to exert residual influence. This paradigm tends to see virtue in light of the domination-subordination motif that has long characterized relations between men and women, colonial powers and the colonized, and rulers and the ruled. Virtue is primarily a matter of reason exerting control over the passions and the unruly body, as well as over impulses to insubordination within social systems. As a result, subordinates are expected to cultivate the virtues of obedience, docility, and loyalty. Moreover, ideals for character tend to be segregated along gender lines, with men trained to think in terms of justice and rights, and women expected to excel in humility, charity, and chastity.

The egalitarian-feminist paradigm, by contrast, is built on the principle of the equal ontological status of women and men, and it emphasizes respect for human dignity and material creation rather than control. Instead of obedience, the central virtue for this paradigm is justice, and it tends to promote gender-integrated ideals for character. Discipline continues to be valued, but is viewed less rigidly than under the patriarchal model. Rather than expecting men to take care of the public sphere and women to keep the fires of charity burning at home, this paradigm sees love and justice as mutually reinforcing norms that should govern both sexes equally. Although the present imbalance of power within the Roman Catholic Church where gender roles are concerned is defended by Vatican authorities on theological grounds, believers influenced by the new paradigm regard these arguments as limited human positions rather than divinely endorsed realities. The two types of virtue paradigms are of course abstractions, and in real life few characters fully embody either one; there is a wide range of "middle" positions along the spectrum from patriarchal to egalitarian-feminist understandings of virtue.

This era of transition has involved dramatic changes, and as a result, persons committed to church service are destined to deal with a good deal of conflict, misunderstanding, and disappointment. This is the case across the board, regardless of gender and whether one's stance is basically patriarchal or egalitarian-feminist. My focus in this chapter has been on the practical difficulties experienced by women religious, who have traditionally been subordinated within Catholic structures, and whose stories have not been widely known in the church precisely because of the sexist ideology and notions of goodness long held by Catholics. Undoubtedly the dramatic decline in membership among communities of women religious in recent decades is partly due to the clash between the ideals of love and justice articulated in church documents and the experience of male domination that remains in Catholic institutions. In 2010 there were 57,544 sisters in the United States, down nearly three-quarters from the peak number of 181,451 in 1966. Women with healthy self-concepts are increasingly skeptical of involvement in an ecclesiastical system where their talents are destined to be circumscribed by a sexist power differential.[17]

Certainly many sisters and laywomen are happily employed in parish or diocesan settings today, but their fate depends on which priest or bishop currently has authority over them, and things could change drastically with a new appointment. As the cases from Brooklyn and Key West show, when conflicts arise between women and their ecclesiastical employers, the power of office enjoyed by clergy of all ranks too often trumps considerations that would otherwise be relevant. There are some exceptions that offer grounds for hope, but in too many instances it happens that women who try to fight this system are destined to lose, at least in the short run.

In these conflictual situations it tends to be the case that women who understand virtue under a patriarchal paradigm will respond by following what may be called a *military obedience and institutional loyalty* model, as did Mother Mary of Lourdes when faced with the ultimatum of the bishop of Brooklyn in 1939. She saw her duty as threefold: protecting the well-being of the sisters by removing them from St James, accepting the resultant ouster from Coney Island,

and keeping the record of events as hidden as possible to protect the image of clerical authorities. In this context she insisted that the sisters should not know they were leaving Coney Island until the last minute, and she forbade them to discuss the true reason for their departure, especially with the parishioners. By contrast, those inspired by an egalitarian-feminist paradigm will be guided by a *personal responsibility and social justice* model, as was the case in Key West fifty years later, when the provincial administrators felt it appropriate to inform the sisters and the laity that the provincial director, Sister Kathleen Griffin, had been unable to obtain a hearing from the archbishop and that the sisters had not chosen to leave.

In recent decades, the church employment scene for women has changed a great deal. Today the majority of church employees are lay, and both laywomen and sisters are usually hired on an individual basis. Nevertheless the cases discussed above are relevant for all women who would minister in the church, since there remains an imbalance of power between clergy and women. In January 2011, the popular *U.S. Catholic* magazine featured Heidi Schlumpf's article, "Femme Fidèle: How Women Who Work for the Church Keep the Faith," which noted that "women virtually run the church in the United States," comprising the "majority of parishioners, volunteers, and staff at the parish level," and "at least half of employees at most diocesan offices."[18] Schlumpf went on to indicate that just employment conditions are not yet in place for many women:

[B]y far the most common concern for women working in the church is a new pastor. Parish employees—as many as 80 percent of whom are women—know they are only a personnel change away from the unemployment line. Talk to a handful of female lay ministers and at least one will tell you how she was unfairly fired or forced out by a new pastor with a new—or often—old vision and different priorities.[19]

Given the tensions of a transitional period, there are three virtues that especially commend themselves to all women who contemplate ministering as church employees: prudence, honesty, and justice. Prudence, which helps in the practical attainment of goals, requires that women enter into ministry situations not only with the idealism of their commitment to the gospel, but also with a good measure of institutional realism. It is not enough to negotiate contracts that provide for just compensation, as the Key West case makes clear. It is also necessary to probe into matters such as where funding for new positions is coming from, how decisions affecting the operation are made, and how the church official in charge tends to handle conflict. One can think of many pastors and a good number of bishops who would have handled the issues that arose in Key West in a much more mutually satisfying way. Just as a diocesan or parish administrator should conduct a background check of references for a prospective church employee, so should a woman undertake some scrutiny of the track record of those for whom she will work. Prudence cannot obviate all possible problems, but it will prevent some.

Honesty is a virtue that has often been sacrificed under the patriarchal model of virtue, for reasons of institutional loyalty, fear of giving scandal, and desire for preserving a measure of status and security. And yet there is still truth in the maxim that honesty is the best policy. Although there was hurt on all sides over the Key West debacle, the pain from having to leave Coney Island abruptly and without a real explanation seems to have lasted much longer, at least for the sisters involved. Certainly the willingness of Sister Kathleen Griffin and her provincial council to state the record of events as the sisters experienced things was appreciated much more by her community than would have been a decision to withdraw without disclosing the reasons, as happened under Mother Mary of Lourdes.

It has taken the tragedy of the clergy sexual abuse scandals, which began to be addressed with appropriate measures only after publicity and lawsuits, to teach those in power that denial of problems does not make them go away. Bringing more honesty into all church employment matters remains a continuing task for Catholic women, who have often been schooled to prefer silence and indirection to confrontation, and as a result may need to cultivate skills of appropriate and effective self-assertion.

Justice is the third virtue commended here, and its meaning needs some clarification in view of the fact that the patriarchal and egalitarian-feminist paradigms interpret it differently. As Margaret A. Farley has observed, under the "old order," which presumed the inferiority of females and understood God's will to require the subordination of women to men, understandings of love and justice did not include the possibility of criticizing sexism. Modern recognition of women's full human dignity, however, is bringing into being a "new order" that requires new interpretations of these traditional principles. With respect to justice she argues that adequate understandings of both individual and common good require a shift from strict hierarchical models of social organization to more egalitarian ones. She notes that ". . . the good of the family, church, etc. is better served by a model of leadership which includes collaboration between [male and female] equals" than one which places a single male leader at the head of the community.[20] In the end, new understandings of justice and love are found to be mutually reinforcing norms for an egalitarian- feminist ethic:

> [I]nterpersonal communion characterized by equality, mutuality, and reciprocity may serve not only as a norm against which every pattern of relationship may be measured but as a goal to which every pattern of relationship is ordered. Minimal justice, then, may have equality as its norm and full mutuality as its goal. Justice will be maximal as it approaches the ultimate goal of communion of each person with all persons and God.[21]

More work needs to be done to translate such insights about the principles of love and justice into new understandings of virtue, but some things are clear already. Justice must be understood not merely as a matter of fulfilling contractual obligations but as one of striving for right relations in all situations. Moreover, especially because many women have been socialized to assume roles of nurturing and self-sacrifice on behalf of others, it is crucial that they include their own well-being among the goods that are rightfully defended against injustice, including that found in the church. The affirmation of gender equality should affect not only general virtues such as justice, but also more specifically ecclesial ones such as religious obedience. Religious cultures must be held to account for the way they promote or inhibit the practice of virtues needed for the ministry to flourish, especially prudence, honesty, and justice. Those ministry settings in which clergy and women do function in just and mutually supportive ways, as seems to have been the case in the flourishing parish on Coney Island in 1939, are harbingers of a future in which an even fuller degree of justice and love will be evident in church administration and ministry. Women and men inspired by the egalitarian-feminist paradigm of virtue today are helping to bring this hope closer to realization.

Notes

1 Kane's words are cited here from Carole Garibaldi Rogers, *Habits of Change: An Oral History of American Nuns,* rev ed. (1996; New York: Oxford University Press, 2011), p. 217. Rogers provides the full text of Kane's greeting to Pope John Paul II at the end of an interview with her conducted in August 1994, "Summoned to Lead," pp. 211–17. See also an earlier interview with Kane, in *The Inside Stories: 13 Valiant Women Challenging the Church,* ed. Annie Lally Milhaven (Mystic, CT: Twenty-Third Publications, 1987), pp. 1–23.

2 For a fuller discussion of the paradigm shift in Catholic understandings of virtue, see Anne E. Patrick, *Liberating Conscience: Feminist Explorations in Catholic Moral Theology* (New York: Continuum, 1996), especially Chapter 3, "Changing Paradigms of Virtue: The Good Life Reconsidered," pp. 76–80 and 94–5.

3 Rogers, *Habits of Change,* p. 215.

4 Ibid, p. 217.

5 I express my thanks here to several Sisters of the Holy Names of Jesus and Mary who provided information about their experiences in the Brooklyn diocese of the 1930s during interviews conducted in Albany, NY, 2–4 July 1998. These women resumed their baptismal names after the Second Vatican Council, but were known by special religious names for decades prior to that: Sisters Marjorie Brainerd (Joan Teresa), Clara Brunelle (Charles Raymond), Edna May Gagnon (Robert Marie), and Anna Martha Murphy (Joan Patricia). All are now deceased.

6 J. F. Powers, "The Lord's Day," *Prince of Darkness and Other Stories* (New York: Image Books, 1958), pp. 11–18.

7 Chronicles of the New York Province, Sisters of the Holy Names of Jesus and Mary. Until 2005 these records were kept at the provincial house in Albany, New York. In 2006 the New York Province joined with four other SNJM provinces to become the U.S.-Ontario Province, with headquarters in Lake Oswego, Oregon. Chronicles and other archival

materials are now maintained at Holy Names Heritage Center there. Subsequent references to chronicles, correspondence, and other unpublished documents are all based on materials in these archives.

8 Eugene M. Quinlan to Kathleen Griffin, 20 January 1989, SNJM New York Province Archives, Holy Names Heritage Center, Lake Oswego, Oregon. Besides drawing on archival documents and newspaper accounts, I have benefited from clarifying conversations with several of the women involved in the case, particularly Sisters Kathleen Griffin, Dolores Wehle, and Eileen Kelleher.

9 Rose Gallagher, "Outline of Key West Events, December 1989–May 1990," SNJM New York Province Archives.

10 Sisters of the Holy Names Provincial Administration to Most Reverend Edward A. McCarthy, D. D., Archbishop of Miami, and Members of St Mary Star of the Sea Parish, 29 March 1990, SNJM New York Province Archives. Besides Provincial Director Griffin, councilors signing the letter were Sisters Rose Gallagher, Rose Christina Momm, and Patricia Brennan. The entire letter was reproduced in a full-page advertisement sponsored by the "Save the Nuns" campaign, which appeared in the *Key West Citizen* on Sunday, 6 May 1990, p. 12-B.

11 Gallagher, "Outline of Key West Events, December 1989–May 1990."

12 Ozzie Osborne, "Pastor's 5-year tenure in Key West to End," *The Miami Herald*, "The Keys", (5 September 1991), p. B-1.

13 "A History of St Mary Star of the Sea Catholic Church," Key West, 1996.

14 Ana Rodriguez-Soto, "A basilica in God's paradise," *Florida Catholic* (Sunday, 3 June 2012), http://www.miamiarch.org/ip.asp?op= Article_1262155656162 (accessed 13 June 2012).

15 Titles reflecting these developments include Léon-Joseph Suenens, *Coresponsibility in the Church*, trans. by Francis Martin (New York: Herder & Herder, 1968); Albert R. Jonsen, *Responsibility in Modern Religious Ethics* (Washington, DC: Corpus Books, 1968); and Dorothee Soelle, *Beyond Mere Obedience*, trans. Laurence W. Denef (New York: Pilgrim Press, 1982).

16 The description below draws on Patrick, *Liberating Conscience*, pp. 77–9.

17 The different values assigned to priestly vocations and those of religious brothers ("lay" by choice or circumstance) and sisters (canonically ineligible for ordination) are shown in the fact that worries about the loss of clergy were articulated much sooner and louder than notice was taken of what was happening to the nonordained religious in the years after Vatican II. The departures of women were considerably more numerous than those of priests, however, and the loss of brothers was also dramatic. It took fifteen years for the drop in the number of priests in this country to approach one thousand, from 59,193 in 1966 to 58,398 in 1981, which represented a decline of just over one percent (795). Meanwhile within the same period religious brothers had declined by more than four thousand (by 1981 there were 4489 fewer brothers, a drop of more than 36 percent from the 1966 figure of 12,255) and nuns had declined by nearly sixty thousand to 122,653 in 1981 (58,768 departures and deaths within 15 years caused a 32 percent drop from the 1966 peak of 181,421 sisters). As the twentieth century drew to a close, there were fewer than 90,000 women religious in the United States, a decline of more than 50 percent from the peak figure. By 2010 this number had dropped to 57,544. Twentieth-century statistics are from P. J. Kennedy & Sons' *Official Catholic Directory*; statistics for 2010 are from the Center for Applied Research in the Apostolate (CARA), http://www7.georgetown.edu/centers/cara/CARAServices/requestedchurchstats.html (accessed 24 July 2012). For contextual background, see Lora Ann Quiñonez and Mary Daniel Turner, *The Transformation of American Catholic Sisters* (Philadelphia: Temple University Press, 1992); and Patricia Wittberg, *The Rise and Fall of Catholic Religious Orders: A Social Movement Perspective* (Albany: State University of New York Press, 1994).

18 Heidi Schlumpf, "Femme Fidèle: How Women Who Work for the Church Keep the Faith." *U.S. Catholic* (January 2011), p. 13.

19 Ibid., p. 15.

20 Margaret A. Farley, "New Patterns of Relationship: Beginnings of a Moral Revolution." *Theological Studies* 36 (1975): 645.

21 Ibid., p. 646.

2

WOMEN AND CHURCH AUTHORITY: A MAP OF RESPONSES TO INJUSTICE

"Catholic women, in their great devotion to the Church and their simultaneous alienation from it, represent the essence of the crisis in the Catholic laity."
—DAVID GIBSON, *THE COMING CATHOLIC CHURCH*[1]

As the cases discussed in the last chapter suggest, the exercise of authority in the church is a thoroughly ethical matter, for it involves the question of right relationships, and matters of justice and injustice. As Catholics we affirm the sacramentality of the church, but this does not mean that ecclesiology should be a branch of theology untouched by the insights of Christian moral wisdom. Instead, ethics should work with other theological disciplines on the question of authority, asking how we may serve our needs for unity, order, and leadership in a way that respects two insights that are having a profound impact on believers today: a conviction of the fundamental equality of women and men, and a deepening appreciation of the fact that God's Spirit dwells in all the faithful, and is not limited to those who hold hierarchical office.

The topic of church authority is closely related to the movement for justice for women. We are beginning to see connections between what women often experience in patriarchal society and what laity, priests, and even bishops sometimes suffer at the hands of domineering religious authorities. The model of domination and subordination that is at the heart of patriarchy expresses itself most clearly in unjust relations between males and females, but it is also seen in many other sorts of unjust relationships. By the same token, a model of mutuality and respect has possibilities for healing relationships not only between women and men but also between Christian communities and their leaders.

One gift the women's movement for justice has brought to the church is the clear recognition that whatever may be true about the catechism description of the church as a "perfect society," the phrase cannot mean what complacent Catholics used to believe that it meant, namely that the church's organizational structure, policies, and procedures are flawless. Indeed, one of the problems of our tradition's emphasis on the sacramentality of the religious institution, on the fact that grace is mediated through the society we call church, has been the tendency to exempt this society from the ethical scrutiny given to other societies. Some have mistakenly held to an ecclesiology that stresses a view of divine foundation and guidance to the point where the human and indeed the sinful aspects of the church are not recognized and properly addressed.

This situation is parallel to the one where believers are reluctant to apply the techniques of literary and historical criticism to biblical texts. The result in both cases can be a style of faith that confuses God with the human realities mediating God's presence, in other words, the classic temptation of idolatry. If Protestants have sometimes succumbed to "bibliolatry," the recurrent temptation for Catholics has been "ecclesiolatry," and the corrective we need is not a rejection of the church or legitimate ecclesiastical authority, but rather a realistic recognition of the humanity of the church, which means that leaders and other members are responsible for the quality of its life and the cogency of its witness. A glance at history confirms that issues of power and justice are sooner or later involved whenever two or three are gathered together in Jesus' name.[2] The fact that we are concerned with an institution with special ties to the sacred does not dispense us from our basic obligation to strive in all contexts of our lives to "discern what God is enabling and requiring us to be and to do," as James M. Gustafson has so aptly described the task of Christian ethics.[3]

Many questions need to be addressed once the decision to draw the ethical implications of accepting the true humanity of the church is made. This chapter focuses on one of these, namely the question of what God seems to be enabling and requiring Catholic women to be and to do in relation to the church at this juncture of its history. Given that Catholicism has reinforced patriarchal values in the past and still continues to do so to a considerable degree despite some progress since the 1960s, what are women choosing to do? And, to put things normatively, what should we be doing? Women's decisions about church membership and involvement are profoundly affecting the religious institution, and one has every reason to think that the trends will be more pronounced as time goes on.

Sociological data on U.S. Catholicism

Shortly before the April 2008 visit of Pope Benedict XVI to the United States, the Pew Forum on Religion and Public Life announced results of a major study showing a dramatic decline in the number of Americans who consider themselves Catholic. Based on interviews with 35,000 adults, the Pew Landscape Survey found that 44 percent of Americans reported some change in their religious affiliation since childhood, and that "Catholicism has experienced the greatest net losses as a result of affiliation change." The report goes on to observe that "while nearly one-in-three Americans (31 percent) are raised in the Catholic faith, today fewer than one-in-four (24 percent) describe themselves as Catholic. These losses would have been more pronounced were it not for the offsetting impact of immigration." The study concludes that approximately 10 percent of the U.S. population is now comprised of former Catholics.[4]

These data support some conclusions of a team of eminent sociologists of Catholicism, who observed in 2007 that "There are signs that commitment to the Church is weakening." The authors of *American Catholics Today*—William V. D'Antonio, James D. Davidson,

Dean R. Hoge, and Mary L. Gautier—noted that "it is widely believed that nonpracticing Catholics are now the second-largest religious group in the United States—second only to practicing Catholics." Moreover, they reported that the Catholics remaining "are not as attached to the Church as previous generations have been."[5] In light of earlier studies, the journalist David Gibson had observed in 2003 that "[within] the Catholic population three groups appear especially vulnerable to alienation: women, Latinos, and young people."[6] The causes of disaffection are multiple, but there is evidence that the status of women within Catholicism is partly to blame. Indeed, the 2007 study by D'Antonio, Davidson, Hoge, and Gautier notes that 38 percent of Catholics consider the fact that "women are not involved enough in Church decision making" to be a serious problem (as opposed to "somewhat of a problem" or "not a problem"). The trend toward increasing discomfort with women's lack of decision-making power seems clear.[7]

Gibson cites data from a 2001 study by D'Antonio, Davidson, Hoge, and Katherine Meyer indicating that there is an erosion of loyalty to the church among Catholic women. Women's rate of weekly mass attendance declined more rapidly than that of men from 1987 to 1999, and the number of women who said they would "never leave the church" fell from 68 percent to 56 percent during the same period. Gibson observes that "the church may be reaching a tipping point when it comes to the loyalty of its most reliable core membership," and quotes the study's authors on the significance of this data:

"Our data, along with data from other research, clearly indicate . . . that women's attachment to the Church is declining. This decline is the result of many forces in society as well as in the Church, including women's perception that their gifts are often overutilized but undervalued. . . . Unless leaders listen to women's concerns and address the conditions underlying them, the risk will be that women's alienation from the Church will turn to indifference and even lower levels of participation."[8]

The 2007 report by D'Antonio and his colleagues points to some significant gender differences with respect to attitudes toward church teachings. Of the four teachings regarded as "very important" by three-quarters of the Catholic population in 2005, more women than men affirmed the importance of these teachings by a significant margin. Thus 91 percent of women said "helping the poor" was very important, compared to 77 percent of men. Similar differences were found with respect to "belief in Jesus' resurrection" (86 percent of women, 81 percent of men), "sacraments" (79 percent of women, 72 percent of men), and "Mary as Mother of God" (78 percent of women, 69 percent of men). However, when it came to the four teachings least often considered "very important" by Catholics, women's percentages were generally lower than men's. Women were less inclined than men to see "teachings that oppose abortion" (42 percent women, 46 percent men), "teaching authority claimed by the Vatican" (39 percent women, 45 percent men), or "a celibate male clergy" (28 percent women, 30 percent men) as very important. Only the teachings that oppose the death penalty were affirmed by a greater percentage of women (37 percent) than men (33 percent). It is especially significant that teachings that were stressed so strongly by Pope John Paul II are regarded as "very important" by fewer than half the Catholic men and women surveyed in 2005. These teachings concern abortion (44 percent) and a celibate male clergy (29 percent).[9]

The erosion of authority is further seen when the study's authors compare the data on how many Catholics placed "final moral authority in Church leaders" on certain sexual questions in 1987 and 2005. In 1987 Catholic men and women registered very similar positions. At that time, "between one in three and one in four Catholic men and women, respectively, continued to see Church leaders as the locus of moral authority on these teachings." However, by 2005 a pattern of gender differences was evident: "women looked more to themselves and less to Church leaders than did men" on a range of sexual teachings. The percentage of Catholics who saw the individual rather than Church leaders as the "proper locus of moral authority" was greater for women than men on several questions:

divorce and remarriage (45 percent women, 38 percent men)
contraception (66 percent women, 55 percent men)
homosexual behavior (51 percent women, 39 percent men)
nonmarital sex (51 percent women, 41 percent men)

The sociologists conclude: "Catholics have increasingly seen authority in individual consciences. As the acceptance of Church leaders as the locus of moral authority declines, individual authority increases."[10]

Comparative data regarding support for women's leadership roles between surveys in 1999 and 2005 is also interesting. Support for women as Eucharistic ministers rose from 83 to 90 percent for Catholics of varying backgrounds and levels of commitment to the Church, as did support for women deacons, from 77 to 81 percent. Support for women priests declined only slightly, from 64 to 63 percent. Highly committed Catholics tended to be less supportive of women deacons and priests than those of low or medium commitment, but the study's authors note that "even among highly committed Catholics, 68 percent expressed support for women deacons and 40 percent supported women priests."[11] The fact that support for women priests has been relatively stable is especially significant in view of the Vatican's having excommunicated the seven founders of the Roman Catholic Womenpriests movement after these women were ordained in an unauthorized ceremony on the Danube in 2002.[12]

It should be alarming to church leaders that many women are experiencing alienation from the religious tradition that once gave meaning to their lives. One might paraphrase a famous remark of the nineteenth-century Anglican churchman Matthew Arnold. Responding to the intellectual tensions of his day, Arnold had declared: "At the present moment two things about the Christian religion must surely be clear to anybody with eyes in his head. One is, that men cannot do without it; the other, that they cannot do with it as it is."[13] Arnold's first premise has surely been discredited, and we must amend his second point to something like, "Whether or not modern persons can do without the church, many women cannot do with it as it is." Arnold was right to see how urgent it was to adapt to the changed intellectual climate of the nineteenth century, and it is equally urgent now for the tradition to adapt to the changed moral climate of today, which takes for granted the full human dignity of females, and assumes that women and men are radically equal in their humanity. As theologian Margaret Farley has pointed out, we are living in an era when "profound conceptual and symbolic shifts have occurred in relation to gender differentiation and sex roles. Indeed, so profound are these changes and so far-reaching their consequences that one is tempted to say that they are to the moral life of persons what the Copernican revolution was to science or what the shift to the subject was to philosophy."[14]

To convey the significance of this change in moral climate, I find it useful to call on metaphor, and to think of the cultural transition now in progress as the ending of a sexist ice age. Recalling what the retreat of the glacier that once covered part of this country has meant for the landscape gives us an analog for grasping what the end of religiously legitimated sexism will entail for Christianity. The ice age metaphor has the merit of helping us realize the scope of the changes involved, but it can be misleading if we imagine that the transition from the old order of injustice between the sexes to a new order of equality and mutuality is an inevitable natural event. Rather we have here an ethical task for all who recognize the truth of the new vision. Moral theologians wisely stress that the first step in discerning moral obligation is to get a picture of the situation calling for a moral response. In other words, we need to interpret what is going on before we can prudently decide what we should be doing about it.

The situation of injustice

When we focus on the question "What is going on with respect to women and the church?" the answers are multiple and complex. But one thing remains true: even today, some degree of oppression persists. Across the board many females continue to suffer unjust discrimination on the basis of sex. The degrees and forms of this sexism vary widely, and not everyone acknowledges the problem, but a good deal of sexism remains even in the dioceses and local congregations known generally as progressive. Nor should this be altogether surprising, for patriarchy has held sway in our culture for millennia, and removing its influence from our structures and our psyches is not something that can be done overnight. By patriarchy I mean a social system biased in favor of maleness, which tends to absolutize male authority and to privilege the class of ruling males.[15] Moreover, patriarchy has been religiously legitimated in Christianity by an overwhelming bias in favor of masculine imagery for the deity.

The child named Sylvia was on to something when she wrote in a letter, "Dear God, Are boys better than girls? I know you are one, but try to be fair." Thanks to the influence of theologians such as Rosemary Radford Ruether and Elizabeth Johnson, there may be fewer children who think this way today than Sylvia did in the 1970s, but her question still reflects the experience of many Catholics.[16]

It is now more than forty years since Mary Daly's 1968 book, *The Church and the Second Sex*, called widespread attention to injustice toward women in the church, and since then efforts have been made, both feeble and strenuous, to mitigate this injustice.[17] And because change has occurred in the ensuing decades, many are puzzled that the pressure for change continues to mount despite the improvements that have occurred. To understand why this is the case, it helps to recognize that oppression is not basically a quantitative phenomenon.

The essence of oppression is not the fact that, say, three hundred unfair things are being done to an oppressed group, so that if twenty-five or fifty, or even two hundred and fifty of these practices were stopped things would really be better. True, things might feel better in a lot of ways. But the very fact that the number of unfair practices is reduced highlights the injustices that remain. The partial remedies make the oppressed wonder all the more, "Why are things this way?" Instead of seeing oppression as simply a collection of unfair practices, it is better to view it in religious terms. Essentially oppression involves a situation where human beings attempt to play God over other human beings. They do this by defining the meaning and purpose of others' lives without respect for the mystery that is basic to human personhood. This is the first stage in what may be termed the process of oppression. The second stage occurs when those whose lives are defined internalize the oppressor's judgment of their purpose and worth. In other words, there are both objective and subjective dimensions to oppression—factors outside the self, and factors within. Psychological oppression is harder to document than the grosser forms of physical oppression such as slavery or the laws of apartheid, but in both forms the mystery and worth of a person are violated by an oppressor's attempting to define what someone else is good for, and not good for. It matters little whether this is done in harsh tones, or in gentler ones, such as by invoking theories of "woman's special nature" or "the feminine role in God's plan." The violation of personhood by others' powers of definition is the issue. Nor should we fail to recognize that there does not have to be someone deliberately causing or acquiescing to the oppression if the social and mental structures of domination and subordination are in place. For the terrible thing about oppression is that once it is internalized, it perpetuates itself without need of deliberate decision or physical force.

In the last several decades awareness about sexism in church and society has spread at a phenomenal rate. Women and men alike are experiencing conflict between their ideals of equality and the discriminatory reality they encounter in worship and other dimensions of church life. And these new perceptions have yielded a range of responses to the new consciousness. Many deserve praise for the ways they have worked to overcome sexism in the church. One thinks of those who first welcomed women to seminaries as students, faculty members, and spiritual directors. One thinks of the priests who signed their names to the charter of Priests for Equality in 1975, thereby dissenting publicly from official Vatican teaching on women's ordination, and insuring that they would not be called to serve as bishops.[18] One thinks of Ray Bourgeois, a Maryknoll priest whose outspoken advocacy of women's ordination led in 2012 to his laicization and dismissal from his religious community after 45 years of membership.[19]

It is crucial, however, not to limit attention to the responses of those already in power in the church, who are still exclusively male, but instead to attend to the responses of women to our growing awareness of being connected by ties of faith to an institution that has been a major culprit in our oppression. I am interested in asking: What is correct "church practice" for female moral agents in view of the institutionalized injustice toward women in Catholicism? What is God enabling and requiring us to be and to do?

A map of women's responses to ecclesial oppression

To approach this question we might begin by considering several types of responses that women are making to the institutional church today. It is useful, in fact, to analyze the relationship between "women" and "church" as a contemporary case of the recurring debate within the Christian tradition that theologian H. Richard Niebuhr probed in his classic study of 1951, *Christ and Culture*. I am suggesting that the same dynamics Niebuhr found in the tension between Christ and culture, or between the gospel and the social environment in which it is lived, are also present in the tension we see today between women and the church. In applying Niebuhr's method to a problem he did not address, I am aware that Niebuhr himself said that the title *Christ and Culture* is a shorthand phrase expressing a recurrent dilemma within the tradition, a debate that has been formulated in a wide variety of terms in the past. He mentions, for example, the relations of Protestantism and capitalism, or Pietism and nationalism, among others. In our day the recurrent debate includes the dialectic between "women" and "church."[20]

As Niebuhr reminds us, the "method of typology" is "historically inadequate," which is to say that the categories are useful as an aid to thinking but should not be applied rigidly to data more complex than any heuristic tool can accommodate.[21] No typology or map can capture the rich variety of life, but properly understood a typology can help to orient those who are searching for answers to ethical questions. We can profitably adapt his typology of responses to the "Christ and culture" tension as a heuristic aid for assessing a confusing contemporary scene. All five of Niebuhr's categories— Christ of culture, Christ against culture, Christ above culture, Christ and culture in paradox, and Christ transforming culture—are useful for answering the question of what is going on with respect to women and the institutional church. Moreover, the fifth model, which Niebuhr called "transformationist," provides what I consider an ideal answer to the question of what should be going on. In other words, women are transforming the church, and to the extent that their energy for reform represents the values of love, truth, and justice, they ought indeed to be doing so.

One of the reasons the map of types of responses cannot do full justice to the complexities involved is that "women" are never simply women in general. Besides being female a woman also belongs to an age group, a racial/ethnic group, and a social/economic class. She lives in a certain geographic region and a certain sort of neighborhood within that region. She works at home or in various other places, or more likely, in both. And her life is colored by all sorts of relationships, including her relationship to religious authorities. However useful our model may be, we still need to keep in mind that the concrete reality of women is much more complex than the abstraction "women" suggests. Furthermore, a full analysis would need to attend to the enormous variety on the "church" side of the relationship, noting, for example, the vast differences among Catholic dioceses as well as among parishes within each diocese. Nevertheless it remains true that an abstract model can shed light on our experience, and it is to this model of five ways in which women are relating to the church that I now turn.

Type 1: Women Against the Church

The dissonance experienced when women discover the gap between Christian ideals of love and justice and the sexism of Christian theology and church practice is often too great to be endured. Four decades ago the president of Church Women United in a major city told me that in her Presbyterian congregation the study group on women in the Bible was the quickest exit route from the church for some women. It is not surprising that women once loyal to the church do an about-face when they apprehend the magnitude of Christian patriarchy's betrayal of gospel ideals. The model of opposition, or "Women Against the Church," expresses their alienation well. Such opposition is evident in the anger of formerly Catholic women who have abandoned the church for neopagan, postchristian, or secular feminist groups or who seek to develop their spirituality exclusively in individualized ways. It is no exaggeration to say that some of these alienated women now regard the faith they once cherished to be a form of blindness or even a destructive addiction akin to alcoholism. One hears now and then the phrase "recovering Catholic" as an expression of such feelings.

The feminist philosopher Mary Daly (1928–2010) was an influential spokeswoman for this type. Although as a young woman Daly had earned doctoral degrees in Catholic theology, and had voiced in her first book, *The Church and the Second Sex* (1968), the hope that women could gain equality in the church, she soon became convinced that all Christian traditions are hopelessly patriarchal. Thus in a dramatic move on 14 November 1971 she led an "exodus" of women from Harvard Memorial Chapel, and in 1973 she articulated her opposition to patriarchal religion in the volume *Beyond God the Father.*[22] The fifth chapter of this book, "The Bonds of Freedom: Sisterhood as Anti-Church," names the response of opposition clearly. It is as if Tertullian's famous question from the third century, "What has Athens to do with Jerusalem?" has been reformulated as "What have women to do with Vatican City?" and answered with a resounding, "Women who respect themselves should have nothing to do with the oppressive patriarchal institutions of Christianity." Exactly how many women have totally rejected the church is difficult to know, but we can be sure there are quite a few, and their numbers are growing. In a volume he wrote with his sister, Mary Greeley Durkin, sociologist Andrew Greeley estimated that as of 1984 between one million and a million and a half Catholic women of all ages did not attend church regularly because of a "complex interplay of imagery" regarding God, Woman, Mother, and Church. He also found emphasis on gender roles to be a significant factor in the nonattendance of some 200,000 young Catholic men.[23] The 2001 study of American Catholics by William V. D'Antonio and his colleagues did not focus so directly on women's anger, but it acknowledged that women "feel increasingly alienated from the organizational life of the Church, in part because of the Vatican's views on women's issues."[24]

Type 2: Women Content with the Church

A second type involves an unquestioning acceptance of patriarchal Catholic culture. Although sociological research suggests that fewer Catholic women today are in full agreement with official teachings and practices regarding women than was the case a generation ago, many can still be called "Women Content with the Church." The sisters associated with communities belonging to the Conference of Major Superiors of Women Religious (CMSWR) tend to reflect this position, as do many laywomen. In many instances their experiences within the tradition have been so positive that feminist complaints are simply not of interest to these women. Some may take inspiration from works such as Genevieve Kineke's *The Authentic Catholic*

Woman, or her website, "Feminine Genius: Authentic Catholic Womanhood." Kineke, who converted to Catholicism in 1984, has enthusiastically endorsed the teachings of Pope John Paul II on women and sexuality, and declared "the very Church I had entered was the paradigm for my own life and the life of every woman."[25] While a critical feminist analysis might speak of their internalized oppression, the women reflecting this type do not see things this way. Rather, they feel comfortable with their subordinate role, which they associate with the divine plan. Because of their willingness to serve in token capacity on boards and committees, and because of their predictable deference to male authority, such women are often hindrances to the reform agenda. It is difficult for feminist women to be patient with their sisters who see things this way, but it ought to be admitted that many feminists once felt fairly comfortable themselves in patriarchal religious culture. Moreover, today's "women content with the church" are responding to many values of traditional Catholicism that have provided hope and meaning to millions over the centuries. In their uncritical esteem for Church authority, they reflect the reaction to secularism and postmodernity that has been named "evangelical Catholicism." Journalist John L. Allen has noted that during the papacy of John Paul II the church became "steadily more evangelical," although in contrast to Protestant evangelicalism the emphasis is on the authority of the magisterium rather than biblical fundamentalism.[26]

Some women content with the church have been troubled by the efforts of Catholic feminists to influence the hierarchy on such matters as inclusive language for liturgy and equal roles for women in ministry and decision-making. They have sought to defend the institution by insisting that the feminists seeking reforms do not speak for all Catholic women. A clear example of this position is found in Helen Hull Hitchcock's 1995 essay about a group she helped to establish in 1984, "Women for Faith and Family: Catholic Women Affirming Catholic Teaching." Organized when the U.S. Bishops were holding hearings as they attempted to prepare a pastoral letter on women's concerns, Women for Faith and Family (WFF) prepared an eight point "Affirmation for Catholic Women" that endorses "the teaching of the Catholic Church on all matters dealing with human reproduction, marriage, family life and roles for men and women in the Church and in society."[27] The statement has subsequently been translated into several languages and circulated in various countries. By 1994 a list of 40,000 names of U.S. Catholic women signers was presented to Pope John Paul II, and the group continues to solicit endorsements and to publish online and print editions of the quarterly journal *Voices*.[28] Although there is strong support for the "Affirmation" among a substantial group of U.S. Catholic women, the sociological surveys indicate that they are not the majority in this country. Their claim, however, is that they are the "orthodox" and "faithful" women, with the clear implication that the dissenters are not.

The rhetoric of WFF has been explicitly anti-feminist, which posed something of a problem when Pope John Paul II advocated in his 1995 encyclical *Evangelium Vitae* the concept of a "new feminism":

> In transforming culture so that it supports life, women occupy a place in thought and action which is unique and decisive. It depends on them to promote a "new feminism" which rejects the temptation of imitating models of "male domination" in order to acknowledge and affirm the true genius of women in every aspect of the life of society and overcome all discrimination, violence and exploitation. (*EV* #91).[29]

Since then one finds in the WFF literature a nuanced willingness to affirm the possibility of a form of Catholic feminism that, in the words of *Evangelium Vitae,* promotes "the flourishing of men and women and children in the culture of love," accompanied by strong reservations about the risks involved in employing terms such as "feminism" and "empowerment," tainted as they are by secular ideas of women's rights. WFF materials continue to use "feminism" as a term for the enemy, although it is sometimes qualified as "ideological feminism," "organized feminism," or "contemporary feminism."[30]

As with Niebuhr's original typology, my first two categories—opposition and agreement, or "Women Against the Church" and "Women Content with the Church"—represent opposite extremes. Those who see perfect consonance between their womanhood and the official church value the tradition uncritically and reject out of hand the feminist critique of religious patriarchy. The "women against the church," by contrast, embrace feminism and reject Catholicism with equal force.[31] The remaining three categories differ from these first two in that they are centrist positions, which accept some elements of both sides of the polarity. That is, they see some validity in the tradition as well as in the feminist critique of Catholicism. Where they differ is in how they respond to the tension.

Type 3: Women Above the Church

This response can be envisioned as the "feminist spiritual community on a pedestal." There is a romantic and sectarian quality to this response. Women who believe the gospel is essentially meaningful and liberating, but whose experience within actual Catholic communities has been oppressive, may well opt for a solution whereby a strain of Christian feminism becomes the "new church" for them. Having been nurtured in a patriarchal faith, they leave their church behind, but not in total angry rejection. Rather, the old religious affiliations are simply cast off like outgrown, constricting garments, and a new circle of worship and discussion celebrates the liberation its members experience from the old ways of internal and external oppression. What distinguishes this model is the tendency to add feminism on top of the Catholic heritage and then to exist as comfortably as possible on the summit, with little concern for the ambiguous church structures below, which are regularly experienced by the unenlightened.

This type is reflected in the words of a Catholic laywoman in her forties, who answered a survey about her involvement with feminist spirituality groups thus:

> "Because I worship in a small community not affiliated with the archdiocese, I am free not to be angry. I am no longer controlled by church authority; therefore I am freer to act, to challenge the church."

One sees it even more clearly in the response of a woman religious, then in her fifties, who replied to the same survey thus:

> "I believe that we women must go our own ways and let patriarchy and its institutions, *all* of them—religious, political, economic—die of their own dead weight! The sooner we let go, the sooner they die. We can do ritual and spirituality, and we don't need males to do it."

Both were among the 7000 women surveyed by Miriam Therese Winter, Adair Lummis, and Allison Stokes in a project funded by the Lilly Endowment in the early 1990s to investigate the situation of U.S. women who had roots in Christianity and also some involvement in feminist spirituality groups.[32]

Another instance of this position is found in an autobiographical essay by Janet Kalven, who converted from Reform Judaism to Catholicism as a young woman in 1937, and has since 1942 been a core member of the Grail, a laywomen's movement based near Cincinnati. Prior to 1970 her faith was oblivious to sexism, but as Kalven encountered feminist writings she grew increasingly critical of "the great gap between the gospel values and the behavior of too many churchmen." As she recalls, "After Vatican II, I began to see the Catholic Church as a way, not the way. I found it harder and harder to attend the local parish and finally stopped going altogether. I find my nourishment, my moments of contact with the sacred, in the various feminist circles I belong to."[33]

Type 4: Women and Church in Paradox

The fourth type involves holding contradictory allegiances to the insitutional church and to feminism. This position is fraught with tension, but a number of women choose to endure the tension because they see value and truth on both sides. Historian Linda A. McMillan has characterized this position vividly:

> Indeed, I sometimes feel like an oxymoron—trying to be both a feminist and a Catholic. I am a woman who can deconstruct the misogyny at the heart of the Roman Church yet still be nurtured by the familiar word and ritual of Sunday mass. I am a historian who can document the struggles of religious women for space and a voice through two millennia yet still actively participate in a local Catholic parish: teaching Sunday school, singing in the choir, and raising my son in this sacramental community. For me, to be a feminist and a Catholic is to live with contradiction and to continue the struggle for a voice in a church that is at times inhospitable but is also the place where my hope of faith is best nourished and supported.[34]

In some instances the tension is more a matter of practice than theory. One finds herself a citizen of two cultures, as it were, alternating between the parish and the women's spirituality group. Many find little or no nourishment themselves in the traditional Sunday worship service, but they continue to attend with their families because they see nothing else in place to help their children. Such women may repair elsewhere to meet their own religious needs, or they may simply let these needs suffer neglect. As a Catholic respondent to the sociological survey *Defecting in Place* by Winter, Lummis, and Stokes expressed it:

> "Right now I struggle with my own spirituality and the responsibility I feel for my children, fourteen and sixteen. Is it right to keep submerging my needs and stay in a community 'for them' which does not address, honor, celebrate my theological beliefs? I'm tired of institutional structures that require more giving. I give all week on the job, at home, and never feel affirmed that my work in education, which is my ministry, is enough. The 'sisterhood' gives so much to each person. I guess this is my church."[35]

There are often complex reasons for holding on to the tension, as is evident in these words of another respondent to the same survey, a woman religious:

> "I sometimes feel I have dropped out of the church. My Hispanic part keeps me in the Catholic Church. My woman part totally disowns the Catholic Church. I do feel the Catholic Church works for the 'poor,' in general for many Hispanics. Yet once the poor are middle-class, women are locked out."[36]

In other instances the tension is sustained with explicit attention to theory, whether theological, philosophical, or anthropological. Theologian Sara Butler, for example, a seminary professor and Trinitarian sister, has argued that the "theology of sex complementarity" promoted by Pope John Paul II "does full justice" to both the equality of men and women and to their different forms of embodiment.[37] She regards sexual difference as "an image of the Trinity" that celebrates the "'genius' or original gifts of both sexes."[38] She holds that the "noninterchangeble sexual roles—husband-wife,

father-mother—are personal, not merely biological, and they are
fundamental ways of fulfilling the vocation to love."[39] In laying out this
Christian anthropology, which she insists respects both equality and
difference, she does not advert to the historical fact that "women's
genius" has not had a voice in setting up the church system that
excludes females from sacramental leadership and ecclesiastical
decision-making. Nor does she seem to be troubled that the papal
insistence on affirming sexual difference has not influenced the
Vatican's position on inclusive language in the liturgy, which prohibits
such attention to sexual difference as would be found in saying, for
example, that "Christ died to save all men *and women*." Indeed, it
is a paradox to claim that women and men are both "equal" and
"complementary" in a system in which the powers of defining the
unique gifts of each and of assigning social and sacramental roles to
women and men rests exclusively with male officials.[40]

Mary Douglas (1921–2007), the eminent anthropologist and
author of *Natural Symbols* (1970), also exemplified a paradoxical
stance insofar as she believed that the role of women in the church
is inadequate, but opposed women's ordination. In a 1996 article, "A
Modest Proposal: A Place for Women in the Hierarchy," she argued
that rather than abandoning the gendered emphasis on the "nuptial
mystery" that has characterized Roman Catholicism, the church would
be better advised to express it more fully by reforming the hierarchy
so as to include a "women's commission" with full authority at a high
level that could balance the authority of the cardinals. Drawing on
the example of African societies that have both female and male
principles of control, with women organized and led by women and at
the highest level "representing the interests of the whole community,"
Douglas proposed that the church should entrust certain matters
to a special "Women's Commission on Doctrine." She saw that the
central issue would be determining the "areas of faith and morals"
to allocate to this commission, which would have "veto power" in its
sphere of responsibility. She suggested starting with areas related to
women's typical concern with life, including "contraception, abortion,
biogenetics, and euthanasia," but added that "it would be a pity to
restrict the range of topics referred to the commission."[41] What is
problematic here is Douglas's assumption that an organization that
has traditionally been so thoroughly patriarchal would be disposed to

create a commission with power to rival its own, much less to avoid restricting its range to a narrow focus on "women's concerns." Her desire to reform a tradition of "nuptial symbolism" in a way that would give women an adequate voice and real power seems unlikely to be fulfilled. Moreover, there are theological problems with the way such symbolism has been interpreted by church officials. As theologian Susan A. Ross has observed, "the Vatican's way of using the term *bridegroom* for both God and Jesus Christ seems to say that female language could never be used of God, and that Christ's maleness is essential to his saving work." Ross objects to this use of metaphor, and asserts, "If we cannot name God as both bride and bridegroom, we do violence to the image of God that each of us is."[42]

Type 5: Women Transforming Church

Women following this fifth model consciously claim both feminism and Catholicism, and they identify with the prophetic strain that has throughout history criticized injustice in the religious community as well as in secular society. Instead of remaining superior and separate, or else existing on a parallel track with the ambigious institutional church, these women see themselves as working to bring about a more just order within the church. Many, though certainly not all, of the women who belong to communities associated with the Leadership Conference of Women Religious tend to reflect this type of position. In some cases, sisters and laywomen who opt for this transformationist model have named themselves as church, and these women gather as such to celebrate their faith, to support each other in the struggle against patriarchy, and to plan ways of remedying injustice in the wider church as well as in society at large.

Whereas some women who seek to transform the church place great emphasis on their Catholic identity and focus their activities directly on church reform, others have moved to the edge of the institution and tend to have little energy for ecclesiastical issues, focusing their activities more broadly on a range of justice concerns. Theologian Sandra M. Schneiders has distinguished these two positions according to their characteristic spirituality, although she acknowledges that the divisions are artificial and most women who are both Catholic and feminist have some affiliation with each trend.

For purposes of analysis, however, Schneiders offers a useful way of distinguishing different impulses within the larger category of "women transforming church." "Feminist Catholics," she observes, are "those who are basically within the mainstream of the Christian tradition and whose spirituality remains recognizably Christian but who are involved in a continuous and radical criticism of the tradition." In contrast, "Catholic feminists" are "those who are still formally within the institutional church but who have, to a large extent, relocated their spirituality into what has been named 'womenchurch.'"[43]

Groups that represent the first impulse include the Women's Ordination Conference, established after the historic 1975 Detroit conference on women's ordination, and the more recent Roman Catholic Womenpriests movement, which began in 2002 with the ordinations of seven women on the Danube, as mentioned earlier in this book. Leaders of this movement explicitly claim Catholic identity, and have generally sought in planning ordination rituals to observe as many details of the official Sacramentary as possible, with a few consciously chosen exceptions required by feminism, such as inclusive language.

Reflective of what Schneiders terms the second impulse are many of those involved in the women-church movement. The designation first became popular after a November 1983 conference called "Woman Church Speaks" drew 1400 participants to Chicago for a weekend of feminist liturgies and workshops. Subsequently the sponsoring organizations established a network of Catholic feminist groups called Women-Church Convergence. Rosemary Radford Ruether, a prominent theologian as well as a leading participant and interpreter of the women-church movement, has accounted for the change to the plural name thus: "Recognizing that women belonged to many ethnic and class contexts, the earlier term 'woman-church' was later changed to the plural in order to avoid the racist, classist implication that there was one group of women (white, middle-class women) who represented normative 'woman.'"[44] There have since been three national women-church conferences, in Cincinnati (1987), Albuquerque (1993), and Chicago (2007). Over the years there have been many developments in the individuals and groups involved, and the movement currently attracts women of various backgrounds, although the national leaders are from Catholic backgrounds. Among the Catholics involved in the movement one can find instances of every type except "Women Content with the Church." A great many, however, exemplify the stance I have designated "Women Transforming Church," and reflect the complementary impulses Schneiders has associated with "feminist Catholics" and "Catholic feminists." They all, in her words, "desire passionately the conversion of the institution from the sin of sexism and know that this requires a full and final repudiation of patriarchy," and they all hope to build "a new religious dwelling for the disciples of Jesus." The "feminist Catholics," she goes on to say, "are struggling to find within the tradition the resources for bringing about this massive transformation," whereas the "Catholic feminists tend, if not to give up completely on the institution, to regard it as not worth their life's blood. For them the best way to bring about a new church is to start being that church now."[45]

Ruether has been a leading spokeswoman for the transformationist response, and in 1986 she published her liberationist ecclesiology in a volume called *Women-Church: Theology and Practice of Feminist Liturgical Communities.* There she discusses the growing phenomenon of women's intentional communities of faith and worship. Such communities are springing up, she notes, because "Christian feminists cannot wait for the institutional churches to reform themselves enough to provide the vehicles of faith and worship that women need in this time." The needs are simply too great to neglect:

Women in contemporary churches are suffering from linguistic deprivation and eucharistic famine. They can no longer nurture their souls in alienating words which ignore or systematically deny their existence. They are starved for words of life, for symbolic forms which fully and wholeheartedly affirm their personhood and speak truth about the evils of sexism and the possibilities of a future beyond patriarchy. They desperately need primary communities that nurture their journey into wholeness rather than constantly negating and thwarting it.[46]

Instead of waiting indefinitely, these women are taking responsibility for meeting their own religious needs.

Linking this development with the biblical heritage, Ruether describes the contemporary women-church movement as an exodus from patriarchy. She argues that historically the church is best understood as a "dialectical interaction" between two elements, namely the "historical institution" and the "spirit-filled community." This analysis lines up well with that of the biblical scholar Walter Brueggemann, who understands the history of the biblical tradition as a constant tension between "royal consciousness" on the one hand and "prophetic consciousness" on the other.[47] Combining the ideas of Ruether and Brueggemann, one might say that Spirit-filled feminist communities are today involved in the sacred task of keeping prophetic consciousness in dialectical tension with the patriarchal or royal consciousness now dominating the historical institution. From a Catholic perspective, however, it is particularly important to recognize the presence of the Spirit in the larger historical institution, and not to mistakenly assume that all truth and goodness reside with self-proclaimed feminists, much less that the latter are immune from error and sinfulness. As is the case with the typology of responses, so also the dialectic of Spirit-filled communities and historical institution is an abstraction that has heuristic value but cannot do full justice to the mystery that is the church.

Ruether is aware that the women-church movement may seem separatist, and indeed that some participate in it on such a basis, but she has argued strongly against any permanent separation from the tradition and she opposes the idea of women-church as an end in itself. Rather, women-church represents a necessary stage on a journey toward an "authentic community of exodus from oppression." She is enough of a realist, however, to know that such widely shared conversion from patriarchy is a long way off. She explains:

Patriarchy is too old and too deeply rooted both in our psyches and in our culture and collective life to be quickly analyzed, rejected and then overcome in new unity of men and women. We must think of Women-Church as a feminist counter-culture to the *ecclesia* of patriarchy that must continue for the foreseeable future as an exodus both within and on the edges of existing church institutions.

This means, Ruether adds, "neither leaving the church as a sectarian group, nor continuing to fit into it on its terms."[48]

From my perspective, this fifth model (Women Transforming Church) is in principle the most adequate one, for it does better justice to the reality of Christianity's ambiguous heritage, which has always combined aspects of liberation and oppression, than do either of the extreme models, those of agreement (Women Content with the Church) and opposition (Women Against the Church). Furthermore, the transformationist model seems to offer over the long term a more realistic and responsible answer to the current dilemma than does the retreat to separatism. Although in some cases a strategic withdrawal may be necessary, the Women Above the Church model tends to lack a principle of self-criticism and to neglect the complex historical and social nature of women's reality, which always includes relationships with men and the next generation. Likewise the transformationist model is usually preferable to the balancing act of the Women and Church in Paradox model, which takes a high psychological toll, and also neglects the task of making Catholicism accountable to its best ideals. Still, there are possibilities and values latent in all five types of response, and women need to discern for themselves which response is most appropriate in their particular circumstances.

Concluding observations

In sum, then, the answer to the question of how women are responding to ecclesiastical patriarchy is that all five sorts of responses are being made today: there are women content with the church, and women utterly opposed to it; there are women who opt for a sectarian solution somewhere above the church, and women who paradoxically maintain church membership on the institution's terms while at the same time claiming feminist values; and finally, there are women dedicated to transforming the church into a community of liberation from patriarchy. On the normative level I have claimed that the fifth is generally the most adequate response, and to conclude I shall sketch what a transformationist response ought to involve.

In the first place, Catholic women who follow the ideals of Women Transforming Church should strive to be as consistently transformationist as possible. This will mean developing a reform movement that flourishes in dialectical, transformative tension with the larger church. They should also strive to be in respectful and loving relationship with the many women in the pews who do not share their feminist vision or agenda.[49] Their movement should be one that beckons the entire Catholic community to be more faithful to gospel ideals of justice and mutuality, and these ideals should be reflected in relationships and organizational structures. Transformationist women need to provide sustenance for their spiritual lives, to integrate feminism with their experiences of the sacred, and to challenge and support one another in the struggle for liberation. They should not, however, retreat permanently to sectarian isolation and complacency, nor be governed by patriarchal definitions of what church membership requires. The task is to claim the Catholic tradition as their own and take responsibility for shaping its future.

And what of the brethren? Transformationist men should share the egalitarian feminist vision. They should support and encourage transformationist women and they should design creative ways to facilitate their own liberation from patriarchy. This will entail respecting the need for female caucuses within the broader feminist community, and sometimes establishing their own male feminist caucuses in which to strategize, sort out, and celebrate their liberation.

Finally, transformationist women and men should be self-critical. Change, even in the right direction, involves loss of some sort, and often has unintended consequences. For this reason, agents seeking change will do well to cultivate patience, respect for tradition and legitimate authority, awareness of the complexity of a global church, and a spirit of careful discernment. Moreover, the transformationist ideal is not easily fulfilled, and there is always the risk of slipping into one of the other responses for less than adequate reasons. In fact, the five types are more than categories for analyzing how women in general are responding; the typology is also a useful tool for scrutinizing one's own inner conflicts and inconsistencies. The shades of thoughtless accommodation, indiscriminate rejection, romantic sectarianism, and timid biculturalism lurk in all our psyches. The Woman Content with the Church surfaces when we repress our anger against oppression or fail to see the injustice in our communities, even the ones we name women-church; the Woman Against the Church emerges when we indulge that anger indiscriminately, or fail to seek constructive alternatives to what we are critiquing. The Woman Above the Church appears when we yield to complacency and let the supportive community of co-feminists become the only group that matters. And the Woman and Church in Paradox is evident in all our failures—whether from timidity, laziness, or plain muddleheadedness—to make the church of Christ the sign of hope to the nations that our just and compassionate God intends it to be.

There is reason, obviously, for even the most committed Catholic feminists, women and men alike, to repent and seek forgiveness for our sins and inadequacies. But in view of what we know of God—whose mercy is above all Her works and who is present with us both to will and to accomplish—there is even more reason to celebrate the liberation from personal as well as from social sin. My next point may already be obvious to many, but it is sometimes necessary to belabor the obvious. Given the fact of this liberation already in progress and coming into its fullness, it is fitting for Women Transforming Church to give thanks—indeed, to preside at Eucharist—and to do this in the name and memory of Jesus, whose ethical ideals, as his followers insisted from the beginning, included the belief that if it came to a choice, one should obey God and not men. Such an insight is attributed to Peter himself in Acts 5, where Luke describes a controversy between early Christian apostles and first-century Jewish leaders. This text has bearing on the present controversy between Catholics with the new moral vision of equality and certain contemporary church officials. Much has changed, but then as now, the issue involves authority:

So they brought them [the apostles] and stood them before the Council; and the High Priest began his examination. "We expressly ordered you," he said, "to desist from teaching in that name; and what has happened? You have filled Jerusalem with your teaching, and you are trying to make us responsible for that man's death." Peter replied for himself and the apostles: "We must obey God rather than men." (Acts 5:27–9)

Today feminist women and men alike are hearing from the high priests of patriarchy, "We do not approve of your teaching." This is said at times with force—not the literal sword that threatened Peter and his companions, but certainly with the bureaucratic sword. And in Acts 5:38–9 we are told of a Jewish thinker whose wisdom stopped the sword on that occasion. What Gamaliel said to the high priest then remains instructive today:

> "[L]eave them alone. For if this idea of theirs or its execution is of human origin, it will collapse; but if it is from God, you will never be able to put them down, and you risk finding yourselves at war with God." (*NEW ENGLISH BIBLE*)

Gamaliel's words did not prevent the flogging and the orders to stop speaking in Jesus' name. But neither did these measures prevent the gospel from being preached.

Notes

1 David Gibson, *The Coming Catholic Church: How the Faithful Are Shaping a New American Catholicism,* rev. ed. (New York: HarperCollins, 2004), p. 75.

2 I discuss this point more fully in Anne E. Patrick, "'Toward Renewing the Life and Culture of Fallen Man': 'Gaudium et Spes' as Catalyst for Catholic Feminist Theology," in *Questions of Special Urgency,* ed. Judith Dwyer (Washington, DC: Georgetown University Press, 1986), pp. 55–78. Leonardo Boff examines the ethics of church practice critically in the light of faith in *Church: Charism and Power* (New York: Crossroad, 1985). For more recent discussions, see Jean M. Bartunek, Mary Ann Hinsdale, and James F. Keenan, eds., *Church Ethics and Its Organizational Context: Learning from the Sex Abuse Scandal in the Catholic Church* (Lanham, MD: Rowman & Littlefield, 2006), and Bishop Geoffrey Robinson, *Confronting Power and Sex in the Catholic Church* (Collegeville, MN: Liturgical Press, 2008).

3 See James M. Gustafson, *Can Ethics Be Christian?* (Chicago: University of Chicago Press, 1975), p. 179.

4 Pew Forum on Religion & Public Life, "Reports: Summary of Key Findings," http://religions.pewforum.org/ reports?sid=ST2008022501236. Accessed 27 February 2008.

5 William V. D'Antonio, James D. Davidson, Dean R.Hoge, Mary L. Gautier, *American Catholics Today: New Realities of Their Faith and Their Church* (Lanham, MD: Rowman & Littlefield, 2007), p. 148.

6 David Gibson, *The Coming Catholic Church: How the Faithful Are Shaping a New American Catholicism* (New York: HarperSanFrancisco, 2003), p. 66.

7 D'Antonio et al., 2007, p. 69.

8 Gibson, p. 69. Gibson quotes here from William V. D'Antonio, James, D. Davidson, Dean R. Hoge, and Katherine Meyer, *American Catholics: Gender, Generation, and Commitment* (Walnut Creek, CA: AltaMira Press, 2001), p. 145.

9 D'Antonio et al., 2007, p. 94.

10 Ibid., pp. 97–8.

11 Ibid., pp. 120–1.

12 Documents from the Congregation for the Doctrine of the Faith include the 10 July 2002 "Warning Regarding the Attempted Priestly Ordination of Some Catholic Women," the 5 August 2002 "Decree of Excommunication Regarding the Attempted Priestly Ordination of Some Catholic Women," and the 21 December 2002 "Decree on the Attempted Priestly Ordination of Some Catholic Women." Cited here from Deborah Halter, *The Papal "No": A Comprehensive Guide to the Vatican's Rejection of Women's Ordination* (New York: Crossroad, 2004), pp. 235–9.

13 Matthew Arnold, *God and the Bible* (Boston: James R. Osgood and Company, 1876), p. xiii.

14 "New Patterns of Relationship: Beginnings of a Moral Revolution," *Theological Studies* 36 (1975): 628.

15 For an historical discussion of this topic, see Gerda Lerner, *The Creation of Patriarchy* (New York: Oxford University Press, 1986). In general, patriarchy may profitably be understood as a social or structural manifestation of the attitude of sexist discrimination against women. For an ethical analysis of "sexism," see Patricia Beattie Jung, "Give Her Justice," *America* 150 (14 April 1984): 276–8. With Jung, I understand the terms "sexism" and "feminism" as dialectically related. I employ "feminist" here in a broad sense to indicate a position that involves (1) a solid conviction of the equality of women and men, and (2) a commitment to reform society, including religious society, so that the full equality of women is respected, which requires also reforming the thought systems that legitimate the present unjust social order. Both women and men can thus be feminist, and within this broad category there is enormous variety in levels of commitment, degrees of explicitness of commitment, and, of course, opinions regarding specific problems and their solutions. For further discussions of "Patriarchy" and "Sexism," see Rosemary Radford Ruether's entries in Letty M. Russell and J. Shannon Clarkson, eds., *Dictionary of Feminist Theologies* (Louisville: Westminster John Knox Press, 1996).

16   Sylvia is quoted from Eric Marshall and Stuart Hample's 1977 book, *Children's Letters to God,* in *Words and Women: New Language in New Times,* eds. Casey Miller and Kate Swift (Garden City, NY: Anchor Books, 1977), p. 70. Corrective theological work is found in such volumes as Rosemary Radford Ruether, *Sexism and God-Talk: Toward a Feminist Theology* (Boston: Beacon Press, 1983), and Elizabeth A. Johnson, *She Who Is: The Mystery of God in Feminist Theological Discourse* (New York: Crossroad, 1992).

17   Mary Daly, *The Church and the Second Sex* (New York: Harper & Row, 1968). Daly subsequently published a revised edition of this work (Boston: Beacon Press, 1975), disagreeing in a new "Postchristian Feminist Introduction" with her former position that equality between men and women in the church is both possible and desirable. Indeed, she offers a chapter-by-chapter critique of her own work, describing the "early Daly" as having been deceived by a cloud of post-Vatican II optimism that prevented her from grasping "the fact that it was not ironic but rather quite consistent with its principles that her church would oppose the liberation of women", 1975, p. 17.

18   Originally published in 1975 with the signatures of 75 Roman Catholic clergymen, the Priests for Equality Charter discusses 17 "affirmations" that include "equal participation in the worship of our Church" and "a right to equal opportunity for ordination to the priesthood" (Quoted here from the 25th Anniversary Edition of the charter, https://www.quixote. org/pfe/pfe_charter.html, accessed 15 October 2008). According to http://cso.quixote.org/pfe (accessed 15 October 2008), by 1979 some 2300 priests had endorsed the statement, including 600 Jesuits. Under the sponsorship of the Quixote Center near Washington, D.C., Priests for Equality has published inclusive language translations of the scriptures: *The Inclusive New Testament* (1994), *The Inclusive Psalms* (1997), and *The Inclusive Hebrew Scriptures: Volume III—The Writings* (1999). The group's eighteen-year project culminated with the publication of *The Inclusive Bible: The First Egalitarian Translation* (Lanham, MD: Roman & Littlefield), 2007.

19   Bourgeois' participation in a 2008 women's ordination resulted in the Vatican insisting that he repudiate his public support for women's ordination or face dismissal from Maryknoll and laicization. Citing the obligation to follow his conscience, Bourgeois refused to do this, and in early 2012 Maryknoll officers reportedly held a vote on his dismissal without obtaining a majority, thus delaying the punishment.

Subsequently the Vatican's Congregation for the Doctrine of the Faith proceeded with a canonical dismissal and laicization on 4 October 2012. See Joshua J. McElwee, "Maryknoll: Vatican has dismissed Roy Bourgeois from order," 19 November 2012, http://ncronline.org/print/news/people/maryknoll-vatican-has-dismissed-roy-bourgeois-order (accessed 21 November 2012). For an account of his position, see Roy Bourgeois, MM, *My Journey from Silence to Solidarity*, ed. Margaret Knapke (Yellow Springs, OH: fxBear, 2012), a PDF version of which is available online at www.roybourgeoisjourney.org.

20 H. Richard Niebuhr, *Christ and Culture* (New York: Harper and Row, 1951), p. 10.

21 Ibid., p. 44.

22 Mary Daly, "The Women's Movement: An Exodus Community," in *Women and Religion: A Feminist Sourcebook of Christian Thought*, eds. Elizabeth A. Clark and Herbert Richardson (New York: Harper & Row, 1977), pp. 265–71. Daly's rejection of her earlier optimism is clearly stated in the claim: "The entire conceptual apparatus of theology, developed under the conditions of patriarchy, has been the product of males and serves the interests of sexist society", p. 267. She developed this claim in her second book, *Beyond God the Father: Toward a Philosophy of Women's Liberation* (Boston: Beacon Press, 1973). For her account of the Harvard Memorial "exodus," see Daly's *Outercourse: The Be-Dazzling Voyage* (New York: HarperSanFrancisco, 1992).

23 Andrew M. Greeley and Mary G. Durkin, *Angry Catholic Women* (Chicago: Thomas More Press, 1984), pp. 41–2, and 49. Greeley makes the following observation in the sociological analysis section of this work. "Obviously it would be desirable to study the situation of women in the Catholic Church from the point of view of a research project which was designed specifically with that goal in mind and which asked a variety of questions to be dictated by such an interest. However, until such a project is funded (and don't anyone hold their breath!) secondary analysis is a useful and valid though somewhat limited technique for understanding the problems of women in the Roman Catholic Church", p.12.

24 D'Antonio et al., *American Catholics*, p. 144.

25 Kineke is quoted here from her web page www.feminine-genius.com (accessed 30 September 2008). See also Genevieve Kineke, *The Authentic Catholic Woman* (Cincinnati: St Anthony Messenger Press, 2006). Since 1998 she has edited *Canticle*, a quarterly magazine for Catholic women.

26 John L. Allen, Jr., "The Triumph of Evangelical Catholicism," *National Catholic Reporter* (31 August 2007): 5. He notes that the movement is

a way of "pitching classical Catholic faith and practice in the context of pluralism, making it modern and traditional all at once." Allen has since discussed evangelical Catholicism more fully in *Future Church: How Ten Trends Are Revolutionizing the Catholic Church* (New York: Doubleday, 2009), pp. 54–94.

27 Helen Hull Hitchcock, "Women for Faith and Family: Catholic Women Affirming Catholic Teaching," in *Being Right: Conservative Catholics in America*, eds. Mary Jo Weaver and R. Scott Appleby (Bloomington: Indiana University Press, 1995), pp. 177–8. During 1983–92 the National Conference of Catholic Bishops held hearings and attempted to publish a pastoral letter on women's concerns. After four drafts and significant Vatican intervention, they failed to reach consensus and instead published the final draft as a committee report. See Thomas J. Reese, SJ, "Women's Pastoral Fails," *America* (5 December 1992): 443–4, and Mary Jo Weaver, *New Catholic Women*, second edition (1986; Bloomington: Indiana University Press, 1995), pp. xiii–xvi.

28 See the organization's website at http://www.wf-f.org/History.html for further information. A conservative Catholic website (http://www. catholicculture.org/culture/reviews), accessed 9 October 2008, comments in its review of WFF's website: "Women for Faith and Family is an excellent organization which represents about 50,000 Catholic women in the United States and abroad who express fidelity to the teachings of the Catholic Church in all matters of faith and doctrine." The WFF website, accessed 13 September 2011, indicates that 50,000 women have signed the "Affirmation for Catholic Women," which was modified slightly following the death of Pope John Paul II in 2005.

29 Quoted here from *Origins* 42: (6 April 1995). See also Ivy A. Helman, *Women and the Vatican* (Maryknoll, NY: Orbis Books, 2012), pp. 8–10.

30 In the Spring 1997 issue of *Voices* Hitchcock reported on a discussion about this matter at a Vatican Conference on Women sponsored by the Pontifical Council on the Laity in Rome in December 2006. She observed that a working group there had failed to reach consensus about using the terms "feminism" and "empowerment," and summarized its report thus: "The majority of the group agreed with Mary Ann Glendon [the Harvard University law professor who had been the Vatican's delegate to the 1995 United Nations Conference on Women in Beijing, and who later served as U.S. Ambassador to the Vatican during 2007–09] when she stated that it is a risk to use these terms and then asked why the Holy Father uses them. We thought that he uses these words as an instrument to reach out to everyone of good will by including those outside of the church." Hitchcock went on to conclude that "Our definition of 'feminism' is not to restrict it only to women, but to integrate the partnership between men and women, taking from *Evangelium Vitae,* 'the flourishing of men and women and children in the culture of love.'" Cited here from http://www.wf-f.org/ Vatican_WomenConference_Dec1996.html, accessed 1 September 2008. Glendon had earlier published her views in "A Glimpse of the New Feminism" in *America* (6 July 2006). There she objected to the "official," "old-fashioned" feminism of the 1970s for denigrating marriage, motherhood, and men; failing to tolerate dissent; and, "inattention to the practical problems of balancing work and family on a day-to-day basis." She voiced hope for a new, "more realistic, less ideological" feminism that will be "responsive, prudent and inclusive" and "radical" in the sense of promoting Pope John Paul II's ideal of a "new civilization of life and love." Cited here from http://www.americamagazine.org/content/article.cfm?article_id=11221, accessed 11 November 2008.

31 Some years ago, when I first applied Niebuhr's typology to the analysis of women and the church, I began by discussing "women content with the church," and then treated "women against the church." However, the former position has grown more complex in reaction to the latter one, and for this reason I have reversed the order here. See Anne E. Patrick, "Authority, Women, and Church: Reconsidering the Relationship," in *Empowering Authority: The Charisms of Episcopacy and Primacy in the Church Today,* eds. Patrick J. Howell, SJ, and Gary Chamberlain (Kansas City, MO: Sheed & Ward, 1990), pp. 17–33.

32 Miriam Therese Winter, Adair Lummis, and Allison Stokes, *Defecting in Place: Women Claiming Responsibility for Their Own Spiritual Lives* (New York: Crossroad, 1994), pp. 89 and 24. The investigators surveyed women "who are or once were within the Christian tradition and who are or once were part of a women's spirituality group", p. 6. They found that alienation was higher among Catholics ("82 percent of the Sisters and 81 percent of the laywomen surveyed often feel alienated from the church") than among Protestants, where "the proportion of women who feel alienated does not exceed 62 percent", p. 102. Their research turns up many more instances of "women and church in paradox" and "women transforming church" than it does "women above the church," and it also suggests that the three centrist positions are less easily distinguishable in practice than the previously discussed stances of "opposition" and "contentment." This may be due to the ambivalence accompanying the tension that Catholic feminists sustain, and it is a reminder that the types are ideal constructs, more useful for heuristic purposes than for historical description.

33 Janet Kalven, "Feminism and Catholicism," in *Reconciling Catholicism and Feminism? Personal Reflections on Tradition and Change,* eds. Sally Barr Ebest and Ron Ebest (Notre Dame, IN: University of Notre Dame Press, 2003), pp. 39, and 44–5. Kalven recounts the history of the Grail movement from an insider's perspective in *Women Breaking Boundaries: A Grail Journey, 1940-1995* (Albany: State University of New York Press, 1999).

34   Linda A. McMillan, "Telling Old Tales about Something New: The Vocation of a Catholic and Feminist Historian," in Ebest and Ebest, op. cit., p. 83. McMillan's essay also reflects the "transformationist" position, discussed below, when she speaks of her vocation as feminist historian: "The work that I have taken up as a historian . . . gives me something to contribute to devising new possibilities", p. 93.

35   Quoted in Winter, Lummis, and Stokes, p. 93.

36   Quoted in ibid., p. 88.

37   Sara Butler, MSBT, "Embodiment: Women and Men, Equal and Complementary," in *The Church Women Want: Catholic Women in Dialogue*, ed. Elizabeth A. Johnson (New York: Crossroad, 2002), p. 36. This essay is Butler's contribution to a dialogue among Catholic women of various perspectives, which took place under the auspices of the Catholic Common Ground Initiative.

38   Ibid., p. 42.

39   Ibid., p. 40.

40   Since the 1980s Butler, who once favored women's ordination, has grown convinced of the cogency of Pope John Paul II's teachings on the complementarity of the sexes and his theological reasons for reserving priestly ordination to men. Her fullest discussion of the topic is published as *The Catholic Priesthood and Women: A Guide to the Teaching of the Church* (Chicago: Hillenbrand Books, 2006). Butler's arguments have been countered by Jesuit theologian Robert J. Egan in a *Commonweal* essay, "Why Not? Scripture, History and Women's Ordination" (11 April 2008), pp. 11–27, with a follow-up discussion by Butler and Egan, "Women & the Priesthood," *Commonweal* (18 July 2008): 8–11. Although I emphasize paradoxical elements in Butler's position here, her stance also suggests a basic contentment with the power differences associated with gender roles in contemporary Catholicism. For further considerations of complementarity and its possibilities for a "new feminism" such as envisioned in *Evangelium Vitae,* see Michele M. Schumacher, ed., *Women in Christ: Toward a New Feminism* (Grand Rapids, MI: Eerdmans, 2004).

41   *Commonweal* (14 June 1996), pp. 14–15. Douglas has discussed these ideas further in "Sacraments, Society, and Women," in *Explorations in Anthropology and Theology,* eds. Frank A. Salamone and Walter Randolph Adams (Lanham, MD: University Press of America, Inc., 1997), pp. 231–44. She believed that the "idea of a high-powered Women's Commission" would have special appeal among

Third World Catholics, and that demand for such a commission would "call [Rome's] gender bluff" (p. 244) while preserving traditions and hierarchical structures she deems essential.

42 Susan A. Ross, "Can God Be a Bride? Some Problems with an Ancient Metaphor," *America* (1 November 2004): 14–15. Ross discusses these issues more fully in *Extravagant Affections: A Feminist Sacramental Theology* (New York: Continuum: 1998).

43 Sandra M. Schneiders, *Beyond Patching: Faith and Feminism in the Catholic Church,* rev. ed. (New York: Paulist Press, 2004), p. 95.

44 Rosemary Radford Ruether, "Women-Church: An American Catholic Feminist Movement," in *What's Left: Liberal American Catholics,* ed. Mary Jo Weaver (Bloomington: Indiana University Press, 1999), p. 50.

45 Schneiders, pp. 108–9.

46 Rosemary Radford Ruether, *Women-Church: Theology and Practice of Feminist Liturgical Communities* (San Francisco: Harper & Row, 1986), pp. 4–5.

47 See Walter Brueggemann, *The Prophetic Imagination* (Philadelphia: Fortress Press, 1978).

48 Ruether, *Women-Church,* pp. 61–2. For another early interpretation of the movement, see Miriam Therese Winter, "The Women-Church Movement," *The Christian Century* (1 March 1989): 227, cited here from http://www.religion-online.org/showarticle.asp?title=849 (accessed 27 September 2008). See also Mary E. Hunt and Diann L. Neu, eds., *Women-Church Sourcebook* (Silver Spring, MD: WATERworks Press, 1993); Sheila Durkin Dierks, *WomenEucharist* (Boulder, CO: WovenWord Press, 1997); and, Mary E. Hunt, "Women-Church," in *Encyclopedia of Women and Religion in North America,* vol. 3, eds. Rosemary Skinner Keller, Rosemary Radford Ruether, and Marie Cantlon (Bloomington: Indiana University Press, 2006), pp. 1243–49. Further information on the women-church movement is available at http://www.women-churchconvergence.org (accessed 23 September 2012).

49 Journalist Peter Steinfels has suggested that Catholic feminism would do well to address two "complications," which were evident to him at the 1993 Albuquerque gathering of Women-Church Convergence, namely "its unreadiness or incapacity to address boundaries and its distance from many Catholic women." See his Chapter 7: "Sex and the Female Church," from *A People Adrift: The Crisis of the Roman Catholic Church in America* (New York: Simon & Schuster, 2003), especially pp. 279–85.

3

A MINISTRY OF JUSTICE: THE 25-YEAR PILGRIMAGE OF THE NATIONAL ASSEMBLY OF RELIGIOUS WOMEN (NAWR/NARW)

"It is not the Gospel that changes; it is we who begin to understand it better. . . . The moment has arrived when we must recognize the signs of the times, seize the opportunity, and look far abroad."

—BLESSED JOHN XXIII, 1963[1]

Within a decade of the Second Vatican Council, Catholic women had brought progressive ideas on ministry to a level undreamed of by the bishops who approved the conciliar schemas. Over Thanksgiving weekend in 1975 a group of such women convened the historic Women's Ordination Conference in Detroit, Michigan, attracting some 1200 persons to consider the topic "Women in Future Priesthood Now." For the first time theologians of both genders gave major presentations on a question that had never been considered in such depth, and participants discussed the issues and prayed about them during liturgies. The gathering was an expression of solidarity among laywomen and women in religious vows (and some progressive men as well), who were united in a desire to open a renewed form of full sacramental ministry to women, but the majority of those who planned and attended the conference were sisters.[2]

The cooperation of many progressive individuals and groups contributed to the gathering's success, and one of these groups, the National Assembly of Women Religious (NAWR), which in 1982 became the National Assembly of Religious Women (NARW) in order to signify the full inclusion of lay members, is of particular interest because its members epitomized the postconciliar vision of Catholic life, and belief in the transforming power of this new vision. They embraced not only the ideals of "women transforming church" described in the last chapter, but also those of transforming secular society in the direction of greater justice for all. NAWR/NARW enjoyed a lifespan of only twenty-five years (1970–95), and its brief history provides a focused case study of the strengths and weaknesses of postconciliar idealism among progressive Catholic women. Religious sisters in the United States had a history of significant achievement—and no little willingness to follow their own lights in the face of hierarchical incompetence when it was encountered—but as we saw in the first chapter, their strategy before the council had been to minimize public expressions of conflict and to proceed with the "quiet grace" and "unshouted courage" of a subordinated class within a male-dominated religious institution.[3] Many sisters, moreover, had internalized the ideology of their own oppression and given the laity reason to think of them as "sweet," "pious," "unworldly," and generally incapable of assertive behavior or criticism of churchmen, much less organized opposition to a longstanding tradition such as the exclusively male priesthood.

In Detroit, however, hundreds of nuns spoke with the authority of their recently acquired graduate degrees in the sacred sciences and the power of their convictions. What accounted for this transformation, this willingness to object publicly to centuries-old practice and to assert their dissonant beliefs with such confidence? In addition to the paradigm shift from patriarchal to egalitarian-feminist understandings of virtue discussed earlier, here I will point to three other factors that contributed to the transformation of U.S. sisters after the council, which may be listed as educational, cultural, and religious.

In the first place, through farsighted planning in some communities, and also the intercongregational efforts of the Sister Formation Conference, women religious in this country were highly educated. Moreover, because most sisters had earned college and graduate degrees while holding jobs in schools or hospitals, habits of continuing education were well established among them. Thus when opportunities to study theology became available after the council, these women found ways to take advantage of them. In addition, many sisters with leadership experience in their own institutions were poised to bring this experience to bear on wider contexts once the council invited all Catholics to leave behind the protective parochialism of the post-Reformation and antimodernity eras and face the contemporary church and world with a new spirit of coresponsibility.[4]

A second factor contributing to the transformation of American Catholic sisters involved the wider cultural context of the United States during the 1960s and early 1970s. Sisters were profoundly affected by the social movements for civil rights, peace, and women's liberation, and many who participated in these struggles applied what they were learning about injustice to their own situation in the church.

Finally, and most importantly, nuns were explicitly religious in their reasons for doing what they did. Their faith in God was quite deep, and this allowed for the winds of change to blow furiously about them without disturbing their bedrock confidence in the Source of their existence. Their habits of prayer and spiritual reading led them to connect the above-mentioned cultural movements with the mandate experienced by biblical prophets to speak out in favor of changes that would bring justice to the oppressed. It was not a great leap to the position voiced by Nadine Foley, OP, at the Detroit conference in 1975: "The conflict between official Church pronouncements and the spirit of the Gospel with its message of freedom of persons through the redemptive activity of Jesus Christ is not merely theoretical."[5]

The 1975 Detroit conference, which was facilitated by other groups in addition to NAWR, took place when NAWR had been in existence five years. It had 103 diocesan organizations of sisters as council or senate members, with direct links to tens of thousands of nuns in these dioceses, and also some 3,500 dues-paying individual sisters as "grassroots" members, along with an unspecified number of clergy and lay associates. Within five years, however, membership had declined dramatically, to 23 sisters' councils or senates and 1,400 individual members, and although some gains were made after laywomen were admitted to full membership, the statistics of the early 1970s were never regained. By 1995 the decline in membership and turnover in the central office staff resulted in an insurmountable fiscal crisis, and NARW disbanded.[6]

Why did this group flourish so briefly? What led to its demise? What does this case signify for American Catholicism, and especially for progressive members of the church? I will suggest idealism as an important factor contributing to the group's decline. This organization's power was due in some measure to the way talented and dedicated women were able to articulate a mission that flowed directly from the Christian gospel, which they expressed in terms of commitment to "a ministry of justice." Once assembled, however, the idealists found it hard to choose among ways of focusing their efforts and structuring their membership. The conciliar spirit of openness and especially the value of inclusivity led them to invite increasingly diverse women into their ranks and governing board, and also led for a time to some unclarity about the Catholic identity of the organization. These changes contributed to the erosion of their original membership base. Although the ultimate explanation of NARW's demise was lack of funds, its collapse seems attributable, at least in part, to the increasing weight of its own idealism.

Despite its brief lifespan, NAWR/NARW's legacy has been enduring, and the group remains an important instance of progressive Catholic approaches to ministry in the United States. Its history illustrates several liberal postconciliar developments, notably an inclusive ecclesiology and a commitment to a feminist vision of social justice. Besides helping establish the Women's Ordination Conference, NAWR/NARW initiated the founding of the social justice lobby NETWORK in 1971 and fostered other local and national efforts for justice in subsequent years.[7] NETWORK, the first women-led Catholic social justice lobby in the United States, celebrated its fortieth anniversary on 14 April 2012. Four days later the organization was named in the Congregation for the Doctrine of the Faith's doctrinal assessment of the Leadership Conference of Women Religious (LCWR) as a group whose collaboration with LCWR the Vatican found problematic. As Simone Campbell, SSS, Executive

Director, has observed, this "catapulted Network into the spotlight along with LCWR," and led to the idea of a bus campaign that would criticize the federal budget that had been proposed by Catholic congressman Paul Ryan for failing to respect the real-life struggles of poor persons, and at the same time draw national attention to the ministries of Catholic sisters among the poor. The "Nuns on the Bus" tours in the summer and fall of 2012 drew widespread media attention to the sisters' campaign for a "faithful budget" that would respect the values of "faith, family, and fairness."[8]

Ministry, social justice, and justice for women

Although women's religious communities had worked in relative isolation from each other prior to the Second Vatican Council, the development of such groups as the National Catholic Education Association (1904), the Catholic Health Association (1915), the Sister Formation Conference (1952), and the Conference of Major Superiors of Women (1956, known after 1971 as the Leadership Conference of Women Religious, or LCWR), as well as diocesan organizations for educators and others, had provided some experiences of collaboration. Women religious built on these experiences with great energy in the years immediately after the council, when ideals of collegiality and coresponsibility gave impetus to the formation of sisters' councils and senates in various dioceses.[9] Nuns who had previously seen the apostolate mainly in terms of their duties in hospitals or schools staffed by their religious communities came increasingly to use the term "ministry" for their activities and grew interested in diverse expressions of apostolic zeal, on an inter-congregational basis as well as with lay colleagues. Sisters with experience in the civil rights movement or in local community-organizing activities were particularly influential in catalyzing the growth of new associations of women religious, first at local and regional levels, and eventually at the national level.[10]

By 1968 aspirations for a group linking U.S. and Canadian sisters' councils and senates were voiced at an assembly in Portland, Maine, and although this international ambition was never realized, the meeting did produce a 44-member task force that convoked some 1,500 U.S. sisters in Chicago the following year. There they endorsed the vision of a national assembly that would allow sisters a corporate voice to "express their stands on issues of concern to the Church in the world."[11] Ethne Kennedy, SH, who headed the task force, was elected chair when 1,800 women religious met in Cleveland in 1970 and ratified the constitution of the new NAWR.

From the first, NAWR's decision to have both corporate members (sisters' councils and senates) and individual members ("grassroots") resulted in ongoing tension between those whose ties to diocesan structures led them to proceed cautiously on controversial questions, and many of the individual members, who were not accountable in the same way to sisters in their home dioceses. Indeed, a progressive group led by Margaret Ellen Traxler, SSND, had already decided in 1969 to found another organization, the National Coalition of American Nuns, precisely to establish the forum for speaking out independently and promptly on issues that NAWR's more cumbersome structures made difficult to achieve.[12]

Twin themes of ministry and social justice have marked the history of NAWR/NARW. From the beginning, its periodical *Probe* devoted issues to particular ministerial topics, and soon after the organization was founded, Kennedy edited two volumes on ministry that provide a rich picture of progressive thought and action on the part of U.S. sisters in the early 1970s. The first book, *Women in Ministry: A Sister's View* (1972), contains articles on such topics as women and ordination, changing attitudes toward church law, ministry to Hispanic peoples, and women doing theology.[13] A year later NAWR published a collection of essays on sisters' new apostolic activities, *Gospel Dimensions of Ministry*. The feminist intent of both books was voiced in Kennedy's 1973 foreword, where she asserts that they show NAWR "taking a stand against discrimination" experienced by women, "whose creative input into civil and ecclesial affairs is negated and blocked by centuries-old prejudice."[14] Prominent in this second book is an essay on "Gospel Ministry" by Marjorie Tuite, OP, then chair of NAWR's Social Concerns Committee. This essay distills some of the material that she and community-relations trainer Sam Easley presented during numerous workshops on justice sponsored by NAWR and other organizations around the country during the 1970s. Tuite's insistence that women religious must "use power creatively—individually and corporately—to discover and empower the human agenda" found resonance among many NAWR members, who adapted community-organizing strategies to various Catholic contexts.[15]

The early books were followed by a number of booklets and resource packets, dealing with such topics as "Lifestyle" (1975), "Models of Ministry" (1979), "Economics: Women's Cry for Change" (1987), "Sexism Is a Sin" (1990), and "Creating Inclusive Community" (1992). The emphasis on education for social justice activism is a consistent theme of this literature, as of other NAWR/NARW activities, including the annual conventions and special workshops. The clientele for these meetings changed dramatically over the years, but the theme of "Empowerment, Justice, and Change," as a 1991 brochure describing several NARW skill training workshops was entitled, remained constant.

Throughout the organization's history members regularly received *Probe*, which started out as a simple typewritten, photo-offset periodical and then adopted a tabloid newspaper format in 1981. Originally subtitled "What are sisters thinking?" *Probe* began as a sounding board for sisters' views on religious life, the contemporary church, and new roles for women. It also provided summaries of convention resolutions and research reports on topics related to the organization's agenda, which had been expressed in terms of a "vision goal" adopted in 1972 by the second House of Delegates assembly, namely to exercise "a ministry of justice by the continuous use of our organized power to effect local and national policy for the liberation of all peoples from oppression."[16]

In 1973 NAWR established a committee on Women in Church and Society, which institutionalized the feminist spirit that had been growing within the group and helped to form a national network of sisters who acted regionally to promote consciousness-raising and feminist activism. A 1971 convention resolution had called for women's ordination to the diaconate, and the following year the delegate assembly had voiced support of women's "full participation in the priesthood." In June of 1974, Mary B. Lynch, the leader of the U.S. branch of the Association of Women Aspiring to the Presbyteral

Ministry, approached me, in my capacity as chair of this committee, about the feasibility of having a national meeting on ordination. We quickly drew up a plan for a small gathering, to be facilitated by NAWR board member Nancy A. Lafferty, FSPA, at the Catholic Theological Union in Chicago on 14 December 1974. It was this meeting of 31 representatives from seminaries, national Catholic organizations, and women's religious communities that led to the historic conference in Detroit the following November, "Women in Future Priesthood Now: A Call for Action," and the subsequent founding of the Women's Ordination Conference organization.

Meanwhile some 650 NAWR members, assembled in St Louis for the annual convention in August 1974, had gone on record overwhelmingly in support of eleven Episcopal women ordained to the priesthood in a controversial 29 July ceremony in Philadelphia. In a telegram sent 14 August, NAWR urged the Episcopal House of Bishops to "affirm and recognize" the ordinations because they are "a sign of hope authenticating the ministry of women in the church and a valid response to the Gospel values of human dignity, service, and justice."[17] NAWR also decided that year to help sponsor the ministry of Patricia Drydyk, OSF, for two years as national coordinator of sisters' efforts in support of the farm workers' movement. Twenty-one years later Drydyk, still National Coordinator of the Farm Worker Ministry, contributed an article to the penultimate issue of *Probe* (Winter 1995) on "Democracy in the Fields."

Membership and the ideal of inclusivity

NAWR membership reached its peak in the mid-1970s, with approximately 100 sisters' councils or senates and some 5,000 individual members.[18] The extension of full individual membership to laywomen in 1978, however, did not increase overall membership. Instead the change in policy and resultant shift in identity were accompanied by a significant loss of the original membership base. In 1980 there were only 23 diocesan organizations of sisters and 1,400 individual members. The name change to National Assembly of Religious Women (NARW) in 1982 signaled more clearly the organization's commitment to inclusivity, and the election of four laywomen to the national board in 1984 brought this commitment to a new level of possibility. By 1985 NARW's board included six sisters and six laywomen, and the board was co-chaired by two of the latter, Maureen Reiff and Pauline Turner, while Marjorie Tuite, OP, served as national coordinator of the organization. Overall membership figures eventually improved, reaching by 1992 approximately 2,800 women who paid dues or contributed services.[19] Although the membership had become one-third lay by 1983, the overall number of sisters had declined, and the statistics of the 1970s were never regained. By 1985 NARW reported 27 local groups of members in 20 states, but the links with diocesan organizations of sisters had been relinquished. As a smaller, less-structured "movement organization," NARW continued to press the inclusivity ideal, and a 1990 report describes the "metamorphosis of NARW" as involving a "change from an organization of predominantly White women in religious congregations into a grassroots organization of women, more than half of whom are lay women and more than 15 percent of whom are African American, Latina, Asian, and Native American women."[20]

The ideal of inclusivity had in fact intensified with time, so that in 1981 the members who convened in Boston opened the possibility of non-Catholic women joining NARW by rephrasing the organization's "vision statement" in general terms: "We are religious feminist women committed to the prophetic tasks of giving witness, raising awareness, and engaging in public action for the achievement of justice."[21] The fact that Tuite, NAWR's national coordinator from 1981 until her death in 1986, was at the same time on the national staff of the largely Protestant group Church Women United provided new opportunities for ecumenical and interfaith collaboration. In 1986, for instance, NARW cosponsored an interfaith conference in Chicago, "Women of Faith: Same Journey, Different Paths," instead of holding its annual convention. A NARW flier from this period describes the organization: "Although the majority of members relate to the Catholic tradition, membership is open to women of all faiths." This enlarged focus continued to complicate NARW's discussions through most of the 1980s, and although by 1990 the group's literature had reclaimed

"Catholic" in its self-description, its last national coordinator, Jan Lugibihl, declared in the final issue of *Probe*: "I'm not Catholic; however, I have in many places in my life . . . been moved and inspired by Catholic women."[22]

By 1985 NARW's justice agenda, long voiced in opposition to racism, classism, sexism, militarism, and clericalism, began to extend also to the areas of heterosexism and environmental concern. Moreover, under the leadership of Judy Vaughan, CSJ, national coordinator during 1987–92, efforts to bring women of diverse economic and racial-ethnic backgrounds into NARW activities were greatly increased. When NARW celebrated its twentieth anniversary at a 1990 conference in Cleveland, more than 120 of the 300 who attended were Latina, African American, Asian, or Native American.[23] The 1992 convention in Spokane, which was designed to counter celebrations of the Columbus quincentenary, was even more markedly multicultural, with particular emphasis on indigenous heritages. By then the inclusivity ideal had been extended also in the direction of youth, so that teenaged women constituted ten percent of the 500 in attendance.[24] Meanwhile Spanish had been introduced into *Probe* in 1987, a reflection of the fact that NARW's vision statement was amended that year to emphasize working inclusively for justice.

Programs, protests, and collaboration

While the antiracism imperative continued to dominate NARW's agenda, by the late 1980s attention to women's economic situation also led to a special focus on homeless women. Workshops on "Undoing Racism," "Creating Inclusive Community," and "Homeless Women: Creating Community, Creating Change" were prominent activities during NARW's final years. During 1989–90, NARW sponsored skill-training sessions for homeless women in eleven cities, and in 1991 the organization was awarded a grant of $50,000 from United Way of Chicago for continuing this work under the program title, "Empowerment, Justice, and Change."

In addition to programs, NARW's commitment to justice was expressed in many protest actions: boycotts in support of farm and factory labor movements, peace marches, vigils to end the violence in El Salvador, and protests against the Persian Gulf War were all part of NARW's public mission. The 1981 vision statement—"We are religious feminist women committed to the prophetic tasks of giving witness, raising awareness, and engaging in public action for the achievement of justice"—committed members to raise awareness and work for change.[25]

The spirit of collaboration evident in these later programs and protests of NARW had been present from the organization's inception, although in the early years NAWR's efforts were directed toward collaboration with official church leaders (e.g., the Bishops' Committee on the Permanent Diaconate) and with groups such as the National Federation of Priests' Councils, the National Assembly of Religious Brothers, and the various national organizations for sisters, especially LCWR, and two groups established for particular constituencies of sisters, the National Black Sisters' Conference (1968), and Las Hermanas (1971). Like NAWR/NARW, Las Hermanas opened its membership to laywomen in the 1970s, whereas the NBSC has, like the National Coalition of American Nuns (NCAN), remained an organization of women in religious vows. Of these Catholic organizations, only Las Hermanas was mentioned in Vaughan's list from the early 1990s of groups that NARW had worked with then, which also included the American Friends Service Committee, Children's Defense Fund, Black Women's Health Network, La Mujer Obrera, United Methodist Women, Coalition for the Homeless, and several others.[26] It is perhaps significant that Vaughan's article omits mention of NARW's participation in the Women-Church movement, discussed earlier in this volume. NARW had been part of the coalition of mainly Catholic women's groups that sponsored national feminist gatherings in Chicago in 1983 and Cincinnati in 1987, but had withdrawn from the Women-Church Convergence in 1992 because preparations for a 1993 assembly in Albuquerque fell short of NARW's antiracist standards. NARW did not publicize the dispute, however, and held a dinner (cosponsored with Las Hermanas, which had also withdrawn from the Convergence) at the nearby Laguna Pueblo during the Women-Church gathering. Although the dissolution of NARW was not anticipated at the time, the Laguna event proved to be its final national gathering, for funding difficulties soon afterward became insurmountable.

Over the course of NAWR/NARW's history, its network of contacts and collaborators had extended in many directions, and increasingly they went beyond the borders of the United States. In 1975 NAWR sent me to Mexico City to represent them as well as Sisters Uniting, an umbrella group of several national sisters' organizations, at the International Women's Year Tribune, a forum held in connection with United Nations meetings there. In 1979 Yolanda Tarango, CCVI, and Mary O'Keefe, OP, represented NARW as participants in "Mujeres para el Dialogo" discussions held in connection with the Puebla meeting of the Latin American bishops' conference (CELAM). In 1982 national coordinator Marjorie Tuite, OP, participated in a peace march in Italy, and the following year she led a study tour to Nicaragua. Seven NARW members participated in Cuatro Encuentro Feminista de Latino America y el Caribe in 1987, and a year later NARW initiated a series of four retreat experiences in Ocotal, Nicaragua. In addition, NAWR's national coordinator, Judy Vaughan, CSJ, was among the official observers of the 1990 Nicaraguan elections.

Factors contributing to decline

The above summary of NAWR/NARW's quarter-century history is only a beginning. A fuller account is needed, one that looks more closely at the inner dynamics of the organization and at its considerable influence through individuals, who gained empowering knowledge and skills under its auspices, as well as through groups such as NETWORK and the Women's Ordination Conference, which resulted in part from its activities.[27] The ideal of a "ministry for justice" that seeks to deepen the analysis of unjust situations and to act in ways that transform power relationships was maintained from the organization's earliest years. This ideal remains vital today for many former members, who continue to work in its spirit.

Undoubtedly there were many factors that contributed to the fiscal crisis that caused NARW to dissolve in 1995. Finances may have been the bottom line, but I believe that six additional factors bear investigation. They are timing, erosion of the original membership base, a distrust of institutions in general, a very fast rate of change, the weighty burden of idealism, and the loss of a shared theological and liturgical tradition.

Timing

Arguably the life and death of NAWR/NARW reflected a unique historical moment. Women religious in this country were poised to appreciate the progressive ideals of the Second Vatican Council and to implement them with great energy. NAWR also gained impetus from the 1971 Synod on Justice, and the organization's peak in terms of membership coincided with a general sense of optimism about the possibilities for continuing reform that lasted through the mid-1970s. The Vatican's explicit rejection of women's ordination in 1976, the distancing of the U.S. bishops from the more progressive results of their bicentennial hearings and the Detroit "Call to Action" conference that same year, followed by the ecclesiastical repression associated with the papacy of Pope John Paul II, all contributed to the alienation of many progressive Catholic women from their own tradition, or if not from Catholicism altogether, from its hierarchical leadership.[28] NAWR/NARW's ambiguity about its relationship to Catholicism in the second half of its existence reflects this alienation, which has been particularly strong among feminists.

This alienation deepened when the Vatican threatened twenty-four women religious with expulsion from their communities because they had signed a statement about the abortion issue, which was published by a lay organization called Catholics for a Free Choice (CFFC) in the *New York Times* for 7 October 1984. This happened shortly before the U.S. presidential election in which Republican Ronald Reagan soundly defeated Democrat Walter Mondale. Geraldine Ferraro, a Catholic congresswoman from New Jersey, had been Mondale's running-mate, and was the first female candidate to be nominated for vice-president in U.S. history. Many Catholics were dismayed by the way some prominent members of the hierarchy had attacked Ferraro during the campaign because although expressing personal opposition to abortion, she assumed a political stance of tolerance in view of its legality. They noted that male Catholic politicians with similar positions, such as Mario Cuomo or Edward Kennedy, had not received the sort of treatment that Ferraro did. Thus as the presidential election neared, CFFC sought to inform voters that Catholic thinking on abortion and related public policy was not limited to the positions of Cardinals Bernard Law or John O'Connor. The prochoice group designed an advertisement based on a 1983 survey they had sent to a number of Catholic thinkers, which included these claims:

> . . . a diversity of opinion regarding abortion exists among committed Catholics: a large number of Catholic theologians hold that even direct abortion, though tragic, can sometimes be a moral choice; [and], according to data compiled by the National Opinion Research Center, only 11% of Catholics surveyed disapprove of abortion in all circumstances. . . . Finally, while recognizing and supporting the legitimate role of the hierarchy in providing Catholics with moral guidance on political and social issues and in seeking legislative remedies to social injustices, we believe that Catholics should not seek the kind of legislation that curtails the legitimate exercise of the freedom of religion and conscience or discriminates against poor women.[29]

Among the ninety-six names published as endorsing this statement were those of twenty-four women religious, including NARW's national coordinator, Marjorie Tuite, OP. Although the statement was the work of lay theologians and CFFC, it was the clergy and members of religious communities among the signers who felt the direct force of Vatican objections to the advertisement. Of these, three men promptly withdrew their endorsement in December 1984 and a fourth had settled by May 1985, but twenty-two sisters held out for nearly two years until they were able to "clarify" their positions in a way that both their consciences and Rome could accept.[30] They had managed, during an arduous process that taxed the energies of signers and community officers alike, to retain community membership without backing down from their claim that signing the statement had been appropriate in view of the political situation in the United States at the time.

The fact that NARW's national coordinator was among these signers not only increased tensions on the NARW board for many months, but also took a considerable toll on Tuite's health, as she gave much time and energy to dealing with the controversy. Tuite reported in May 1986 that her case with Rome had been closed, and a few weeks later she was hospitalized for surgery. A diagnosis of cancer was soon confirmed, and she died on 28 June 1986.[31] The entire episode, which also involved other prominent NARW members (including Judy Vaughan, CSJ, who eventually succeeded Tuite as national coordinator), further distanced many progressive Catholic women from the Vatican.

Another factor related to timing involves the less well-publicized personal situations of many of NAWR's original members. The organization's early days coincided with their decisions about changing from traditional works in schools and hospitals to a variety of new ministries, and as these women became educated to new professions such as law or theology they brought the organizational know-how obtained through NAWR to new settings, both professional groups and groups focused on church reform. Also, a number of NAWR members were eventually chosen by their religious congregations for internal leadership, and before long some NAWR officers and board members were moving among the ranks of the Leadership Conference of Women Religious (LCWR). Indeed, the commitment of LCWR to social justice concerns, which became increasingly evident with time, seems attributable in part to the influence of NAWR/NARW.

Erosion of original membership base

The communities of women religious whose members first organized sisters' councils or senates and then established national organizations like NAWR were at their peak of numerical strength immediately after the Second Vatican Council, with 1966 statistics showing 181,421 sisters in the United States. But the years of renewal and adaptation saw many departures from religious communities, and by the time NAWR was founded in 1970 the overall number of sisters had dropped by more than 20,000, to 160,931. The steep decline continued, so that in 1978, when NAWR first welcomed laywomen as full members, there were 129,391 sisters in this country. Four years later, in 1982, when the organization's name was changed to NARW, there were 121,370 sisters, nearly one-third fewer than immediately after Vatican II. Indeed, the number of sisters continued to fall throughout the period of NAWR/NARW's history, with a count of 92,107 (a drop of nearly 50 percent since 1966) at the time the organization folded in 1995.[32] Thus, one can read the difficulties of the group's later years to some extent as reflecting the situation of U.S. sisters more generally. Not only were the sisters fewer in number, but they were also aging and increasingly burdened with financial worries about funding their retirement needs without a strong base of younger members. These congregations could no longer afford to subsidize ventures like NARW at the level needed when the staff were drawing even modest salaries at the national office. Funding was more dependent on grants and donations than on membership dues, and when these were not available, the organization could not sustain its programs.[33]

Distrust of institutions

An attitude discernible among many progressives is the impatience with which they sometimes regard structure and institutions. There is often more energy for critique and dismantling of structures than for rebuilding. NAWR originally had a Structures Committee and gave attention to a constitutional document that provided for regional representation and regular change of the national leadership. Ironically, as the group sought to express the ideal of inclusivity more fully (and also to model a nonhierarchical team approach to leadership), it allowed its organization-maintenance (especially among the original base) to diminish. Also, the notion of regular replacement of national leadership was seemingly forgotten after 1981, when for reasons that warrant study NARW allowed itself to become an organization increasingly identified with a single leader, Tuite from 1981 to 1986 and Vaughan from 1987 to 1993.

The rate of change

The many changes that NAWR/NARW implemented in its relatively brief existence led to gains, especially as women from more varied backgrounds learned of its ideals and activities, but also resulted in losses, particularly in continuity and stability of membership. Many women did not continue to pay dues after their initial interest had been sparked by a convention or other event. One may ask whether the rate of change itself was a factor in this turnover of members, who may have related to aspects of NARW's identity that were eclipsed as the group's focus shifted. The loss of a sense of shared history was evident during what turned out to be its final gathering, in Laguna, New Mexico, in April 1993. The after-dinner program there featured a performance by children from the pueblo and a farewell ritual honoring Vaughan, who was leaving the Chicago office after nearly six years as the organization's national coordinator. The ritual expressed well the gains that NARW had made in terms of racial-ethnic inclusiveness, but the new members who toasted Vaughan that evening were apparently unaware that the organization's early leaders were among the women who packed the community hall that evening. No acknowledgment was made of the presence, for example, of Ethne Kennedy, SH, NAWR's first national chair, or of Mary Rehman, CHM, and Maggie Fisher, SCN, whose virtually volunteer labors in the Chicago office had helped the fledgling organization begin to implement the ministry for justice agenda established at the 1972 Minneapolis assembly.

The weight of ideals

Committed to a ministry of justice, NAWR/NARW felt the burden of injustice keenly, whether in the church, in the wider society, or in its own ranks or those of its collaborators. With many justice issues constantly on the table, and various programs, protest activities, and strategies for change under discussion, tensions often ran high. The effort to institutionalize justice through bringing representatives of formerly excluded women onto the board assembled an increasingly different set of interests and experiences. Perhaps more might have been done to deal directly with the tensions resulting when these differences were voiced. It may also be asked whether NAWR/NARW's prophetic stance (articulated explicitly as such in the 1981 assembly) aimed at such a perfection of justice that the journey itself became too difficult for most members to sustain over a long period of time. Also, the multi-issue approach that had always characterized NAWR/NARW led to a certain diffusion of energy, and it is likely that many women who initially benefited from the approach moved on in time to concentrate on specific local projects or became involved in national organizations with more limited but focused agendas.

Loss of shared theological and liturgical tradition

NARW gained immensely from experiencing the variety of religious wisdom and women's ritual leadership available when it discontinued traditional Catholic celebrations of Eucharist at its gatherings. One may ask, however, if the loss of a worship tradition that included occasional attention to the Christian doctrine of sin and forgiveness as matters of daily life may have been contributed to the organization's inability to hold members. Aspirations to prophecy and perfection can sometimes result in a moralism that brings discouragement and disunity. Psalms and Eucharistic prayers, which some feminists may abandon because of their historic links with sexism, have served as reminders of divine transcendence and of human limitations.

Conclusion

Financial difficulties and a relatively small membership base, however, were the principal reasons for NARW's demise, and it is likely that had some major grants or donations been available, the organization might have survived. Also, if women's economic situation were generally better, dues could have been raised well beyond the $20 asked of individual members annually in the 1990s. Finally, if the 1994 convention had taken place and been successful, that might have generated enough income to allow time for the organization to develop better long-range ways of staying solvent.

One can of course only speculate about these and other unrealized possibilities. What is not a matter of speculation, but rather one of historical record, is the fact that thousands of women in this country were inspired by NAWR/NARW's vision of a ministry of justice.

Through *Probe*, resource packets, books, conventions, workshops, and especially through personal contact with others who shared the ideals of liberation and empowerment, these women gained knowledge, experience, skills and a wide network of associates who could be tapped for assistance with countless activities in behalf of justice and peace. The influence of this short-lived organization has continued well into the future.

Among the virtues characterizing the women who felt called to participate in NAWR/NARW were zeal for the reign of God and hunger and thirst for justice. With time and experience many of these generous idealists also gained a new sense of humility and patience as they came to grips with the organization's and their own limitations. This appreciation of finitude did not diminish their zeal, but it did prove an asset for subsequent efforts to speak and act prophetically. As NAWR/NARW's short history was drawing to a close, women religious were starting other organizations and movements with more focused agendas. Among many examples are the Intercommunity Peace and Justice Center established in 1991 in Seattle, and the "Sisters of Earth" network, whose first conference drew some fifty sisters working in earth ministries to discussions at St Gabriel's Monastery in Clark's Summit, Pennsylvania in 1994.

In 1991 the leaders of four women's congregations in the Pacific Northwest founded the Intercommunity Peace and Justice Center (IPJC), which has since drawn support from eleven other women's communities and the Oregon Province Jesuits. The center's founding vision was one of "collaboration among individuals, churches and organizations to build community and create change for the common good."[34] According to Linda Haydock, SNJM, who has been executive director of the Seattle-based center from the beginning, this vision was focused on three activities: community organizing, especially among marginalized women; education for peace and justice; and efforts for corporate social responsibility. Haydock had attended the final NARW convention in Spokane in 1992, and was disappointed when the national organization went out of existence. Although she had found its agenda too diverse and unfocused, she observed in a 2012 interview that NARW's "model of ritual, study, and action" was influential.[35] One can see traces of this influence in the highly successful women's convocations IPJC has sponsored at four-year intervals in Seattle, and in its other conferences, events, and educational activities. Because IPJC has strong connections with its sponsoring and affiliated communities, most of which are in the Northwest region, it has had sufficient funding to conduct a wide range of activities for education and advocacy, and although its organizing focus remains regional, it now uses technology to make some of its programs available nationally and internationally. For example, "Justice Cafés" now gather young adults monthly in locations in the United States and Africa to "build community, act for justice, and deepen their spirituality," with local hosts using materials provided on the internet by IPJC, and participants able to follow up on blogs and social media.[36]

While the women, both vowed religious and their collaborators, involved in IPJC and in other such centers were responding to the call to act prophetically on behalf of justice and peace, others were hearing and answering an even more specific call, which they describe as a summons from the earth to promote ecology and sustainable living. Sarah McFarland Taylor has documented the movement associated with the "Sisters of Earth" network in a 2007 study, *Green Sisters: A Spiritual Ecology.* In this ethnographic history Taylor characterizes "green sisters" as "environmentally activist Roman Catholic vowed religious women" who in devoting themselves to earth ministries have combined their heritage with new ideas and thereby become "active producers and transformers of new varieties of culture and spiritual expression."[37] In contrast to NAWR/NARW, which was organized nationally from the first, and to IPJC, which was founded by regional leaders of religious congregations, the Sisters of Earth movement began with individual projects such as an organic garden or an ecological learning center, often started by just one or two sisters. By 1993 some of these women religious felt it was time to gather with others similarly involved, and a small group led by Mary Southard, CSJ of LaGrange, Illinois, planted the seed that grew into the decentralized "Sisters of Earth" network.[38] Nearly two decades later there are several hundred participants in the network, which is open to all women "who share a deep concern for the ecological and spiritual crises of our times and who wish to support one another in work toward healing the human spirit and restoring the Earth's life support systems."[39] Taylor's volume includes a list of some fifty centers of earth ministries established by sisters across the United States and Canada. These locally based projects are linked by strong, spiritually motivated social networks, and they have significant impact as well as an appeal to the youthful "Generation Green."[40]

While maintaining the zeal that has long characterized active women's religious communities, these twenty-first-century activists have learned to focus their energies and to concentrate on building effective relationships with collaborators of various backgrounds. In part the success of their ventures seems due to a tempering of the ambitious idealism of the early post-Vatican II days with a patience gained from experience. The IPJC concentrates on issues where sisters and the hierarchy agree, rather than pressing for reform of church structures and practices, thereby gaining many allies for their endeavors. Sisters of Earth have learned patience and persistence from contemplating nature, and have developed strategies for dealing with conflict that stress humility and empathy as well as courage.[41] As Taylor observes, "Respectfully but nimbly finding a path between authority of institution and authority of conscience, the sisters, row by row and community by community, simply continue their work of planting 'seeds of change.'"[42]

What the earlier activists of NAWR/NARW have in common with the peace and justice leaders and the "green sisters" of today is the sense of being called to dedicate their lives wholeheartedly to the values of God's realm, and thus to act prophetically and influence history for the well-being of all God's creatures. Whether the emphasis is on hearing that divine summons in the cries of human victims of violence and injustice, or in the call of the earth for healing, their sense of vocation is central to the contributions they are making.

Notes

1 Quoted as Blessed John XXIII's "final message to the church," uttered from his deathbed, in Robert Ellsberg, *All Saints* (New York: Crossroad, 1997), p. 244.

2 See Anne Marie Gardiner, SSND, ed., *Women and Catholic Priesthood: An Expanded Vision: Proceedings of the Detroit Ordination Conference* (New York: Paulist, 1976). In the opening chapter, "Who Are These

Women?" Nadine Foley, OP, stresses the fact that canonically all women are "lay," noting that the conciliar document *Lumen Gentium* (#43) "stratifies the Church as composed of bishops, clergy and laity", (p. 6). The event was first proposed by a lay social worker, Mary B. Lynch, who at the time was the U.S. representative to the International Movement of Women Aspiring to the Presbyteral Ministry and editor of the movement's newsletter, *The Journey*. Foley chaired the task force, however, and 17 of its 21 members were sisters. More than three-quarters of those attending the meeting returned surveys at its conclusion, and nuns' surveys (676) outnumbered those of laywomen (142) nearly five to one. The statistics on women desiring ordination were comparable for both groups, however; just over one-third from each group answered affirmatively when asked, "Do you wish to be ordained?" See Patricia Hughes, "Who Are These Women? The Answer Takes Shape," in Gardiner, pp. 174–5.

3   These phrases are borrowed from Katie Geneva Cannon's groundbreaking study, *Black Womanist Ethics* (Atlanta: Scholars Press, 1988), and used analogously here. Historian Jay P. Dolan writes in *The American Catholic Experience* (Garden City, NY: Image, 1985) that sisters ". . . were the Catholic serfs, having fewer rights and fewer options than priests, brothers, or lay people", p. 289.

4   Sisters were notably influenced by the work of the Belgian Cardinal Léon-Joseph Suenens, *Coresponsibility in the Church*, translated by Francis Martin (New York: Herder & Herder, 1968).

5   Foley, "Who Are These Women?", p. 4.

6   "The National Assembly of Women Religious (NAWR) — 1968–1975" (1975), and *Probe* (Summer 1995). The 1975 brochure includes a diagram showing the organization's complex structure at that time. The national executive board included representatives of fourteen geographic regions spanning the entire country, chairs of seven national committees, and three officers.

7   A comprehensive historical study of NAWR/NARW has not yet been done. The organization's archives are at the University of Notre Dame. Also important are the papers of Marjorie Tuite, OP, a key figure in NAWR from its inception until her death in 1986, which are stored in the Women and Leadership Archives at Loyola University in Chicago. Mary Henold includes some material on NAWR/NARW in *Catholic and Feminist: The Surprising History of the American Catholic Feminist Movement* (Chapel Hill, NC: University of North Carolina Press, 2008), and Ann Carey looks critically at the organization in *Sisters in Crisis: The Tragic Unraveling of Women's Religious Communities* (Huntington, IN: Our Sunday Visitor Publishing Division, 1997), pp. 243–51. Of particular help for my research were Judy Vaughan, CSJ's article,

"National Assembly of Religious Women (NARW)," in *U.S. Women's Interest Groups: Institutional Profiles,* ed. Sarah Slavin (Westport, CT: Greenwood Press, 1995), pp. 283–7, and the historical data given in the final issue of NAWR/NARW's periodical *Probe,* 23, 2 (Summer 1995). I was a board member of NAWR from 1972 to 1975, and consulted several other leaders in doing research for this chapter. My thanks go to the late Ethne Kennedy, SH, and to Rosemary Rader, OSB, Merle Nolde, OSB, Pauline Turner, and Judy Vaughan, CSJ, for information provided in interviews about their experiences with the organization. Kennedy chaired and Rader served on the task force that created NAWR during 1968–70, and Kennedy was NAWR's first elected leader, from 1970 to 1973; Nolde was a codirector of the national office during 1978–81; Turner, one of the first laywomen to be elected to the national board, served during 1984–86; and Vaughan succeeded Tuite as national coordinator from 1987 to 1993.

8   Simone Campbell, "If We Stay Faithful," NETWORK *Connection* (Third Quarter 2012), p. 4. As Stephanie Niedringhaus has noted in a 2002 article, NETWORK was founded as the result of a December 1971 meeting of 47 women religious who gathered at Trinity College in Washington, DC, to discuss "working for social justice through legislative advocacy." There Carol Coston, OP, proposed that "sisters form a 'network' for political action and education," and the motion passed with 43 affirmative votes, three opposed, and one abstention. In the spring Coston opened the office with a budget of $185, and she served for ten years as Executive Director. Niedringhaus traces the origins of NETWORK to an October 1971 board meeting of the Catholic Committee on Urban Ministry (CCUM), when NAWR national board member Marjorie Tuite, OP, discussed with Mary Reilly, RSM, Claire Dugan, SSJ, and Monsignor Geno Baroni "the idea of a workshop for sisters interested in political activism." See Stephanie Niedringhaus, "Celebrating 30 Years Action on Behalf of Justice: The Evolution of NETWORK," NETWORK *Connection* (May/June 2002), p. 3. I believe the beginnings can be traced back even further, to a meeting of the local Washington, DC, unit of "grassroots" NAWR members, which I attended on 16 September 1971 at the residence of Josephine Dunne, SHCJ, on Tunlaw Road. Dunne, who later returned to lay life and has since died, was at the time president of the local NAWR unit and also administrative assistant to Msgr. Baroni, then head of the U.S. Bishops' new program, the Catholic Campaign for Human Development. The idea of political ministry was raised during brainstorming at that September meeting, and I think Dunne should be credited with taking it back to the office and helping nurture it through and beyond the crucial CCUM board meeting. The link between NETWORK and LCWR began informally early on, and was solidified at the 1972 LCWR assembly

in Seattle, when "more than 350 sisters endorsed the network and pledged financial support," according to Maureen Kelleher, RSHM, "Politics as Ministry," in *Gospel Dimensions of Ministry,* ed. Ethne Kennedy (Chicago: NAWR Publications, 1973), p. 116.

9   Ethne Kennedy, SH, reviews this early history in "The Changing World of Women: 1972," the foreword to her edited volume, *Women in Ministry: A Sisters' View* (Chicago: NAWR Publications, 1972), pp. 9–18. Also valuable is the historical summary by Hildegarde Marie Mahoney, SC, "Sisters Councils: Their Beginnings," *Probe* (September-October 1981), pp. 13–14, which gives an account of events leading to NAWR's establishment.

10   In addition to Marjorie Tuite, OP, notable instances of women who brought experience with civil rights activism to the new organizations of sisters include Margaret Ellen Traxler, SSND, founder of the National Coalition of American Nuns (NCAN), and Carol Coston, OP, the first executive director of NETWORK. Traxler's and Coston's stories are found in a volume edited by another NCAN leader, Ann Patrick Ware, SL, *Midwives of the Future: American Sisters Tell Their Story* (Kansas City, MO: Leaven Press, 1985), pp. 129–39 and pp. 146–60. See also Carol Coston, OP, "Women Religious Invest Their Lives," in *Journey in Faith and Fidelity: Women Religious Shaping Life for a Renewed Church,* ed. Nadine Foley, OP (New York: Continuum, 1999), pp. 198–217.

11   Quoted here from the 1975 NAWR brochure, "The National Assembly of Women Religious (NAWR) — 1968–75."

12   A tenth anniversary membership renewal form reflects NCAN's outspoken approach to justice advocacy: "During the 70s NCAN analyzed issues; took unpopular stands . . . published study guides on relevant issues; badgered, barraged, and buffeted the bishops." NCAN's newsletter had supported the Equal Rights Amendment, disarmament, civil rights for homosexuals, gender-inclusive language, and "'home rule' for nuns," along with other progressive causes of the 1970s. NCAN remains a small, efficient, and outspoken group today.

13   Kennedy, ed., *Women in Ministry,* 1972.

14   Ethne Kennedy, ed., *Gospel Dimensions of Ministry* (Chicago: NAWR Publications, 1973), "Foreword," p. 9.

15   Tuite, in Kennedy, *Gospel Dimensions,* p. 7.

16   Quoted here from the 1975 NAWR brochure, "The National Assembly of Women Religious (NAWR) — 1968–1975."

17   *St. Louis Globe-Democrat,* 16 August 1974, p. 8-A.

18   "The Spirit Continues to Live," *Probe* (Summer 1995), p. 3

19   Judy Vaughn, CSJ, who was national coordinator during 1987–92, provided this information in a telephone interview, 30 December 1996.

20 "NARW Annual Report: August 1989-July 1990," p. 2.

21 *Probe* 11 (September–October 1981), p. 1. This is the first issue published in tabloid newspaper format.

22 "I Am Sad About the Loss of Possibilities," *Probe* (Summer 1995), p. 3.

23 NARW Annual Report (August 1989–July 1990), p. 1.

24 The ideal led next to the decision that "At least two young women will be invited to be part of the 1994 Conference Planning Committee," according to the NARW Annual Report (August 1992–July 1993), p. 4. This intended gathering on the theme, "Celebrating Women's Sexuality: Healing Ourselves, Healing the Earth," never took place because of NARW's financial difficulties.

25 *Probe* (September-October, 1981), p. 1.

26 Vaughan, in Slavin, p. 286.

27 Vaughan describes NARW as a "cofounder" of these groups, as well as of "Call to Action, Chicago Religious Task Force on Central America, and the Interfaith Task Force on Central America," in Slavin, p. 284.

28 For sociologically grounded accounts of this alienation, see Andrew M. Greeley and Mary G. Durkin, *Angry Catholic Women* (Chicago: Thomas More Press, 1984), and Miriam Therese Winter, Adair Lummis, and Allison Stokes, *Defecting in Place: Women Claiming Responsibility for Their Own Spiritual Lives* (New York: Crossroad, 1994).

29 The full text is reprinted in *Origins* 14 (6 December 1984), immediately following a 15 November 1984 statement of Archbishop John R. Quinn, then chair of the U.S. Bishops' Committee on Doctrine, "Abortion: A Clear and Constant Teaching," which criticizes the CFFC statement, pp. 413–14. I have discussed this episode of the "Vatican 24" more fully in Patrick, *Liberating Conscience*, pp. 118–28 and 134–43.

30 Two of the original twenty-four, however, came to advocate a "pro-choice" position, and eventually decided to leave their congregation, the School Sisters of Notre Dame. See Barbara Ferraro and Patricia Hussey (with Jane O'Reilly), *No Turning Back: Two Nuns Battle with the Vatican over Women's Right to Choose* (New York: Poseidon Press, 1990). For further analysis of the controversy from the perspective of CFFC, see Mary E. Hunt and Frances Kissling, "The New York Times Ad: A Case Study in Religious Feminism," *Journal of Feminist Studies in Religion* 3/1(Spring 1987): 115–27.

31 Tuite's life was celebrated in a special issue of *Probe* (September/October 1989) and in a 1989 videotape produced by NARW, *¡Presente!* In addition, the book by Ferraro and Hussey, *No Turning Back,* gives particular attention to Tuite's influence.

32 These statistics are from P.J. Kennedy & Sons' *Official Catholic Directory.* See also Chapter 1, n. 17.

33 Stipends for nuns in the NAWR/NARW office had been quite low through the early 1980s. Ethne Kennedy, SH, and Merle Nolde, OSB, both mentioned an annual compensation of $4000 during the 1970s, which Kennedy recalled not always taking in full. Judy Vaughan, CSJ, reported that sisters and lay staff were compensated equally from 1987 on, with salaries beginning at about $18,000 then and approaching $24,000 toward the end. Meanwhile NARW's annual budget had grown from $32,000 in 1970 to $200,300 by 1992–93.

34 "Intercommunity Peace & Justice Center: Building Community, Creating Change," descriptive brochure published by IPJC, 1216 NE 65th St, Seattle, WA 98115. Fuller information on IPJC and the Northwest Coalition for Responsible Investment, which IPJC founded in 1994, is available at www.ipjc.org.

35 Linda Haydock, SNJM, telephone interview with Anne E. Patrick, SNJM, 26 March 2012. Haydock indicated that originally four women's communities—Sisters of the Holy Names, Tacoma Dominicans, Edmunds Dominicans (now Adrian Dominicans), and Sisters of St Joseph of Peace—provided seed money for the venture. They were soon joined by Sisters of Providence (Mother Joseph Province) and the Jesuits of the Oregon Province, and later by the Sisters of St Francis of Philadelphia. These seven sponsoring communities all have a representative on the IPJC governing council, and nine additional women's communities are formally affiliated with the center, which collaborates with many other organizations in its programs and activities.

36 http://ipjcjusticecafe.ning.com/ (accessed 31 March 2012).

37 Sarah McFarland Taylor, *Green Sisters: A Spiritual Ecology* (Cambridge: Harvard University Press, 2007), p. ix.

38 Taylor names four Sisters of St Joseph associated with the beginnings of the movement—Southard, Evelyn Sommers, Toni Nash, and Mary Louise Dolan—all of whom had collaborated at a Hudson Valley center in 1993. She also notes that Southard objected to being described as a "founder" of the movement, preferring instead to speak in agricultural terms: "It was more like noticing a seed, planting it, and seeing it grow", p. 303 n. 6, and p. 24.

39 http://sistersofearth.wikispaces.com/ (accessed 4 April 2012).

40 Taylor, p. 275.

41 Ibid., p. 277.

42 Ibid., p. 279.

4

"FRAMEWORK FOR LOVE": TOWARD A RENEWED UNDERSTANDING OF CHRISTIAN VOCATION

"The word of the Lord came to me thus: 'Before I formed you in the womb I knew you, before you were born I dedicated you, a prophet to the nations I appointed you.'"
—JEREMIAH 1:4-5, *NEW AMERICAN BIBLE*

Earlier we have seen how a transformed sense of what is virtuous has led some Catholic women to respond to perceived injustice with new forthrightness and energy in the late twentieth-century. Both the episode of the Sisters of the Holy Names in Key West during 1989–90 and the efforts of NAWR/NARW during 1970–95 to transform church and society involved women with a strong sense of calling, indeed of mission. Although the perceptions of what is going on in church and society differ greatly among Catholic women, as we saw in Chapter 2, the idea of vocation is something shared by virtually all of them.

In this chapter, I explore the theological meaning and ethical implications of this shared concept. I do so in the hope of further clarifying the choices that confront the consciences of Catholic women as they discern how to serve in tomorrow's church. The meaning of vocation has to some degree been put in question by the fluctuations of our fast-paced social context. Most of us can put names on the statistics mentioned in the last chapter concerning departures from the religious life, and we all know persons who have ended marriages, sometimes more than once. Moreover, the pace of technological change has quickened to the point where many young people can expect to have two or three careers, and medical progress gives them hope of living with good health and energy well into their eighties. In such an age, some may wonder what value remains with the notion of vocation. Is the concept hopelessly destabilized by the many instances of changing commitments on the part of persons who married or made religious vows, by our postmodern culture that prizes spontaneity and independence? Or is the notion a potential resource for living a centered and productive life in an increasingly unstable world?

John W. Gardner, who founded the citizens' movement Common Cause, observed decades ago that in a world of constant change, "[t]he only stability possible is stability in motion."[1] Can the theological idea of vocation help us to achieve such equilibrium, such empowering stability in the course of a lifetime "in motion"? I suggest that an affirmative answer is possible if we are willing to confront the myth and mystery of vocation with discerning minds and generous hearts. My title, "Framework for Love," is inspired by the work of theologian Margaret Farley, a Sister of Mercy who taught from 1971 to 2007 at Yale Divinity School. Although she has been well known to Christian ethicists and church professionals, she came to widespread international attention in 2012 when her 2006 study *Just Love: A Framework for Christian Sexual Ethics* was censured by the Vatican Congregation for the Doctrine of the Faith (CDF) for departing from official Catholic teaching on certain topics in sexual ethics, as I have mentioned in the Introduction.[2] Farley has written extensively on commitment and on justice, with particular attention to the concerns of women. Her work does not focus directly on the idea of vocation, but her reflections on commitment and related issues offer help for thinking in new ways about this concept, which retains great potential as a resource for the Christian life.[3]

By vocation I refer not only to the special states of life such as marriage, the priesthood, or membership in a vowed religious community, but also to such secular callings as that of artist, teacher, doctor, or politician. I refer as well to the fundamental call to respond to the Good News of salvation by living a holy life, which the Second Vatican Council emphasized in the *Dogmatic Constitution on the Church*: "Thus it is evident to everyone that all the faithful of Christ of whatever rank or status are called to the fullness of the Christian life and to the perfection of charity" (*Lumen Gentium* #40). I believe that vocation involves both a story-saturated symbol of tremendous power and a mystery that eludes any attempts at full certainty about what one should be doing with one's life. Furthermore, both the symbol and the mystery are religious in the general sense of being associated with the human experiences of ultimacy and transcendence, whether or not specific language about the sacred is employed.

The myth of vocation

In his volume *Stories of God* theologian John Shea describes religious myth as a story that shapes consciousness, encourages attitudes, and suggests behaviors. "Myth," he observes, "is that story or formulation which establishes the world within which we live and out of which we act."[4] It is in this rich sense that one can speak of the myth of vocation. As Andrew Greeley stresses in *The Jesus Myth*, "There is nothing more real than [human] symbols and myths," understanding the latter in the sense of narratives that convey the fullest possible truth about the meaning of our existence.[5] For persons influenced by the Christian tradition, the idea of particular callings in life is grounded in many biblical accounts of God or Jesus summoning people to tasks and indeed to life-projects. The early chapters of *Genesis* establish a pattern whereby God speaks with human beings, and this metaphor of conversation between Creator and creature often extends to stories of a special divine summons. The story of the Covenant with Israel is a prime example, as is the episode where the prophet Jeremiah is called to be a prophet. Likewise the gospels portray Jesus calling fishermen to abandon their nets and become "fishers of men," offering discipleship to a rich young man who is unable to leave his possessions, summoning a tax-collector to abandon that work and become an apostle, and sending Mary Magdalene to tell the disciples the news of his resurrection.

From such narratives has arisen the notion of vocation, the idea that individuals have a life task they are destined to figure out and fulfill. The concept is deeply etched into western consciousness, affecting believers and nonbelievers alike, although in different ways. Fundamentalists tend to speak confidently of being or expecting to be called by God as if it were an actual summons, as if there were a "thing" called vocation out there somewhere to be experienced and known. Less literal Christians may not expect such clarity or certainty, but often they operate under the assumption that there is a calling specifically designed for them. Even when people no longer interpret biblical narratives as literal accounts of events but rather understand these stories as theological interpretations of the significance of something that happened in the past, their imaginations have been profoundly affected by stories of God's summoning individuals for particular tasks in life. Moreover, religious and secular persons alike still speak of being called by the community, or by the times, or by one's deepest self, to undertake this or that life-project. And once language of vocation is adopted, ethical judgments soon follow, particularly judgments about fidelity and infidelity. The good person is faithful to the demands of her calling, the good parent puts the welfare of the child above his own, the good artist is true to her vision.

The mystery of vocation

The powerful myth that there is such a thing as a life-calling should be balanced by a counterweight, namely the recognition that the meaning and purpose of any life is ultimately a religious mystery, to be discerned gradually over the course of one's earthly existence. The biblical stories of callings and the subsequent literature of vocation are misleading if they are not interpreted in the full context of the Mystery that created us and sustains us in being. Since God transcends our knowledge, and since the meaning and purpose of our lives are finally bound up in our relationship with God, there can be no complete resolution of the question of our particular life-calling within the finite frame of our existence. What this means is not that the idea of vocation is worthless, but simply that our process of discernment must proceed with an appropriate degree of humility. The question of vocation amounts to a collection of repeated articulations of what theologian James M. Gustafson has identified as the basic question of Christian ethics: "What is God enabling and requiring me to be and to do?" not just in this or that particular moment of my life, but for a significant portion of my life, and maybe even the rest of my life.[6]

Furthermore, although everyone's vocation is ultimately a religious mystery, there remains value in doing the hard work of conceptual and ethical analysis about the matter. As Margaret Farley has indicated, "It is possible . . . to enter more deeply into the questions—to take a lantern, as it were, and walk into what may ultimately be a mystery to us, but which we do not deserve to call a mystery until we have entered it as far as we can go."[7]

An individual's vocation can be analyzed as a composite that involves three sorts of callings. For everyone there is the basic summons to holiness, which is a succinct way of stating the biblical command to love God with our whole heart and soul and strength and our neighbor as ourselves (Matt. 22:37–9). Beyond that is the sense of being invited to focus love and creativity (and sexual energy) in a particular life-context. This is the meaning that vocation has had for most Catholics. They are accustomed to link the idea with the sacraments of matrimony and holy orders, or with a call to practice celibacy in community or individual life, speaking of these various "states of life" as things that God invites one to enter. Finally, there is the matter of the many possible occupations that become vocations to the extent that they are seen as more than mere jobs. This third sort of calling, to productive secular activity, was emphasized especially by the reformers Luther and Calvin, who felt that the Roman Catholic stress on the clerical and vowed religious states had tended to obscure the baptismal vocation to holiness that belonged to all believers.

The distinction between a vocation in this occupational sense and a mere job depends on factors that are elusive but nonetheless real. A given occupation fits somewhere on a continuum that is defined at one extreme in terms of economic utility ("what I do to earn a living") and at the other in terms of meaning and fit with one's unique capacities and inclinations ("the work I was born to accomplish"). Frederick

Buechner's oft-cited characterization of vocation as "the place where your deep gladness meets the world's deep need" describes the latter very well.[8] This occupational sort of vocation goes beyond what we think of as a job or career to include our sense of being called to devote time and energy to various persons, projects, and causes. Whether through a career or through an avocation in this latter sense, one's experience of meaning and "fit" (with one's particular gifts and talents) in the way one spends one's hours contributes significantly to overall meaning and satisfaction in life.

The three sorts of vocations outlined above—the fundamental call to holiness, the call to a state of life such as marriage or the religious sisterhood, and the call to particular occupations, activities, or causes—are intimately connected with each other. Each concerns the love of God and neighbor, which is the fundamental obligation of every human being. The call to holiness is another way of stating this universal commandment to love God with one's whole heart, mind, soul, and strength, and one's neighbor as oneself. A vocation to a "state of life" such as marriage or celibacy establishes a focus and context for interpersonal love and sexual expression or abstinence. And a vocation to an occupation, cause, or enterprise establishes the setting for labor suffused with love. The responses to these multiple callings can be separated out for purposes of analysis, and there are often conflicts over which demand takes precedence on a given day, but ultimately they are united in the will to love.

Having established the three basic types of callings and their common relationship to love, we still face many questions about this matter of vocation. What is it that lends such solidity to the amorphous idea of vocation? What gives it power and substance, the ability to demand countless small deeds of fidelity over years and even decades of a lifetime? What is it that dissolves that substance and frees one from a formerly felt sense of obligation, or perhaps instead realigns that sense of obligation? I believe that the power attaching to the concept of vocation depends on a quality of relationship developed by a process that combines the passive experiences of attraction and insight and the active response of commitment. The former involves the reception of a gift, known theologically as a "grace," and the latter a series of decisions in response to this gift, including the choices to attend to what is attractive, to affirm the love that is evoked, and to promise future deeds of love. The power builds from the interaction of the passive and active aspects of the experience, sustained by a religious conviction that the ultimate source of the inclination is God, the creator of one's very life. In embracing a vocation one feels that this will be the appropriate context in which the faithful practice of neighbor love can be substantively linked with a loving response to the gifts of God. Furthermore, in the Christian religious context the notion of vocation operates by analogy, that is, by a thought process that recognizes both similarities and differences between what the contemporary believer experiences and what certain biblical personages experienced. What is happening to me in this attraction, this sense that here indeed is the situation where my own "deep gladness meets the world's great need," is like what those first disciples of Jesus experienced when they heard him say, "Come, follow me." And at the same time it is an altogether different experience, unique to my circumstances today.

Farley's "ethics of commitment" and the reconsideration of vocation

Although Margareet Farley's writings do not deal explicitly at length with the concept of vocation, her insights constitute a rich resource for ethical reflection on this topic. Most obviously relevant here is her important study from 1986, *Personal Commitments*, which can be read as a highly successful reinterpretation of the ethical significance of vocation that derives its power in part from an avoidance of this theologically freighted term. Nowhere does Farley directly reject the rhetoric of vocation, and there are occasional references to "calling" and "vocation" in this book as well as in her other writings, but these are rather rare for an author so centrally preoccupied with commitment.

One may speculate that several factors contribute to Farley's tendency to give the rhetoric of vocation a rest. In the first place, Roman Catholic understandings of vocation as a state of life have been linked with a problematic tendency to moral absolutism, especially where sacramental marriage is concerned. The longstanding tendency to absolutize the "marital bond" even in abusive situations has caused suffering and scandal for many Catholics, which the post-Vatican II liberalization of the annulment process has not fully remedied. It is precisely this situation of a tradition imposing impossible demands on individuals that *Personal Commitments* is designed to counter.[9] In an article on sexual ethics published in 1983 Farley had made brief reference to "weariness with the high rhetoric that has traditionally surrounded human covenants," seeking to replace it with a more "limited" rhetoric that recognizes that "commitment is itself only a means, not an end."[10]

Moreover, Roman Catholic teaching has historically relegated marriage to a lesser status than that of virginity chosen "for the sake of the Kingdom." An effort was made by the Second Vatican Council to offset this elitism by stating in the *Dogmatic Constitution on the Church* that all members of the People of God share "a common dignity" and "the same vocation to perfection."[11] Nearly two decades after the Council, however, Farley lamented the fact that the Church's recent emphasis on the universal call to holiness had not altered an entrenched elitism. "Twentieth century efforts in the Roman Catholic tradition to move beyond a ranking of higher and lower ways of Christian living," she observed in 1983, "are countered still by largely unanalyzed beliefs which hold the family to an inferior place."[12] Instead of making an explicit argument against vocational elitism in *Personal Commitments*, Farley takes what marriage and religious or priestly vows have in common, namely the formal promise of binding oneself to future deeds of love within a particular framework, and she analyzes these commitments on an equal basis. Her choice to treat examples from various walks of life on the same plane is a subtle but effective way of countering the elitism to which she objects. Furthermore, Protestant understandings of vocation have been associated with debates about matters such as the extent to which biblical meanings have been misapplied to worldly concerns and Christian moral energies have been co-opted by secular powers.[13] Important as they may be, these debates are not central to Farley's purpose, and it makes sense to avoid engaging them by employing new language.

Finally and most importantly, both Roman Catholic and Protestant understandings of vocation have been implicated in the sort of gender injustice that Farley's feminist ethic so strongly opposes. For all of church history Christian women have suffered under male definitions of their vocational possibilities and duties. These range from literal applications of the Pauline exhortation, "Wives should be submissive to their husbands as if to the Lord" (Eph. 5:22), to claims that only men are called to the priesthood. In her 1983 essay on "The Church and the Family: An Ethical Task," Farley observed:

> Women, unlike men, have received a double message about vocation to marriage and family life. On the one hand, the call to transcend it has been given to them . . . [and] on the other hand, they have been taught that they have a special call to the family. The family is a refuge for men, and hence the object of *eros*, a selfish love. But it is the responsibility of women, and hence the place of self-sacrificial love, of unlimited Christian *agape*.[14]

Several years earlier Farley had called for a revolution in patterns of relationship between women and men. Writing in *Theological Studies* during 1975, which the United Nations had designated International Women's Year, Farley declared that patriarchal family and church structures are "inadequate, based on inaccurate understandings of human persons, preventive of individual growth, inhibitive of the common good, conducive to social injustices, and in the Christian community not sufficiently informed by or faithful to the teachings of Christ." Then, in a carefully reasoned discussion of what authentic love and justice require, she went on to conclude that both family and church are "better served by a model of leadership which includes collaboration [of men and women] between equals."[15] These ideals of mutuality and collaboration, however, were far from realized in 1986, when Farley published *Personal Commitments,* and the situation is hardly better today.

In light of all this, there is considerable wisdom in Farley's move to consider the issue of vocational obligations in fresh language. In *Personal Commitments* the term she employs instead of "vocation" is "framework for love." This phrase respects two realities that an uncritical application of the concept of vocation otherwise obscures: the role that our own freedom plays in contributing to the sense of bundled obligations that a particular calling entails, and the ultimate mystery of the divine-human relationship that grounds all our responsibilities. A framework is useful but provisional, and so are the settings in which human beings are meant to respond to God's love for us. The frameworks have moral weight, but they are not ultimately binding in themselves, because God alone is the proper object of an absolute love.[16]

Farley's book on commitment is an excellent example of the process that philosopher Paul Ricoeur (1913–2005) commended to our age in his hermeneutical theory of "second naïveté." This process involves the task of rethinking the classical religious symbols and stories that provide meaning for our lives in the light of new, "critical" knowledge. In articulating this theory at the close of *The Symbolism of Evil*, his cross-cultural investigation of ancient stories about such figures as Adam and Eve, Pandora, and Oedipus, Ricoeur distinguishes three possible ways of relating to traditional myths. There is in the first place an unquestioning acceptance of the story as literally true, which he characterizes as "primitive naïveté." Typical for children, fundamentalists, and many premodern thinkers, this approach to myth assumes that the things narrated in biblical accounts happened just as they are told, whatever degree of fiction may be involved in myths from pagan sources. The reward for this stance is a high level of meaning, although the sort of simplicity entailed here cannot stand up to the new gains of knowledge brought by modern history, science, and philosophy.

Thus, there often emerges a second attitude to myth, which Ricoeur calls "criticism." Here the story is again understood literally, but this time it is judged as false. The character Sportin' Life from Gershwin's *Porgy and Bess* captures this attitude well in his song about biblical stories, "It Ain't Necessarily So." In naming this attitude, Ricoeur had in mind such great critics of religion as Nietzsche and Freud, thinkers who made significant gains of truth at the expense of meaning. Finally, Ricoeur proposes a way to get beyond the "meaning versus truth" impasse that modernity had reached with respect to biblical narratives. He does this by describing the possibility of a third stance toward myth, which combines aspects of the first two stances, "primitive naïveté" and "criticism." This third stance he calls "second naïveté." His use of the word "naïveté" here is paradoxical, for this stance involves a sophisticated ability to interpret the story symbolically rather than literally, and thus the adjective "second" is crucial to the concept. Ricoeur's reason for retaining the term "naïveté" in this secondary sense is to convey that some of the immediacy and power felt by those who relate uncritically to myth can be regained if educated persons will undertake a dialectical process. The first step in this process toward second naïveté is to make a sort of Pascalian wager that the narrative offers significant truth about human existence. Following this act of trust, one seeks to embrace all that criticism can supply by way of scientific or factual knowledge relevant to this myth. Ricoeur envisions a continuing dialectic in which the powers of imagination are unleashed by the wager of trust and then informed by the knowledge gained through critical thought and research so that *both* meaning *and* truth are realized. He offers the image of a "hermeneutical circle" to describe the ongoing dialectical process by means of which the truth available in the myth is discovered "in and through criticism."[17] Farley's endorsement of the possibility and desirability of reaching "second naïveté" understandings of key theological ideas is clear from what she says at the outset of *Personal Commitments*:

> [J]ust as special revelations (whether through sacred scriptures or through the voice of the community or through whatever sources) may illuminate all of our commitments and enable us to covenant forever, so our philosophical reflection on our experience of commitment can, as Paul Ricoeur testifies, "set off the horizon of significance where [God's word] may be heard."[18]

And her skill in navigating the hermeneutical circle is evident in the book's final chapter, which takes the biblical myth of God's Covenant with Israel in precisely this fashion.

The preceding chapters of *Personal Commitments* involve the descriptive and normative analysis of the human experience of commitment, and Farley waits until the book's conclusion to unpack its religious presuppositions in a chapter entitled, "Commitment, Covenant, and Faith." Her espousal of a second naïveté approach to the biblical myth of God's Covenant with Israel is apparent when she acknowledges the critical insight that the Covenant tradition is ambiguous and problematic. To begin with, there are conflicting interpretations, and the tradition of these interpretations and the theologies shaped by them has displayed "an alarming potential for the oppression of groups and individuals—in spite of its remarkable possibilities for liberation and for life." She cites the scandals of religious chauvinism and anti-Semitism, as well as the tradition's acceptance of atrocious violence and its "massive dependence" on imagery of domination, as in "lord-servant and husband-wife relationships." Nevertheless she proceeds to make her Pascalian wager on the fundamental truth of the symbol: "Despite all of these difficulties, however, the Covenant tradition can, I believe, illuminate important aspects of commitment. If it is interpreted with sufficient caution, it retains a power to express the convictions of a fundamentally strengthening and freeing faith."[19]

Farley recognizes the narrative basis of faith claims concerning God's love and fidelity to human beings. She prefers the terms "story" or "narrative" to "myth," but there is no doubt that Farley is well acquainted with the critical literature of biblical studies regarding Covenant stories, citing as she does figures from Gerhard von Rad through Katherine Doob Sakenfeld. She speaks of a "narrative kernel" that continues through biblical accounts of creation and the covenants with Noah, Abraham, and Moses. What the people receive in various instances, she observes, is God's "promise of a relationship, a promise of unconditional love and ongoing presence: 'I will be your God. You shall be my people.'"[20] In Ricoeur's terms, it is this symbol of God's Covenant of unconditional love and care for humanity that has "given rise" to Farley's own thought on analogous human commitments in the book's earlier chapters. She ends the work by affirming that the "Covenant story provides a context and a ground for all our commitments to love."[21]

Embedded but not developed in this chapter is the language of call, which Farley links directly with God's promise: "God's promise is addressed to human persons in a way that takes account of their reality as persons and that thereby calls for and makes possible a responding personal and communal commitment."[22] Indeed, the fact that the chapter subsequently speaks of calls to love, action, and responsibility suggests that a theology of vocation is present here at a deep level:

> Out of the relationship that is the substance of the Covenant, then, emerges the call and the responsibility to oppose the forces of evil in the world, to nurture the sources of human well-being, to

form structures that respect human dignity. Whatever can serve this labor falls within the scope of the Covenant. Always any given labor may end in exile, or in destruction of the land, or in death. Yet the word remains; the relationship holds; hope, and responsibility can continue.[23]

Mercy vocations and Farley's theological ethics

If Farley had reason for keeping explicit references to vocation to a minimum when she published *Personal Commitments* in 1986, the situation today is different. In recent years there has been a resurgence of this rhetoric in U.S. Christian circles, in part because of the generous funding the Lilly Endowment has provided for religious scholars and college educators and students to probe this theme. There is now a vigorous discussion of vocation among Catholic and Protestant scholars, and although Farley herself has not been involved in this discussion, the ethical insights she has developed over the years can contribute much to it.[24]

Farley's ideas on commitment and related topics are particularly useful for the contemporary reassessment of Christian vocation because she understands both Catholic and Protestant experiences so well and because she has integrated feminist insights so thoroughly into her work. A Catholic Sister of Mercy who taught for thirty-six years in a historically Protestant seminary at a secularized university (Yale Divinity School), Farley was trained in philosophy before undertaking studies of Christian Ethics under James Gustafson at Yale. Gustafson, a path-breaking Protestant scholar who later taught at the University of Chicago and Emory University, brought an ecumenical spirit and openness to diverse disciplines and methods to his theological and ethical work, and encouraged his students to pursue projects related to their backgrounds and interests. Farley began teaching full-time in New Haven in 1971, shortly before Gustafson moved to Chicago, and during her tenure at Yale Divinity School she was an active participant in important vocational struggles involving herself and other Sisters of Mercy.

Experiences during the period just prior to the publication of *Personal Commitments* in 1986 included tensions with the Vatican over demands that the sisters (elected leaders and many members) found inimical to their sense of what God was calling them to be and do. Three cases were profoundly significant for these women religious: a 1982 Vatican directive to the Mercy General Administrative Team halting consideration of whether their hospitals should provide tubal ligations; a 1983 ultimatum that Sister Agnes Mary Mansour should resign as Director of the Michigan Department of Social Services; and various pressures brought on Farley herself during 1984–85 to disavow a judgment concerning diversity among Catholics on the abortion issue. This last instance had involved the advertisement published in the *New York Times* just prior to the 1984 U.S. presidential election, which was discussed in the last chapter. As we saw, by late 1984 Farley and twenty-three other Catholic sisters faced the possibility of being dismissed from their communities if they did not publicly disassociate themselves from the advertisement. Each of these cases involved complex issues and a "trial by fire" of the vocations of the sisters affected. Their ideals, intelligence, faith, and staying power were tested by pressures from within and without.

Mercy hospitals and tubal ligations (1982)

Farley offered an analysis of the tubal ligation crisis to colleagues at the June 1982 convention of the Catholic Theological Society of America under the title, "Power and Powerlessness: A Case in Point." She explained that concern for the well-being of patients in hospitals operated by the Religious Sisters of Mercy of the Union had led the elected leaders of the community to sponsor a theological and ethical study of the policy banning tubal ligations in Catholic hospitals. These officers were persuaded by the study to recommend that tubal ligations should be made available in Mercy hospitals, which then comprised the largest network of private nonprofit hospitals in the country. This put them in a position of dissent from hierarchical authorities, since the policy had been established by the National Conference of Catholic Bishops. Although the Mercy General Administrative Team did not order a change in hospital policy, they informed hospital administrators of their belief that tubal ligations should be available "when failure to provide [them] would cause unjust injury to persons," and they expressed their "desire to draw concerned persons into dialogue on the issue." After some discussion between Sisters of Mercy and U.S. bishops on the matter, a directive of Pope John Paul II ended the dialogue with an ultimatum that the Mercy officers should withdraw their letter to the hospitals and accept magisterial teaching on tubal ligation. This Vatican directive posed a crisis of conscience for the Mercy leadership team, which they resolved in favor of submitting to Church authorities. Their submission entailed informing the Vatican officials on 11 May 1982 that although "they had personal disagreements" with official teaching on tubal ligations, "they would not in the light of present circumstances take a public position in opposition to it" and "they would withdraw their letter to the Community's hospitals."[25]

Farley's analysis of the reasons for this submission is instructive for a theology of vocation. She points out that three values were at stake—ministry, truth, and community—and all three had to be respected in the decision. Recognizing that public standoffs between the Vatican and women's religious congregations had led to the dissolution of American communities of sisters in the recent past, and knowing that not all Sisters of Mercy shared their own vision, the officers judged it prudent not to "take this Community 'to a wall' on this particular issue forced to a time-line by external authorities."[26] Their concern for community survival was not about preserving community for its own sake but about preserving the conditions for the possibility of continuing a healing ministry in their hospitals and maintaining a corporate voice capable of raising the question of truth again in a more favorable time. To employ the metaphor from *Personal Commitments*, they were willing to compromise their vision of truth and justice in order to preserve the "framework for love" that had served ministry so well in the past and still had such promise for the future.[27] Their capitulation was justified by Farley in terms of a traditional moral principle that allows for material cooperation in evil for the sake of a "proportionate good," with a proviso that the decision needs ongoing assessment from within and beyond the Mercy community. "[T]his story is unfinished," she concludes. "The wisdom of the decision of the Sisters of Mercy may become manifest only when their voice is once again heard."[28]

Agnes Mary Mansour and Mercy political ministries (1982–83)

Shortly after the tubal ligation case had been temporarily resolved, Mercy leaders were again confronted with Vatican pressures overriding their authority, this time with regard to appointing sisters to ministerial positions. The case of Sister Agnes Mary Mansour, a member of Farley's own Detroit Province of the Religious Sisters of Mercy, involved complex issues of political ministry, government service, and abortion. In 1982 Mansour had been President of Mercy College of Detroit for eleven years, and with the support of provincial leaders she decided to implement Mercy chapter statements about justice and systemic change by accepting a political appointment by the governor-elect of Michigan, James Blanchard. Sister Helen Marie Burns, Provincial Administrator, wrote that she "telephoned Archbishop [Edmund] Szoka who expressed his approval for the appointment and reflected his concern—should it be the Department of Social Services—for a clear stand relative to the abortion issue."[29] Mansour spoke with Szoka on 29 December, the day the governor-elect announced her appointment, and felt uncertain of the archbishop's support. It was clear, however, that he wanted her to state her opposition to abortion and to Medicaid payments for abortions, although her post would require her to uphold the law that mandated them. Burns quoted a 31 December 1982 *Detroit Free Press* article that indicated to her the archbishop's support for Mansour was "clear and firm":

> "A lot is being made about the fact that the [Department of Social Services] (uses Medicaid funds) to pay for abortions," [Szoka] said. "It's creating a problem where there is none. . . . As a sister, Sister Mansour must be in accord with the church. But in her job she has to follow the laws of the state, even if she doesn't agree with them. . . . The fact that her appointment encompasses so many of the areas women religious have traditionally worked in— poor, foster children, welfare—could give a powerful witness to the Christian dimension of the D.S.S."[30]

Between the Governor-elect's announcement and the 8 March confirmation hearing, however, pressure from right-to-life groups led Archbishop Szoka to ask Mansour to relinquish the appointment unless she made a clear statement against Medicaid funding for abortions. Mansour was decidedly against abortion, but she had reached a more nuanced view of the Medicaid situation than would allow her to comply with Szoka's wishes, which she subsequently described thus:

> I'm opposed to abortion and consider it a violent solution to a human problem. I don't consider myself pro-choice; I am pro-life. I also recognize that those who are pro-life need to be more convincing in changing attitudes than in controlling what is done in a pluralistic society. Living in a morally pluralistic society, one must respect the fact that other people may conscientiously come to other decisions regarding abortion. We should not attempt to control their decisions through public policy when no consensus exists. Neither do I feel it would be appropriate to withdraw resources for the poor as long as abortion is legal in our society. It would be illegal to withdraw [M]edicaid funds for abortion.[31]

On 23 February Szoka called for Mansour to resign the position, and Mercy leaders then sought in various ways to gain time to consider the issues. Burns and her administrative team named these issues in a 5 March press release: "'(a) the religious community's traditional involvement in social services; (b) their support for Sister Agnes Mary Mansour in accepting the appointment as Director of Social Services; and (c) their respect for the Archbishop's authority.'"[32] Church authorities, however, took swift action to address what they regarded as a simple matter of obedience and insisted that Mercy leaders confront Mansour with a stark choice. On 23 March the apostolic delegate, Archbishop Pio Laghi, gave Mercy general administrators Sister M. Theresa Kane and Sister Emily George a letter indicating that the Vatican Congregation for Religious and Secular Institutes (CRIS) required Kane to order Mansour to resign or else face dismissal from the congregation. After extensive consultation the Mercy leaders (provincial and general) sought an alternative solution to the dilemma. On 11 April Kane requested formal reconsideration of Rome's decision, with a provision that Mansour would be granted a leave of absence from the Sisters of Mercy during her term of political

office, effective 20 April 1983. The leadership team expected there
would be time for discussion of this alternative with the Holy See, but
instead their authority was bypassed by Roman officials, who sought
a direct confrontation with Mansour.

CRIS had delegated Bishop Anthony Bevilacqua of Brooklyn, NY, to
"approach Sister Agnes Mary directly and to require, in the name of the
Holy See and by virtue of her vow of obedience, that she immediately
resign as Director of the Department of Social Services," and he did
this during a momentous meeting on 9 May 1983.[33] The Mercy sisters
in attendance—Agnes Mary Mansour, Helen Marie Burns (the Detroit
provincial leader), and Emily George (a Detroit Province member then
serving on the general administrative team)—were surprised by the
nature of this meeting, having expected an opportunity to discuss
the issues with church authorities. Mansour knew that Bevilacqua
had been delegated by Pope John Paul II to convey the Holy See's
decision concerning her government appointment, but neither she
nor the Mercy leaders realized she would be expected to come to an
immediate decision about her future as a woman religious.

On 9 May at the Mercy provincial house in Detroit, Bevilacqua
presented a long document from the Holy See to Mansour. This
"formal precept" summarized the Vatican interpretation of events
since December and the official policy on leaves of absence, and
concluded with the following points:

> 3. In virtue of this mandate and as *ad hoc* delegate of the Holy See,
> I hereby require, in the name of the Holy See and by virtue of your
> vow of obedience to the Holy Father, that you immediately resign
> your position as Director of the Department of Social Services in
> the State of Michigan.
> 4. Should you refuse to obey this precept to resign imme-
> diately . . . I shall be compelled to initiate immediately the
> canonical process that subjects you to the penalty of imposed
> secularization entailing dismissal from the religious Congregation
> of the Sisters of Mercy and the loss of your canonical status as a
> Religious Sister.[34]

Mansour later observed that the meeting offered "no due process"
and "there wasn't even a full understanding of my rights." She feared
dismissal from her community and scandal.

Burns' account of the meeting's outcome accords with that of Mansour:

> After discussion, argumentation, reflection, and prayer, Sister Agnes Mary regretfully requested dispensation from her vows. She had asked what alternatives were open to her and was offered none. She had stated that she did not wish to be in defiance of the Holy Father and did not wish to be dismissed. She asked for dispensation, then, as the only means possible to avoid resigning from a position she felt was in accord with the mission of the Sisters of Mercy and to avoid defiance of the Holy Father by forcing the Holy See to dismiss her from the Sisters of Mercy.[35]

Bevilacqua had brought to the meeting an official document of dispensation from vows, which Mansour and he signed, along with Mercy leaders Burns and George.[36] Mansour left the meeting officially separated from the religious community to which she had belonged for thirty years.

Later efforts by Mercy leaders to have the case reconsidered because the process had impinged on Mansour's freedom without benefit of canonical legal advice proved unsuccessful. In the fall of 1983 the Eleventh General Chapter of the Sisters of Mercy of the Union voiced deep concern over the matter, objecting to the lack of mutuality and due process in the Vatican's handling of Mansour's case.[37] Mercy general administrators soon faced further difficulties concerning political ministry, this time involving two sisters from Rhode Island, Arlene Violet (who was running for state Attorney General) and Elizabeth Morancy (who sought a fourth term in the state legislature). Although Bishop Louis Gelineau of Providence had given Morancy a diocesan award in 1981 for her "work with the handicapped," including "her successful sponsorship of two bills providing subsidy programs for parents of handicapped children," by 1983 he opposed the political ministries of both Morancy and Violet.[38] Each sister sought ways of continuing political work without leaving the congregation, and the Twelfth General Chapter sent a formal petition to the Holy See for an indult that would allow Morancy to remain a legislator, which Rome denied.[39] By the time Theresa Kane completed her term as General Administrator of the congregation in July 1984, both Violet and Morancy accepted dispensations from their vows in order to continue political ministries originally undertaken in response to Mercy chapter decrees.

Margaret Farley and the *New York Times* advertisement (1984–86)

These developments had meanwhile alerted other women religious to issues of Vatican power and due process of canon law, and the Mercy cases were kept in mind during a third critical confrontation between Rome and U.S. sisters, which took place during 1984–86. This involved the case of the twenty-four women religious who had signed the statement on abortion and public policy that had been published by Catholics for a Free Choice (CFFC) in the *New York Times* on 7 October 1984. This case, which has been discussed briefly in the last chapter, affected a number of religious congregations, including the Sisters of Mercy.[40] Farley, like many other signers, had responded to a 1983 CFFC survey without knowing that the document would eventually be published as an advertisement.

The case put pressure as well on the officers and staff of the Leadership Conference of Women Religious (LCWR), the national organization of elected leaders of women's communities. LCWR called for a day of prayer and fasting in March 1985 on behalf of "a just and peaceful resolution to the situation," and supported the officers by trying to communicate with the Vatican behind the scenes. The organization also sought to educate its members by focusing the program of its September 1985 convention in New Orleans on ethical decision-making, inviting Margaret Farley as a plenary speaker. Despite the fact that two prominent members of the hierarchy cancelled their plans to attend and celebrate the liturgy because Farley was speaking, LCWR went ahead with their program.[41] Farley's presentation, "From Moral Insight to Moral Choice: Decision-Making in the Christian Community," was a general one that did not mention her own situation as a signer, although in discussing natural law she declared that "'authority' to teach is the power to evoke consent, the power to enable to see. Truth . . . does not come in the form of extrinsic imposition, in the form of juridical power."[42] Neither the Mansour case nor that of the Vatican 24 has been the subject of an ethical essay by Farley comparable to her treatment of the tubal ligation case in 1982. These three cases, however, were unfolding during the years she prepared *Personal Commitments* for publication in 1986. They have informed her subsequent work as well, including an essay occasioned by the Vatican's removal of moral theologian Charles Curran from his tenured position at the Catholic University of America in 1986. In that 1987 essay, "Moral Discourse in the Public Arena," Farley observed that "[w]e have had long centuries in which to learn the counterproductiveness of coercive measures when the issue becomes not truth but power."[43]

Farley waited until the occasion of her presidential address to the Catholic Theological Society of America in 2000 to make a full statement of her reasons against the hierarchy's "overwhelming preoccupation" with abortion policies and its effort to control internal debate on moral questions. Arguing that these approaches are counterproductive and scandalous, she recommended that opposition to abortion "should be removed from the center of the [church's political] agenda until the credibility gap regarding women and the church is addressed."[44] Although abortion policy should remain part of the agenda, Farley invited speculation on gains to be made if racism or welfare rights were to become the central focus instead.[45] She also argued that efforts by the hierarchy to curtail debate among theologians are unhelpful. Not only do they diminish the "effectiveness of the Church's voice in the public political arena," but they also cause confusion among the faithful and discourage the "best and the brightest" from pursuing a "vocation in theology."[46] The aim of Farley's critique is to restore the possibility that the church can bring a prophetic witness to the public arena. In her estimation, a reconfigured agenda and a reasonable degree of tolerance for theological diversity will allow the church to regain credibility in the wider society. This will permit its voice to summon everyone "to the imperatives of justice and the respect and care of those among us who are wounded or ignored." The tradition itself, in its enduring respect for reason and human freedom and its ideal of love for one another, has the resources needed to restore trust between those "whose vocation is theology and those whose vocation is church leadership."[47] The willingness of Pope John Paul II to pray for forgiveness at the Western Wall in Jerusalem during Lent of the Jubilee Year 2000 exemplifies the sort of "humility, respect, and deepest compassion" required for the church in the United States to influence the wider society for the good.[48]

As one looks back over the tensions between the Sisters of Mercy and the hierarchy that affected Farley so profoundly during the 1980s and then observes the appreciative way she invokes the image of papal leadership while seeking to deflect the U.S. bishops from a counterproductive public strategy, there are several things to note. In the first place, Farley's theological work is so thoroughly Catholic, shaped by the characteristic conviction that tensions between faith and reason, authority and freedom, individual conscience and the common good, are creative and enduring ones. The vocations of theologians and church leaders are different, and each role affords a different vision of what circumstances require. Although church officials should have the last word, this word will be the wiser if leaders listen well to the wide range of church members' experiences before teaching on controversial issues.

Also noteworthy is the irony that the Vatican made such strong efforts in the early 1980s to control the behavior of women religious, whose political actions and statements issued from concern for the poor and marginalized, and whatever one thinks of their wisdom, were legal and well-meant. Church officials did this, however, during the very years when they missed the opportunity to stem the sexual abuse crisis by taking strong action against the criminal behavior of priests. If only the wrath of Rome had fallen on abusive priests with half the force expended on Agnes Mary Mansour or Elizabeth Morancy!

Finally, it is intriguing to note that although Farley regularly stresses that women's experience is a crucial resource for feminist ethics, she has rarely written about the experiences of herself and other Sisters of Mercy. The brief treatment of the tubal ligation case she presented to colleagues of the CTSA in 1982 was exceptional in this regard. Nevertheless these experiences inform her choice of topics and the ethical insights she reaches, and they undoubtedly contribute as well to the theology of vocation that grounds her work. Although she does not often employ the rhetoric of vocation or call, the occasional instances are telling, perhaps none more so than the following passage from her 1985 address to LCWR, offered in a discussion of conflicts of value:

> When it comes to making radical choices—choices that involve explicit decisions about what we will love absolutely and how we will integrate all of our other loves and all of our actions in relation to our absolute love—we need a method of discernment that goes beyond rational assessment of situations and consideration of principles. We need a method that enables us to discern the call of God—a call not always able to be understood only as a call to "right" rather than "wrong," or even "good" rather than "evil," but a call to the way along which we are to go if we are to be faithful to what we love above all else.[49]

This ideal of fidelity to the divine call, we may infer, is what enabled the various Sisters of Mercy to sacrifice different finite goods and loves, even their treasured identity as members of this religious congregation, when confronted with an ultimatum that would take them off the path their consciences had discerned as the way of fidelity to God, who called them to care especially for the poor and marginalized. Farley said as much at the 21 December 2004 funeral of Agnes Mary Mansour:

> It was a painful truth that she had to leave [the Sisters of Mercy], that the church declared her officially not a member. There was suffering in the community, and also for her. When she left she was quoted as saying that she would always be a Sister of Mercy in her heart. And that has absolutely been the case. She continued in works of mercy all her life.[50]

Farley's vocational metaphor from 1985 of the "way along which we are to go" seems to anticipate the metaphor of "framework for love" associated with her largely implicit theology of vocation in *Personal Commitments*. Both metaphors suggest the idea of a context for living as a Christian, one capable of allowing the agent to relate finite loves appropriately to their divine Source.

Insights contributing to a theology of vocation

With these experiences and writings of Farley in mind, we are now in a position to draw out some implications of her ethics for today's discussion of vocation. As was mentioned earlier, in recent years there has been a resurgence of interest in the topic of vocation in the United States, thanks in part to funding from the Lilly Endowment. Two works of note that Lilly has supported are Sandra M. Schneiders' trilogy *Religious Life in the New Millennium*, of which the first two volumes (*Finding the Treasure* and *Selling All*) were published in 2000 and 2001, and the third (*Buying the Field*) is expected in 2013; and Douglas J. Schuurman's 2004 study, *Vocation: Discerning Our Callings in Life*.[51] The former is a masterful treatment of the Catholic vowed religious life, with particular attention to the situation of contemporary women who have chosen this "organic lifeform," to use Schneiders' language. The latter is a more general exploration of the topic of vocation from a Protestant perspective. Each makes a distinctive contribution to contemporary understanding of the religious reality of vocation, and both can be effectively complemented by some ethical insights Farley has developed over the years. Among the ideas from Farley's ethics that are particularly useful for the contemporary discussion of vocation are the following: active receptivity and the framework for love; the value of institutions; egalitarianism and a new natural law sexual ethic; the reciprocal relationship of justice and love; and attention to the problems of postmodernity for love and commitment.

Active receptivity and framework for love

The metaphor of framework, derived from the human activity of building, takes away the "mystique" of vocation and assigns human responsibility properly. Frameworks are humanly built. This metaphor counters the passivity of precritical understandings of vocation and highlights the active dimension of the experience, which is recognized by Schneiders, Schuurman, and others. Farley has also written on the notion of "active receptivity," an idea that offers philosophical and theological grounds for recognizing our role as cocreators of our own vocations, and helps us to demystify the experience. Schuurman, for example, stresses that it is a "misconception" to think of vocation as providing a "blueprint" for life or an "unmistakable, miraculous call." Rather the "call" is mediated in "numerous and quiet ways," and is essentially a matter of employing "one's God-given gifts to be of use to the broader community."[52] Schneiders is similarly concerned to minimize miraculous interpretations of the imagery of the call to a religious vocation. Faith in God's presence and guidance does not require that this call must occur outside normal processes of attraction and influence. Far from being a thunderclap from the sky, the experience of vocation involves a

> convergence of interior factors such as attraction, talent, interest, experience, desires, ideals, and even realistic fears and awareness of personal limitations, with exterior factors such as people I admire, work that interests me, opportunity presenting itself, needs that move me, structures that facilitate exploration, invitation from another. This convergence is usually a rich mixture that is both confusing and exciting and leads a person to begin to explore what this might mean.[53]

What Farley has observed concerning the "active receptivity" involved in the love of God and neighbor is indeed congruent with what these contemporaries are noting about the experience of Christian vocation: " . . . [A]ll this receptivity at the heart of Christian existence is not in any way only passivity. . . . The receiving which is each human person's from God, and from one another within a life shared in God, is an active participation in the active receptivity of Christ, awakening, growing, reaching to the coincidence of peak receptivity with peak activity."[54]

The value of institutions

As structures, frameworks are valuable and necessary; they are not mere scaffolding. Keeping them serviceable is a worthy task, and whenever possible the frameworks for love should be preserved and strengthened. The Mercy leaders who decided in 1982 to submit to a Vatican directive they judged to be wrong did so with the awareness that this "material cooperation with evil" seemed necessary to prevent greater harm, namely the loss of the institutions that expressed the Mercy ministry. Schneiders prefers an organic metaphor for the institution of vowed religious life, treating it as a "lifeform" at some risk in a postmodern era, one whose evolution (or possible extinction) is in large measure in the hands of religious themselves. Farley's structural metaphor complements this organic one nicely, inviting awareness of the ways that institutions are needed to support life, just as skeletal structures are needed for complex organisms.

Egalitarianism and a new natural law sexual ethic

Although official Catholic teaching no longer promotes an elitist view of celibacy as superior to marriage, the magisterial positions on sexual ethics have not kept pace with these developments in ecclesiology. The classic Christian ethic has tended to view celibacy and marriage as islands of grace in a sea of sexual sin. Farley is a leader in developing a more adequate sexual ethic, one that respects the complexity of sexual sin and grace and the diversity of human beings. Proposing that justice is a better norm for sex than either the traditional "taboo morality" or the vague subjectivism of "love," she argues that sexual relations, to be just, must respect the "concrete reality, actual and potential" of the partners, which she analyzes in terms of their autonomy and relationality. This leads her to develop several criteria for judging the appropriateness of sexual relations: avoidance of unjust harm, free consent, mutuality, equality of power, commitment, fruitfulness, and social justice. The list comprises a stringent set of norms that apply equally to heterosexual and homosexual couples.[55]. The pioneering work Farley has done in the area of same-sex relationships is also a resource for vocational exploration by homosexual and other differently gendered persons, including the increasingly wide sanctioning of gay marriage.

The reciprocal relationship of justice and love

Contrary to the stereotypical gendered assignment of love to the private sphere and justice to the public sphere, Farley argues persuasively for a unified understanding, which sees that justice and love are dialectically related. In an important essay from 1975, "New Patterns of Relationship," she examines the historical reasons for bringing a new feminist approach to the question of justice and love, and insists that "justice itself is the norm of love," while love (mutuality, communion) is the goal of justice:

> What is required of Christians is a just love, a love which does indeed correspond to the reality of those loved. . . . Minimal justice, then, may have equality as its norm and full mutuality as its goal. Justice will be maximal as it approaches the ultimate goal of communion of each person with all persons and with God.[56]

Farley's detailed analysis of justice as a norm for love would be especially helpful as a complement to Schuurman's discussion, which emphasizes love as "vocation's guiding moral norm" and shalom as "its orienting ideal." Schuurman recognizes that a proper understanding of vocation ought to "criticize hierarchies—whether based on gender, race, or class" and "transform asymmetric relations." A fuller treatment of what constitutes a love that is *just* would enhance this discussion considerably.[57] Farley's 1975 analysis of *agape*, equal regard, self-sacrifice, and mutuality in light of the recognition of women's full human dignity offers ways of advancing the revolutionary changes required in intimate and public relationships alike if the aims Schuurman expresses are to be achieved.[58]

Attention to the problems of postmodernity for love and commitments

Farley returned to the analysis of love and justice with new force and insight in her 2002 Madeleva Lecture, *Compassionate Respect:*

A Feminist Approach to Medical Ethics and Other Questions.
This time the analysis is conducted mainly in conversation with
philosophical ethics and theories of postmodernity rather than
Christian texts, with particular attention to the current debate
between schools of ethics emphasizing care and those stressing
autonomy, respect, and justice. She argues that the debate
between these schools is misconceived, and maintains that when
care is thought of in terms of compassion it becomes evident
that "only if they [compassion and respect] are integrated, each
requiring the other, will their full meaning be conceptually clear
and practically useful in moral discernment."⁵⁹ She describes
compassion as "a way of 'seeing' that evokes a moral response,"
and maintains that this way of seeing brings a "stronger affect"
to the notion of care because it attends to the concrete reality of
suffering human beings.⁶⁰

Attention to the concrete reality of suffering human beings is
a theme threaded through Farley's writings. Postmodernity, she
is quite aware, has challenged traditional understandings of the
unified self and posed philosophical problems for claims about
reality, and the possibility of commitment and love. And yet, she
maintains, the seemingly decentered postmodern self ("no longer
preoccupied with self-certainty in settled truth") is paradoxically
"freed for relationship," particularly when it is willing to respect the
destabilizing experiences of beauty and the pain of others, and to
respond with reverence and compassion.⁶¹ However attenuated our
freedom may be, it remains the case that human beings have some
ability to focus our attention and bind ourselves to future deeds of
love. Indeed, as she argued in *Personal Commitments*, it is precisely
the instability of our experiences of desire that leads us to bind up
our futures by making commitments, for commitment is "love's way
of being whole when it is not yet whole, love's way of offering its
incapacities as well as its power."⁶² Schneiders' treatment of the
need for "perpetual commitment" to Jesus Christ in Religious Life is
explicitly dependent on this work of Farley, although she does not
probe the factors that can sometimes justify seeking a dispensation
from religious vows once the commitment has been publicly
expressed. Further conversation with Farley on this matter seems
warranted, as well as on the connections between Farley's claim

that only God is to be loved absolutely and Schneiders' assertion that "[t]he commitment that constitutes Religious Life is absolute, total, and unconditional, whereas the implicated commitment to the congregation is relative, partial, and conditional" because the essence of religious life involves "the commitment to love Jesus Christ totally, absolutely, and forever and to express and embody that love . . . in the complete and exclusive self-gift of consecrated celibacy."[63]

Schuurman's discussion of vocation would likewise benefit from more explicit attention to the demands and limits of commitment, for it is more concerned with arguing the value and possibility of vocation than with pondering what constitutes fidelity to vocation once it is embraced. He shares the basic position of Farley and Schneiders that one's ultimate relationship is with God, and this leads him to recommend always being "open to the possibility that God will call us to other forms of paid work, to new social relations, to a different marital status, to different roles in our churches and communities."[64] One senses that he would welcome the sort of clear criteria Farley provides for changing "frameworks for love" as a way to balance the openness to change that his theological position commends.

Schuurman and Schneiders both share with Farley the recognition that the Christian's vocation is linked with concern for the needs and sufferings of others, and their discussions can be enriched by Farley's increasingly explicit emphasis on the call to "drink the cup" of suffering, and to combat vigorously the "unnecessary" suffering that is caused by injustice, including injustice for which the Christian tradition bears some responsibility.[65] In her recent work Farley has elaborated this concern in terms of the need to see how religions, particularly fundamentalist versions, are putting the health of persons, especially women, at great risk. The inability of most Catholic bishops to tolerate the use of condoms as part of a comprehensive program to prevent spread of the AIDS virus is surely a factor in Farley's articulating this concern about fundamentalist religion. Undoubtedly her earlier experience of tensions over health care issues between the Vatican and the Sisters of Mercy contributes to her insistence that the suffering we see in the global HIV/AIDS pandemic should inspire Christians to examine their own attitudes and actions in light of the gospel mandate to imitate God's mercy:

> Like God's mercy, genuine human mercy is formed by respect for what God has made—for human freedom, relationality, embodiment, historical and cultural formation, uniqueness, and the potentiality of fullness of life in an unlimited future. Like God's mercy, genuine human mercy is made true by its justice.[66]

Mercy, we do well to note, is the distinctive charism of her religious congregation, and there is no doubt that her years of contemplating this particular gift have contributed to Farley's insights on what works of mercy and justice are demanded in our time. We should hardly be surprised that her writings argue so strongly that attention to the sufferings of others is essential to love, in a postmodern or any other world, or that poised as she is between the world of the Religious Sisters of Mercy and that of the secular academy, she has probed, again and again, the connection between compassion/care and rationality. She has further enriched the contemporary discussion of vocation by her occasional remarks on the Christian vocation to prophecy, something Schneiders claims is central to the "organic lifeform" of Religious Life, and by her own willingness "to speak the truth in love" to a wide audience of secular and religious readers, including church authorities who might encounter her works.[67]

The stakes for rethinking the meaning of vocation in a world of systemic violence and injustice are as high today as ever. Farley's ideas on "frameworks for love," on the relation between justice and compassion, on how to love justly in a postmodern world, and on the process and obligations of personal commitments constitute an invaluable resource for this task.

Notes

1   John Gardner, *Self-Renewal: The Individual and the Innovative Society*. New York: Harper & Row, 1963, p. 7. Gardner credits Peter Drucker's *Landmarks of Tomorrow* (New York: Harper & Brothers, 1959), chapters 1 and 2, as the source of this insight.

2 Margaret A. Farley, *Just Love: A Framework for Christian Sexual Ethics* (New York: Continuum, 2006). See also Introduction, p. 25n. 46.

3 Farley's discussion of "framework for love" (pp. 36, 98, and elsewhere) has given me the title for this chapter. See especially Margaret A. Farley, *Personal Commitments: Beginning, Keeping, Changing* (San Francisco: Harper & Row, 1986).

4 John Shea, *Stories of God: An Unauthorized Biography* (Chicago: Thomas More Press, 1978), p. 52.

5 Andrew M. Greeley, *The Jesus Myth* (Garden City, NY: Doubleday & Company, 1971), p. 13. Greeley's prefatory note begins with a defense of his title: "The word 'myth' is used in the title of this volume in a specific and definite sense. A myth is a symbolic story which demonstrates, in Alan Watts' words, 'the inner meaning of the universe and of human life.' To say that Jesus is a myth is not to say that he is a legend but that his life and message are an attempt to demonstrate 'the inner meaning of the universe and of human life.'" I concur with Greeley's judgment that there is great value in employing this term that is so "common among historians of religion, literary critics, and social scientists," and that Christians should overcome their fear of the word "myth" and appropriate it as a valuable tool for understanding their faith, p. 12.

6 James M. Gustafson, *Can Ethics Be Christian?* (Chicago: University of Chicago Press, 1975), p. 179.

7 Farley, *Personal Commitments*, p. 11.

8 Frederick Buechner, *Wishful Thinking*, 1993, p. 119. Cited here from Parker J. Palmer, *Let Your Life Speak: Listening for the Voice of Vocation* (San Francisco: Jossey-Bass Publishers, 2000), p. 16.

9 Farley, *Personal Commitments*, pp. 22, 84, 92, 99, and elsewhere.

10 Margaret A. Farley, "An Ethic for Same-Sex Relations," in *A Challenge to Love,* ed. Robert Nugent (New York: Crossroad, 1983), pp. 103–4.

11 Vatican II, *Dogmatic Constitution on the Church (Lumen Gentium)* #32. All citations from the Second Vatican Council are from Walter M. Abbott, ed., *The Documents of Vatican II* (New York: America Press, 1966).

12 Margaret A. Farley, "The Church and the Family: An Ethical Task," *Horizons* 10 (1983): 56.

13 For a full treatment of Protestant discussions, see Douglas J. Schuurman, *Vocation: Discerning Our Callings in Life* (Grand Rapids, MI: William B. Eerdmans, 2004).

14 Farley, "The Church and the Family," p. 63.

15 Margaret A. Farley, "New Patterns of Relationship: Beginnings of a Moral Revolution," *Theological Studies* 36 (1975): 628 and 645.

16 Farley, *Personal Commitments*, p. 120.

17 Paul Ricoeur, *The Symbolism of Evil*, trans. Emerson Buchanan (Boston: Beacon Press, 1967), p. 351.

18 Farley, *Personal Commitments*, p. 10. Farley is quoting here from Ricoeur's *Essays on Biblical Interpretation*, ed. Lewis S. Mudge (Philadelphia: Fortress, 1980), p. 97.

19 Farley, *Personal Commitments*, p. 112.

20 Ibid., pp. 114, 116.

21 Ibid., p. 134.

22 Ibid., p. 117.

23 Ibid., p. 133.

24 In addition to other vocation-related grants to scholars, seminaries, and divinity schools, the Lilly Endowment awarded $176.2 million to 88 church-related colleges and universities during 2000–02 through its Programs for the Theological Exploration of Vocation (PTEV) initiative. According to the PETV website, the purpose of these grants was to help the schools "establish or strengthen programs that (1) assist students in examining the relationship between faith and vocational choices, (2) provide opportunities for gifted young people to explore Christian ministry, and (3) enhance the capacity of a school's faculty and staff to teach and mentor students effectively in this area" (http://www.ptev.org/history.aspx, accessed 28 April 2004). Since 2010 information is available at a new site, for the Lilly-funded Network for Vocation in Undergraduate Education, or NetVUE: http://www.cic.edu/Programs-and-Services/Programs/NetVUE/Pages/default.aspx (accessed 29 September 2012).

25 Margaret A. Farley, "Power and Powerlessness: A Case in Point," *CTSA Proceedings* 37(1982): 116–7. I have discussed these issues more fully in Anne E. Patrick, *Liberating Conscience* (New York: Continuum, 1996), pp. 41–8.

26 Farley, "Power and Powerlessness," p. 118.

27 In making this decision Mercy leaders were vividly aware of two cases from the late 1960s in which women's religious communities had been drastically reorganized after hierarchical interventions short-circuited internal debates on post-Vatican II renewal. In both cases (Glenmary Sisters and Sisters of the Immaculate Heart of Mary of Los Angeles) the majority of sisters had responded to Vatican interventions by reluctantly requesting dispensations from their vows and forming noncanonical religious organizations. For accounts of these events, see Helen M. Lewis and Monica Appleby, *Mountain Sisters: From Convent to Community* (Lexington, KY: The University Press of Kentucky, 2003), and Anita M. Caspary, *Witness to Integrity: The Crisis of the Immaculate Heart Community of California* (Collegeville, MN: Liturgical Press, 2003).

28 Farley, "Power and Powerlessness," p. 119. The eminent moral theologian, Richard A. McCormick, SJ, had been involved in the study originally commissioned by the Mercy leaders, and with bioethicist Corrine Bayley, CSJ, had published some findings in "Sterilization: The Dilemma of Catholic Hospitals," *America* 143 (1980): 222–5. He later commented in *Health and Medicine in the Catholic Tradition* (New York: Crossroad, 1984) that "In 1980 I coauthored . . . an article in *America* arguing that some sterilizations were morally defensible. A bishop friend of mine remarked to me, 'I can name you at least one hundred bishops who agree with you—but none who will say so publicly.' That is, of course, profoundly saddening for anyone who treasures the free flow of information in the Church", pp. 103–4.

29 Helen Marie Burns, RSM, "Case Study: The Experience of Sisters of Mercy of the Union in Public Office," in *Authority, Community, and Conflict*, ed. Madonna Kolbenschlag (Kansas City, MO: Sheed & Ward, 1986), p. 5.

30 Quoted in *ibid.*, p. 6. Archbishop Szoka's account of events in December differs from that of Burns, according to his letter of 23 February 1983, which is reproduced as an appendix to Kolbenschlag, *Authority*, pp. 155–7.

31 Agnes Mary Mansour, interviewed by Annie Lally Milhaven, ed., *The Inside Stories: 13 Valiant Women Challenging the Church* (Mystic, CT: Twenty-Third Publications, 1987), p. 66.

32 Burns, "Case Study," p. 8.

33 Ibid., p. 12.

34 Kolbenschlag, *Authority*, p. 173. The full text of the formal precept is found on pp. 168–73.

35 Burns, "Case Study," p. 12.

36 The Indult of Secularization is reprinted in Kolbenschlag, *Authority*, p. 174.

37 Burns, "Case Study," p. 15.

38 The diocesan award is mentioned in a lengthy Petition from the Twelfth General Chapter of the Sisters of Mercy to CRIS, included as "Document 29" in Kolbenschlag, *Authority*, p. 201.

39 See "Document 29", pp. 196–205 and "Document 30", pp. 205–6, in Kolbenschlag, *Authority*. Priests and religious brothers were also required to leave political office at this time. A notable example was Robert F. Drinan, SJ, who had been a congressman from Massachusetts during 1971–81, but did not seek reelection in 1980.

40 See Chapter 3, pp. 97–99, and p. 109n. 29.

41 Archbishop Pio Laghi, Papal Pro-nuncio to the United States, and Archbishop John R. Quinn of San Francisco cancelled plans to attend the LCWR convention, but Archbishop Philip Hannan of New Orleans did celebrate the liturgy there. See Florence Herman and Jerry Filteau's story in the Washington, DC, *Catholic Standard* for 12 September 1985, "Archbishops Boycott Meeting Because of Abortion Ad Signer." Former executive directors of LCWR, Lora Ann Quiñonez and Mary Daniel Turner, describe the careful thought involved in LCWR's convention decisions in *The Transformation of American Catholic Sisters* (Philadelphia: Temple University Press, 1992), pp. 133–40. Along with Farley, I was also a keynote speaker for this convention, giving a presentation on "The Moral Decision Maker: 'From Good Sisters to Prophetic Women.'" My subtitle was taken from Jeannine Gramick, "From Good Sisters to Prophetic Women," in *Midwives of the Future: American Sisters Tell Their Story*, ed. Ann Patrick Ware (Kansas City, MO: Leaven Press, 1985), pp. 226–37.

42 Margaret A. Farley, "From Moral Insight to Moral Choice: Discernment and Decision-Making in the Christian Community" (unpublished typescript, 1985), p. 11.

43 Margaret A. Farley, "Moral Discourse in the Public Arena," in *Vatican Authority and American Catholic Dissent: The Curran Case and Its Consequences*, ed. William W. May (New York: Crossroad, 1987), p. 184. See also Margaret A. Farley, "Ethics, Ecclesiology, and the Grace of Self-Doubt," in *A Call to Fidelity: On the Moral Theology of Charles E. Curran*, eds. James J. Walter and Thomas A. Shannon (Washington, DC: Georgetown University Press, 2002), pp. 55–75.

44 Margaret A. Farley, "The Church in the Public Forum: Scandal or Prophetic Witness?" *CTSA Proceedings* 55 (2000): 89–92.

45 Ibid., p. 95.

46 Ibid., pp. 96–7.

47 Ibid., pp. 98–9.

48 Ibid., p. 101.

49 Farley, "From Moral Insight to Moral Choice," p. 9.

50 Margaret A. Farley, quoted in Arthur Jones, "She Answered to Her Conscience: Agnes Mary Mansour, Who Left Mercys at Vatican Ultimatum, Dies at 73," *National Catholic Reporter* (7 January 2005), p. 7.

51 Sandra M. Schneiders, IHM, *Finding the Treasure: Locating Catholic Religious Life in a New Ecclesial and Cultural Context*, vol. 1 of *Religious Life in a New Millennium* (New York: Paulist Press, 2000), *Selling All: Commitment, Consecrated Celibacy, and Community in*

Catholic Religious Life, vol. 2 of *Religious Life in a New Millennium* (New York: Paulist Press, 2001), and *Buying the Field: Religious Life in Mission to the World*, vol. 3 of *Religious Life in a New Millennium* (New York: Paulist Press, 2013); and Douglas Schuurman, *Vocation: Discerning Our Callings in Life* (Grand Rapids, MI: Wm. B. Eerdmans Publishing Company, 2004).

52 Schuurman, *Vocation*, pp. 127 and 164. The mediated quality of vocation is also emphasized in Edward P. Hahnenberg's recent study, *Awakening Vocation: A Theology of Christian Call* (Collegeville, MN: Liturgical Press, 2010), pp. 193–5.

53 Schneiders, *Selling All*, pp. 12–13.

54 Farley, "New Patterns of Relationship," p. 639.

55 *Just Love*, pp. 215–31. Some of Farley's conclusions differ from official Catholic teaching, as the CDF censure in 2012 made clear, but they are grounded in a natural law ethic, in this case one that is informed by scripture and tradition. Among other Catholic moral theologians whose writings on sexual ethics received ecclesiastical censure earlier are Charles E. Curran, André Guindon, Anthony Kosnik, Todd A. Salzman, and Michael G. Lawler. Bradford E. Hinze discusses recent interventions in "A Decade of Disciplining Theologians," in *When the Magisterium Intervenes: The Magisterium and Theologians in Today's Church*, ed. Richard R. Gaillardetz (Collegeville: Liturgical Press, 2012), pp. 3–39.

56 Farley, "New Patterns of Relationship," pp. 643 and 646.

57 Schuurman, *Vocation*, pp. 79 and 114.

58 Farley, "New Patterns of Relationship," pp. 632–46. See also Farley, *Just Love*, pp. 196–206.

59 Margaret A. Farley, *Compassionate Respect: A Feminist Approach to Medical Ethics and Other Questions* (New York: Paulist, 2002), p. 4.

60 Ibid., p. 40. Hahnenberg likewise stresses the importance of attending to others' suffering: "God calls us through the suffering of others. Our vocation is found in and through the world's pain," *Awakening Vocation*, p. 201.

61 Margaret A. Farley, "How Shall We Love in a Postmodern World?" *The Annual of the Society of Christian Ethics* (1994): 17–18. This was her presidential address to the Society.

62 Farley, *Personal Commitments*, p. 134.

63 Schneiders, *Selling All*, p. 80.

64 Schuurman, *Vocation*, p. 162.

65 Margaret A. Farley, "History, Spirituality, and Justice," p. 335; and *Compassionate Respect*, pp. 69–79. In the latter work Farley draws attention particularly to the unjust suffering associated with the worldwide HIV-AIDS pandemic and maintains that patriarchal religions must be challenged about their role "in making women invisible" if there is to be a "compassionate response to the crisis of AIDS", p. 17.

66 Farley, *Compassionate Respect*, p. 79.

67 See, for example, Farley, "The Church in the Public Forum," pp. 98–9. Schneiders maintains that "as an essentially prophetic vocation and state of life in the Church, Religious Life should constitute a continual call from within the Church to ongoing reform and increasing fidelity to the Gospel." See her *Finding the Treasure*, pp. 252–3.

5
VOCATION IN A TRANSFORMED SOCIAL CONTEXT

"Since the late 1960s, a Catholic woman in American society has had vastly more opportunities for education and meaningful work outside church structures than within them. But from the mid-nineteenth century until the late 1960s, quite the opposite was true."

—KATHLEEN SPROWS CUMMINGS, 2009[1]

"In our [U.S. Catholic] parishes, 80 percent of the lay ecclesial ministers are women, as are the great majority of lay ministers. . . . The women involved in ministry are a leaven in the churches, bringing change."

—ZENI FOX, 2008[2]

Just how high are the stakes involved in rethinking Catholic women's church vocations became evident in the spring of 2012, when the Vatican Congregation for the Doctrine of the Faith (CDF) moved to take control of the Leadership Conference of Women Religious (LCWR), the organization of leaders of approximately 400 U.S. congregations, representing more than eighty percent of the 54,000 sisters in this country. As was mentioned in the Introduction, on 18 April 2012, the CDF pronounced LCWR deficient both doctrinally and pastorally, and called for its reform under the supervision of Archbishop Peter Sartain of Seattle, assisted by Bishop Thomas John Paprocki of Springfield, Illinois, and Bishop Leonard Blair of Toledo.

The CDF announcement in April drew widespread attention in the secular and religious media, and sparked the rallying of many U.S. lay Catholics in defense of the sisters. When on 4 June the CDF also condemned *Just Love: A Framework for Christian Sexual Ethics*, the 2006 study by Sister of Mercy Margaret A. Farley mentioned in the last chapter, fuel was added to the controversy that had erupted in the U.S. church over the status and role of women religious. These developments in early 2012 came in the wake of an unprecedented "visitation" to investigate the "quality of life" of sisters in all noncloistered congregations based in the United States, which has also been described in the Introduction.

The visitation of noncloistered women's communities and the investigation of the sisters' leadership organization were attempts by Rome to gain control of women who have lived out their vocations conscientiously for decades. This they have done without financial support from the hierarchy, and in some respects beyond the administrative reach of church officials, although communities have complied with canonical requirements that their constitutions be approved by the Vatican, and sisters employed by the church have generally cooperated with its policies.

CDF and LCWR tensions come to a head

The timing of CDF's disciplinary action against LCWR in 2012 only added to the public relations difficulties of the hierarchy, who have been beset with scandals over finances, sexual misconduct, and cover-ups. A triptych of news stories from the *National Catholic Reporter* in January 2012 indicates the context in which sisters have been subject to scrutiny. On one page is a story noting that Mother Mary Clare Millea had completed the visitation process and submitted her report to Rome, and suggesting that personnel changes at the Vatican could portend better relations with American sisters.[3] Framing this story on the right is an article about a Canadian bishop (Raymond Lahey) freed after serving eight months in prison for importing child pornography, and on the left one about the resignation of the auxiliary bishop of Los Angles, Gabino Zavala, after acknowledging that he fathered two children.[4] Months later, as the news of the CDF action against LCWR was being absorbed in the spring of 2012, Monsignor William Lynn was convicted 22 June in Philadelphia of child endangerment for his role in protecting priest-predators while serving as secretary for clergy under the late Cardinal Anthony Bevilacqua. Only death prevented the indictment of the Cardinal, whose orders Lynn had carried out. Meanwhile Bishop Robert Finn of Kansas City-St Joseph had been ordered on 5 April to stand trial in Missouri for failing to report suspected child abuse, in "the first criminal case against a Catholic bishop in the decades-long sex-abuse scandal."[5] Also that spring the Vatican was weathering public relations difficulties of its own, notably on account of the leaking of papal documents that culminated with the arrest of a papal butler in late May.

It is small wonder, then, that editorials supporting LCWR and American Catholic sisters in general appeared in the secular and religious press in the spring of 2012. The *New York Times* observed on 19 April that the Vatican's "reining in" of LCWR seems to misread the accomplishments of American sisters and their leaders, who "continued to bolster the reputation of the Roman Catholic Church even as it suffered one of its greatest scandals in the sexual abuse of schoolchildren by rogue priests and the cover-ups by diocesan authorities."[6] *Commonweal*'s editors declared on 1 May that, "The CDF action is certain to be a pastoral disaster, another instance of the hierarchy acting in an imprudent and counterproductive fashion." While acknowledging the role of the hierarchy in preserving and conveying "the fundamentals of the faith," which includes "correcting doctrinal error," they asked: "But wouldn't the bishops be more effective in that task if they did not confuse disagreement about public policy with doctrinal dissent—and if the experience and judgment of women were given an honored place and a decisive role in the church's governance?"[7] The mention of public policy refers to the fact that LCWR was associated with support for the Affordable Care Act of 2010, the health care reform law that had been opposed by the U.S. bishops' conference.

To be sure, there were also statements in more conservative outlets that strongly supported the CDF action. Columnist George Weigel, for example, expressed satisfaction in *National Review Online* that "the Vatican had finally acted decisively, after three decades of half-hearted (and failed) attempts to achieve some sort of serious conversation with LCWR about its obvious and multiple breaches of the boundaries of orthodoxy."[8] And Mother Mary Assumpta Long, OP, superior of the Dominican Sisters of Mary, Mother of the Eucharist, voiced the hope that the CDF action will "awaken" LCWR "to once again 'think with the Church,'" and thereby "rediscover and wholly embrace their vocation in its integrity at the heart of the church."[9] Mother Long, and the even more outspoken critics of LCWR such as Donna Bethell, who chairs the board of Christendom College, and journalist Ann Carey exemplify in this discussion the position described in Chapter 2 as "Women Content with the Church," whereas LCWR and its supporters are closer to the position "Women Transforming Church."[10] The former believe that the role of publicly identified "women of the church" requires full conformity with official teachings and enthusiastic support of positions regarded as important by the hierarchy. The latter understand the responsibilities of vowed women religious differently.

Theologian Sandra M. Schneiders has articulated a transformationist position on the role of sisters at length in her 2011 book, *Prophets in Their Own Country: Women Religious Bearing Witness to the Gospel in a Troubled Church,* most of which was written as a series of articles for the *National Catholic Reporter* during the visitation in 2009 and 2010. "Religious," she writes, "are not 'mini-clerics,' that is, agents of the institution. They are not a work force whose job is to indoctrinate or discipline their fellow believers. Their vow of obedience is made only to God."[11] Although she acknowledges that before the post-Vatican II renewal, sisters had often been venerated as quasiclergy, Schneiders maintains that the spiritual elitism and subordinate church-worker status of that era have been left behind by most U.S. communities of women religious. She believes that the sort of community represented in LCWR has evolved from an earlier stage of hybrid monasticism-and-apostolate to a "new form of Religious Life," which she designates as "ministerial" and "prophetic": "Our whole life is affected by our ministerial identity: searching out the places (often on the margins of the Church and society) where the need for the Gospel is greatest (which may be in Church institutions but often is not); living in ways that are conducive to our ministry; preaching the Gospel freely as Jesus commissioned his itinerant, full-time companions to do."[12] Indeed, she goes on to observe, "Jesus, in prophetic word and work, not in institution maintenance, is the model of ministry for Religious."[13] Schneiders understands the prophetic task as "announcing the Reign of God, good news to the poor." In proclaiming the end of oppression and injustice, "[t]he prophet is acting out the universal compassion of God by practicing and empowering people to a practice of justice that will make God's compassion the normal state of affairs, God's reign on earth as it is in heaven."[14]

In contrast to the clergy, who promise obedience to ecclesiastical superiors, ministerial religious "are *not agents of the institutional church* as Jesus was not an agent of institutional Judaism."[15] Although like other Catholics ministerial religious should respect church authority and represent official positions accurately, they are not responsible for enforcing them, or for stopping discussion of controversial questions. "Jesus knew and respected the Law and the official teachers of Judaism," she writes, "[b]ut sometimes he gave priority to other equally valid and important considerations such as the suffering of individuals, the inequity of human laws, the fallibility of human interpretation of God's will even on the part of officials."[16] Schneiders acknowledges that the prophetic calling frequently involves tension with institutional authority, and thinks that such tension is "at the heart of the current struggle between Religious and the Vatican."[17] Moreover, it is her conviction that this struggle over the role of sisters is part of a larger "power struggle" in Catholicism "between the promoters of the renewal initiated by Vatican II and a program of Tridentine restoration."[18] At issue, in other words, is the way power is exercised in the church, a matter of concern to bishops, clergy, religious, and laity alike.

Complicating the picture

While the CDF calls for reform of LCWR and conformity to its ideas of what "good sisters" and their leaders should be like, arguably the greater need is for the Vatican to reform *its* structures and procedures. Indeed, an eminent member of the American hierarchy, Archbishop John R. Quinn, made just such a case in his scholarly volume from 1999, *The Reform of the Papacy.* Written in response to the request of Pope John Paul II for suggestions about how the papacy could become "a service of love recognized by all concerned," Quinn's book offers the perspective of a former president of the U.S. bishops' conference about ways the modern papacy can improve.[19] He writes: " . . . in the exercise of the papacy two things, more than others, are the greatest problem for the Church and for Christian unity. The first is centralization; the other, the need for reform of the Roman Curia [the Vatican bureaucracy]."[20] Although written more than a decade earlier, these words of Quinn's have bearing on the tensions between CDF and LCWR that became public in the spring of 2012:

> If the curia does not change, and decentralization does not take place, there will ensue great disorder in the Church because of its inability to respond to changing situations with sufficient rapidity, and the inability of an omnicompetent central bureaucracy to have an adequate grasp of swiftly changing, multicultural situations. It will be the paradox of the insistence on central control being, in reality, the loss of control.[21]

Clearly the issues are larger than the role of women in the church, but the changed status of women does seem to be one situation that Vatican structures have not been able to address adequately. Women who have been influenced by Vatican II's declaration that ". . . with respect to the fundamental rights of the person, every type of discrimination, whether . . . based on sex, race, color, social condition, language, or religion is to be overcome and eradicated as contrary to God's intent" are increasingly troubled by a church structure in which all women religious are ultimately subject to male control.[22]

That having been said, it is also important to recognize that the polarization evident in the dispute between the Vatican and LCWR covers over the diversity of positions within both groups: LCWR leaders and congregations are a complex social reality, and so are the members of the hierarchy. LCWR members come from communities representing a wide range between the monastic-apostolic and ministerial-prophetic types that Schneiders has sketched, and the leaders themselves have different theological positions and priorities. Likewise there are important theological and political differences among the hierarchy. Other bishops besides Archbishop Quinn have objected to the curtailing of collegiality and the weakening of national and regional bishops' conferences that took place during the long reign of Pope John Paul II, and several have expressed a desire to discuss topics the pope declared off-limits, including clerical celibacy, women's ordination, and sexual ethics.[23] The reforms called for by Archbishop Quinn and desired by a number of other bishops are unlikely to occur very soon, because they "do not have the votes" at this time, and episcopal appointments are currently made with little or no input from anyone but clerical elites. For this reason I see wisdom in the decision of LCWR leaders to choose a prayerful, contemplative approach to the dilemma posed by the ultimatum from CDF, and to seek a "third way" of responding that was neither capitulation nor noncompliance. As LCWR President Pat Farrell, OSF, said in an interview shortly before the organization's 2012 assembly, her hope was "to see if we can somehow, in a spirit of nonviolent strategizing, look for some . . . third way that refuses to just define the mandate and the issues in such black and white terms." What was most important to Farrell is that LCWR "respond with integrity . . . however we proceed."[24] It is in light of this ideal of integrity that they went forward with plans to honor Sister Sandra Schneiders, IHM, with the 2012 LCWR Leadership Award, although that award would not likely have been favored by CDF.

Integrity was also central to the measured response to Rome that the organization announced at the close of its annual assembly on 10 August 2012. A press release explained that after three days of "sustained prayer and dialogue," LCWR members had commissioned their officers to begin a conversation with the Vatican's delegate, Archbishop J. Peter Sartain, with the expectation that "open and honest dialogue may lead not only to increasing understanding between the church leadership and women religious, but also to creating more possibilities for the laity and, particularly for women, to have a voice in the church." Clearly the group avoided for the moment the extremes of capitulation and noncompliance, and only time will tell whether LCWR succeeds in its hope of maintaining its "official role representing US women religious in the Catholic Church" and at the same time fulfilling its "role as a voice for justice in the world."[25]

New context for women's vocations

There is no doubt that the events of 2012 have further complicated the context in which Catholic women of the future will make decisions about their vocations, especially where church service is concerned. Already that context had changed dramatically since the mid-twentieth century, when women religious in the United States were more than two-and-a half times as numerous as priests and religious brothers.[26] Many factors account for this transformation, such as demographic trends toward smaller Catholic families, technological advances, and cultural developments, including greatly increased opportunities for women in society generally. Also significant is the paradigm shift in Christian ethics from an ethic of obedience to an ethic of responsibility. This shift, discussed in Chapter 1, has meant that contemporary women are more willing to look critically at the institutional contexts of their lives than were women of the mid-twentieth century. Indeed, as we saw in Chapter 2, some women have been critical enough to leave the church entirely, contributing to an exodus that would have reduced the overall Catholic population significantly had the decline not been offset by immigration. According to a 2008 Pew Forum study of the U.S. Religious Landscape, one-third of those raised Catholic no longer identify with the tradition, and "former Catholics" now comprise ten-percent of the American population.[27]

Undoubtedly the reasons for this exodus are many and complex, but we can safely assume that two factors are especially important for women. One involves the perception of injustice, which has been discussed at length in Chapter 2. A second involves the anti-institutional bias that has been a recurrent theme in American culture, and is especially pronounced today. Catholic women who seek to discern what God is calling them to do with their lives conduct this discernment within a social context that regards both government and religion with considerably more skepticism than prevailed at the time of the Second Vatican Council.

Sociologist Patricia Wittberg has noted that the longstanding tendency of Catholic women to be more active in the church than Catholic men has recently been reversed in this country. Although for centuries "[m]ore than twice as many women as men . . . entered their era's version of religious life," today this is no longer the case.[28] In 2009, she reports, 1396 men were in U.S. religious formation programs compared to 1206 women, and in 2010 statistics for Philadelphia showed "173 men preparing to be priests, brothers, and deacons, but only 30 women preparing to be sisters." Wittberg finds the drop in church involvement to be especially pronounced among younger women, both those born during 1962–80 ("Generation X") and those born during 1981–95 ("Millennials"), with the latter "even more disaffected" than the former. Millennial women, she observes, are "the first generation of American Catholic women" who are "more likely than Catholic men their age to say that they never attend Mass," and who are considerably "less likely than their male counterparts to say they have ever considered a religious vocation."[29]

The sociological data about young women's diminishing church involvement bears out what many have been reporting anecdotally. For example, Loretto sister Maureen Fiedler stated in an open letter to the committee appointed by the Vatican to investigate U.S. women's religious congregations in 2010: "Many young women I know would never consider religious life because they see women being relegated to subordinate roles in the church."[30] Wittberg acknowledges that those learning about the fact that young men's dedication to Catholic institutions is overtaking that of young women are likely to interpret the data in various ways. Some will see it as warranting expanded leadership roles for women, including ordination, while others will find it calls for a stronger voicing of the conservative version of "feminism" favored by Pope John Paul II, and still others will opt for letting things simply take their course. However, not to address the changed situation, she maintains, will result in "fewer young women, and likely fewer of their children, remaining in the Catholic Church" and thus a significant decline in the church's influence in the wider society.[31]

My own position is that canon law should be revised so that the equal dignity of women is fully affirmed in a meaningful way. Baptized women should be eligible for all ministries of the church, including sacred orders. This is essentially the position that Teresa Kane recommended to Pope John Paul II in 1979, and it is finding increasing support in the Catholic community despite Vatican efforts to close discussion on this topic. The main theological reason for this change is to respect the freedom of God to call whom She wills to sacramental ministry and official leadership. Certainly no one has a right to a particular vocation, but until women who feel called by God to exercise full pastoral ministry have the same possibilities as men do to have their vocations tested and affirmed, claims of church officials to regard women as equal will sound hollow to many. I have long believed that the ordination of women is actually a "conservative" move, one that respects sacraments, church order, tradition, and, of course, women, who are now seen as fully equal to men, although at the time canon law was developed women's humanity was thought to be inferior to that of men. Time has only reinforced my sense that the values in tension—sacraments, church order, tradition, and women—can all be affirmed if the fundamental law of the church is changed, and that delaying the change puts these values at risk.[32]

Currently the sacramental life of U.S. Catholics is affected by diminishing numbers of priests, who are rapidly aging. According to the Center for Applied Research in the Apostolate (CARA), in 1965 there were nearly 59,000 priests serving a Catholic population of 45.6 million, and only 549 parishes lacked a resident pastor. By 2012 there were about 43,000 priests serving 65.6 million Catholics, and more than 3400 parishes had no resident pastor.[33] Many of these parishes have sisters and laywomen as administrators, and their duties are often described as, "she does everything the priest did except the sacraments."[34] Such pastoral administrators, and many other Catholic women in ministry, have felt the sacramental discrimination intensely, and some have concluded that their gifts are better utilized beyond the official Roman Catholic Church. In some cases they have been ordained for Protestant churches, in others for schismatic Catholic groups, and in still others as part of the Roman CatholicWomenpriests movement, which pushes the boundaries but hopes to avoid outright schism.[35] These developments are affecting the unity and order of Roman Catholicism, and the simple condemnation of such actions by the hierarchy does nothing to address what is causing them.

Tradition: A contested reality

For many years the Vatican has invoked "tradition" as a chief reason not to admit women to sacred orders. However, as theologian Anne Carr (1934–2008) observed in 1988, "two traditions" are discernible in Christian history where women's ministry is concerned, an early egalitarian one and a later subordinationist one. She noted that scholars have found evidence from the beginnings of Christianity that women were "apostles, prophets, deaconesses, disciples, witnesses, and servants in the ministry of the gospel." Indeed, there was a "vigorous female ministry in which women played an active and public role in the life of the early churches." Gradually, however, this tradition of female ministry was "suppressed by the second tradition, which, in conformity with the prevailing cultural patterns, relegated women to the more private spheres of Christian life and allowed public ministry only to men."[36] The conclusion that Carr drew from this research is that tradition has adapted to changed cultural circumstances in the past, and should do so again today: "It is clear that the developing tradition of the church and its ministry should be correlated with the experience of contemporary women in such a way as to legitimize the ordination of women."[37] Such a change, she argued, would represent the Catholic tradition at its best, which has in the past broken with outmoded practices and teachings on matters such as the persecution of heretics, slavery, and crusades: "Going against traditional practice has been called for many times and is called for especially now in a church newly conscious of its sinfulness past and present, of the times it has sided with the rich and powerful over the poor and powerless, with vested interest over truth in scholarship."[38]

In recent years further research has only strengthened the historical claims made by Carr decades ago. For example, in 2005 Kevin Madigan and Carolyn Osiek published *Ordained Women in the Early Church: A Documentary History*, which provides strong evidence of women clergy and concludes that "[e]choes of women in clerical office continued into the medieval period in both East and West, as witnessed by the sacramental powers and symbols of early medieval abbesses, who wore elements of priestly vesture in procession, gave blessings, and received the confessions of their nuns." Still, they report that "for the most part, the highest level of church office for women was on the decline already by the end of the sixth century." Various reasons account for the decline, including a growing interest in "cultic purity," which saw women's menstrual and childbirth functions as contaminating, and became "the biggest argument against women presbyters," and the transition from adult baptisms by immersion to infant baptisms, which lessened the need for female deacons for that sacrament.[39]

More recently, in *The Hidden History of Women's Ordination: Female Clergy in the Medieval West* (2007), historian Gary Macy has demonstrated that a significant change in understanding the meaning of ordination had occurred by the end of the twelfth century, and this led to the phasing out of most clerical roles for women:

> Ordination in the early Middle Ages did not have the same meaning that it would come to have after the twelfth century. Rather than the bestowal of a particular power and authority connected to the Eucharistic liturgy and limited to those offices that performed that liturgy, ordination referred to the process by which one was chosen for a particular ministry or service in the church. Further, the term "ordination" was more or less interchangeable with the term "consecration" or "blessing" or even "making" or, in the case of nuns, "veiling." Many different ministries were considered to be ordained, including several ministries reserved for women.[40]

Macy places great significance on a creed adopted at the Fourth Lateran Council of 1215, which attempted to quell debates about the Eucharist by introducing the term transubstantiation and insisting that the sacrament can only be effected by "the priest who has been duly ordained in accordance with the keys of the Church, which Jesus Christ Himself gave to the Apostles and their successors." He differs with scholars who assume that this statement about ordination "merely represents the standard orthodox position of the time," holding instead that it can be seen as "a magisterial intervention to settle theological and pastoral discussions of real importance." As a result of Lateran IV, there emerged a "very different church from that which preceded the council." He insists that "the concentration of sacramental power into the hands of the priest did not occur until the end of the twelfth century," and prior to that "both the men and women who constituted the leadership within their communities perform[ed] sacramental and even sacerdotal functions."[41] The changes evident in the decrees of Lateran IV were part of an effort to distinguish the clergy more clearly from the laity, and to centralize power in the hands of the former.

In a lecture elaborating on this research, Macy indicates that until this change in understanding and practice had taken place, ordination had simply been "the process by which an individual moved into a new role or vocation (*ordo*) in both ecclesial and lay society." Thus in the church, "anyone who moved into a new ministry or vocation in the community was 'ordained' to that new ministry." This included everyone in minor orders, "as well as abbots, abbesses, deacons, deaconesses, priests, nuns, monks, emperors, empresses, kings, and queens." And most importantly, "there was no distinction made between the ordination of priests, for instance, and abbesses . . . All were equally sacramentally ordained."[42]

Suggestions for new roles

The complex history of Catholic tradition on ordination is glossed over by recent magisterial assertions against ordaining women, but as an educated laity grows more aware of past practices and understandings, debate is emerging about history as well as about women's roles in the future. This climate is surely an important aspect of the context in which women of tomorrow will discern their vocations. As stated earlier, I believe that church law should be reformed so as to match the magisterial rhetoric of women's equality, and thus to lay a legal foundation for opening all ministries and offices to baptized candidates of either sex. I recognize, of course, that implementing so great a change for Catholicism will require a good deal of time, and it should be done with appropriate sensitivity to different cultures in the world church. Although I believe full equality of opportunity for sacramental service and leadership is the goal to aim for, I recognize wisdom in suggestions for improving the situation in incremental ways.

The editors of the Jesuit weekly *America*, for example, suggested in 2011 that laity should be involved in church governance, perhaps by being admitted to the College of Cardinals, or else by constituting advisory councils at diocesan and international levels. In the latter case they envision a situation where laity would comprise "at least half" of each ordinary's principal advisors, and where in time a new "international council of laypersons" would share three functions with an equal number of cardinals: "administer the Vatican offices, advise the pope and select his successor." Membership on the council would reflect the diverse global population of Catholics, and participants would be chosen for limited terms on the basis of recommendations by "grass-roots representative caucuses of clergy and laity."[43]

An even more practical suggestion is to ordain women deacons. With ample evidence that this was once an ordinary practice in both eastern and western Christianity, and with churches whose orders are recognized by Rome (Orthodox Church of Greece and Armenian Apostolic Church) currently approving women deacons, such a change would involve restoration more than innovation for Catholics. Furthermore, in contrast to the question of women priests, there is no official teaching against the possibility of women deacons, and some members of the hierarchy have gone on record in their favor.

Theologian Phyllis Zagano has thoroughly researched this possibility, carefully thought through the implications that such a development would mean for the church, and published her findings in both scholarly and popular venues.[44] She believes there is a great need to ordain women deacons today for the sake of the church's evangelical mission, which is currently compromised by the exclusion of women from official ordained service. "[R]eopening the diaconate to women and admitting ordained women to proper governance and ministry would have a startling effect on the public perception of the official church, now suffering from an increasing erosion of moral authority."[45] Furthermore, the people of God throughout the world "hunger for the diaconal ministry of the Word, the liturgy, and charity," especially from women. They also need the witness to women's equal dignity that sacred orders and sacramental roles of women deacons would mean. "It is no secret," she writes, "that women are ill-treated in many Christian territories. Ordination, which further configures the individual to Christ, serves as a reminder of the Catholic teaching that all are made in the image and likeness of God."[46] Although current doctrine against women's ordination to priesthood emphasizes the inability of women to be icons of Christ as head of the church (*in persona Christi capitis Ecclesiae*), there is no teaching preventing women from being icons of Christ as servant (*in personae Christi servi*), and Zagano is among those who insist on keeping a strong separation between the questions of diaconate and priesthood for women, for theological and practical reasons.[47]

Zagano recognizes that in the United States today there are many thousands of women, both apostolic women religious and lay ecclesial ministers, who "serve the church in diaconal roles," particularly by their charitable works, but "do not formally minister in the liturgy or through the Word as preachers," and do not serve their bishops "in any direct, permanent manner."[48] Indeed, one may discern in the tensions between the Vatican and the Leadership Conference of Women Religious an implied longing for women deacons on the part of the Congregation for the Doctrine of the Faith. Had the women of the LCWR communities been deacons, they would have promised obedience to the bishops and served directly under their authority. But in fact the apostolic women religious are not ordained to serve as part of the clergy, and their vows are made to God according to the constitutions and spiritual gifts of their congregations. Zagano correctly notes that if the diaconate is restored to women, this could complicate life for congregations of sisters by adding clerical members to what had been an entirely lay community, and new forms of religious life may need to be developed.[49]

Becoming the change they seek

Also affecting the setting in which Catholic women will discern their vocations in the future is the small but influential reform movement known as Roman Catholic Womenpriests (RCWP), which has been mentioned earlier in this book. Since 1975 there has been a nationally organized women's ordination movement in the United States, the Women's Ordination Conference, and in 1996 the network called Women's Ordination Worldwide was founded in Austria.[50] The first international conference of Women's Ordination Worldwide took place in Dublin in 2001, and one year later seven women took matters a step further and were ordained priests on the Danube River by two bishops no longer in communion with Rome. These seven are the founders of Roman Catholic Womenpriests: Pia Brunner, Dagmar Celeste, Gisela Forster, Christine Mayr-Lumetzberger, Iris Müller, Ida Raming, and Adelinde Theresia Roitinger.[51] It is important to note that RCWP members report that they have also been encouraged and assisted by some bishops in good standing with Rome, whose identities have not been disclosed. When Pope John Paul II excommunicated the "Danube 7," they sent a formal response declaring their refusal to accept this status and claiming full membership in the Catholic Church. Since then the male bishops who support RCWP have secretly ordained several womenpriests as bishops, carefully following official procedures and depositing documents, films, and photos with a notary public. These women bishops claim apostolic succession and have themselves gone on to ordain deacons, priests, and bishops.[52]

In ten years RCWP has grown from a small symbolic movement into a fledgling organization, with websites that articulate its vision and structures and describe its members and their ministries. Not surprisingly, RCWP has been attacked from the right and the left, with some objecting to its disobedience and others to perceived inadequacies in its members, and it has also experienced internal tensions among its expanding membership. Nevertheless, despite declarations of excommunication by the hierarchy, despite critical essays by feminists who find the movement wanting for various reasons, and despite internal differences of vision and strategy, RCWP continues to affect Catholics young and old, and to attract new members.[53] Figures for mid-2012 show an international membership of more than 130, including priests, bishops, deacons, and candidates for ordination, with three-fourths of them in the United States. There are also members in Canada, Austria, Germany, France, and Colombia, South America. For its tenth anniversary (29 June

2012), RCWP prepared a directory listing its members according to the year of ordination, and describing 55 U.S. and 9 Canadian communities where members regularly lead worship for groups of various sizes. Most communities have chosen names, such as "Mary Magdalene Apostle Catholic Community," "Living Water Inclusive Catholic Community," "Mary Mother of Jesus Catholic Community," or "Oscar Romero Church," but some are simply designated "house church." While some celebrations are held in private homes, many take place regularly in Protestant churches or other large facilities. Directory entries for the communities provide information about worship schedules and other ministries, and one notes plans to have a weekly Mass streamed on the internet to reach the sick and others unable to attend.[54]

The original draft constitution prepared by the European founders of RCWP had stated: "The goal of the group: 'RC Womenpriests' is to bring about the full equality of women in the Roman Catholic Church. At the same time we are striving for a new model of Priestly Ministry. When these goals are reached and Can. 1024 CIC [the law requiring that ordinands be baptized males] has been changed [to recognize baptized persons], the group 'RC Womenpriests' will be dissolved." They also declared that the movement does not see itself as working against the church: "It wants neither a schism nor a break from the Roman Catholic Church, but rather wants to work positively within the Church." After describing their governing structures and listing various issues for discussion, the group noted that they see themselves as "worker womenpriests," financially independent of the church, who "practice our church functions in an honorary capacity except for reimbursement of our expenses."[55]

Ten years later, the 2012 Constitution of Roman Catholic Womenpriests-USA, Inc., shows an evolution to greater complexity of structures and does not mention any expectation of completing its work. It does, however, continue to affirm the vision of a "new model of ordained ministry in a renewed Roman Catholic Church." RCWP-USA characterizes itself as "a prophetic organization within an international progressive movement in the Roman Catholic Church," whose mission is "to prepare, ordain in apostolic succession, and support primarily women who are called by the Holy Spirit and their communities to a renewed priestly ministry rooted in justice and faithfulness to the

Gospel." The constitution describes the roles of deacons, priests, and bishops; outlines structures of governance; and provides a code of ethics. Among the principles voiced in the constitution are the beliefs that "there is no intrinsic connection between priesthood and mandatory celibacy" and that "we are called to operate on the principles of subsidiarity and democratic process."[56] In practice, the movement has ordained women, and a few men, without regard to marital status or sexual orientation; most of their names are listed on the RCWP website, though in several cases the priests or deacons are listed as "catacomb" or "confidential" ordinands, often because of concerns about their employment.

Although the RCWP movement is influential, the practical difficulties of trying to institutionalize a prophetic movement are considerable. If members and supporters can seek justice with a view to eventual reconciliation they will enhance the prospects of an outcome that avoids the sort of violent breaks that occurred between traditional Jews and Jewish Christians in the first century, and between Protestants and Catholics in the sixteenth century. The jury is still out on whether in a century or two the leaders of this movement will be thought of as more like Catherine of Siena or Martin Luther, and my belief is that the words of Gamaliel concerning the preaching of Peter are relevant to their situation: "For if this idea of theirs or its execution is of human origin, it will collapse; but if it is from God, you will never be able to put them down . . ." (Acts 5:38–9).[57]

Lay ministries and lay ecclesial ministers

At the opening of this chapter are quotations from two scholars, which offer complementary perspectives on the transformed social context in which Catholic women are making decisions about church vocations today. In view of the fact that women are now established as leaders in politics, medicine, business, and many other fields of endeavor, historian Kathleen Sprows Cummings rightly observes that "Since the late 1960s, a Catholic woman in American society has had vastly more opportunities for education and meaningful work outside church structures than within them. But from the mid-nineteenth century until the late 1960s, quite the opposite was true."[58] Her observation helps to account for the dramatic decline in young women's interest in vocations to the Catholic sisterhoods. Nevertheless, in view of the enhanced role of the laity since the Second Vatican Council, theologian Zeni Fox is also right in noting that "In our [U.S. Catholic] parishes, 80 percent of the lay ecclesial ministers are women, as are the great majority of lay ministers. . . . The women involved in ministry are a leaven in the churches, bringing change."[59]

Fox's words imply a distinction between "lay ministers" and "lay ecclesial ministers" that needs attention, for the terminology has some ambiguities that can be confusing, especially because "lay," which is traceable to the Greek word *laos* ("people"), can mean *both* "nonordained" (which includes vowed religious sisters and brothers) *and* "neither ordained nor in religious vows." In general, the term "lay ministry" uses "lay" in the second sense, and refers to Gospel-inspired activity undertaken by women and men who are neither clerics nor members of vowed religious communities. It can be done on a volunteer basis, or with compensation, and it may involve distinctively religious service (lector, catechist, church musician, etc.) or secular activity undertaken to advance the Reign of God, such as working for social justice or peace. The term "lay ecclesial minister" has a more precise and specialized meaning, and it uses "lay" in the first sense, meaning "nonordained." In the 2005 document *Co-Workers in the Vineyard of the Lord*, the U.S. bishops describe lay ecclesial ministry as a distinct form of service that is based in the Sacraments of Initiation (Baptism and Confirmation) rather than Ordination. It is characterized by:

- *Authorization* of the hierarchy to serve publicly in the local church
- *Leadership* in a particular area of ministry
- *Close mutual collaboration* with the pastoral ministry of bishops, priests, and deacons
- *Preparation and formation* appropriate to the level of responsibilities that are assigned to them.[60]

As theologian Edward P. Hahnenberg has indicated, lay ecclesial ministers receive, in addition to the universal call to become disciples and take part in the church's mission, a special "call to minister on behalf of the church in a public and professional way," indeed to "minister in the name of the church."[61] The phenomenon of lay ecclesial ministry has evolved especially on account of the drop in numbers of priests available for parish ministry, and the resulting appointment of lay persons and religious sisters and brothers, along with a growing number of permanent deacons, to positions on parish staffs. In many instances lay ecclesial ministers serve as "parish life coordinators" or "pastoral administrators" in the absence of a resident pastor.[62] As theologian Susan K. Wood, SCL, has noted, such a ministry is permitted by church law (Canon 517 §2), but is "considered to be extraordinary and temporary since the norm is for an ordained priest to provide the pastoral care of a parish." As examples of lay ecclesial ministries that are "ordinary," because they are clearly rooted in Baptism and Confirmation, Wood mentions being a director of liturgy or of faith formation, or managing the material goods of the church.[63]

Citing the research of David DeLambo, the bishops' document from 2005 (*Co-Workers*) describes the situation of lay ecclesial ministry as continuing to "grow and develop":

Today, 30,632 lay ecclesial ministers work at least twenty hours per week in paid positions in parishes. An additional 2,163 volunteers work at least twenty hours per week in parishes. The number of paid lay parish ministers has increased by 53% since 1990, while the percentage of parishes with salaried lay ecclesial ministers has increased from 54% to 66%. In 2005, the percentage of lay women is 64%; laymen, 20%; religious women, 16%. Religious educators (42.5%) and general pastoral ministers (25%) account for two thirds of all parish ministers.

The document goes on to state that as of 2004–05, "more than 2,000 lay persons ministered in the name of the Church in hospitals and health care settings, on college and university campuses, and in prisons, seaports, and airports."[64] More recently, journalist Tom Roberts indicates that as of 2008 some ten thousand persons were preparing to become lay ecclesial ministers, and in 2009–10 the Center for the Applied Research in the Apostolate (CARA) had "identified 266 active lay ecclesial ministry formation programs that were of at least two years duration."[65]

The burgeoning of lay ministries in general, and of lay ecclesial ministries in particular, is a highly significant and promising development in contemporary Catholicism. The fact that so many individuals who are neither ordained priests nor vowed religious have experienced a vocation to ministry and had that call affirmed by the church is cause for celebration. Moreover, from a feminist perspective it is encouraging to see opportunities for women's gifts, especially for leadership, so widely recognized. Insofar as church employment is concerned, however, these vocations are subject to the discretion of the pastor or bishop, and a change in administration can signal an abrupt end to someone's ministry, regardless of professional competency, spiritual gifts, and sacrifices made in order to become qualified. As a matter of justice, the church needs to provide structures and rules that respect the vocations it has encouraged. As canon lawyer Lynda Robitaille has put it, "If lay ecclesial ministry is recognized as being important for the church, then such ministry needs to be protected with canonical norms to promote its stability, to give confidence to the ministers and those who are served by them."[66] In the meanwhile, women who serve in these ministries must walk a fine line if their sense of women's possibilities does not match the roles currently available within Catholicism. Many such women of faith are flourishing in ministry today and giving hope to others despite the limits of the "stained-glass ceiling."[67]

Concluding reflections

It is indeed a complex scene that women with a sense that God is calling them to church vocations face today, especially if they hope to use their talents for preaching, sacramental ministry, and church governance.[68] Perhaps the diaconate will soon be restored as a possibility for women, but there is clearly a difference between the Vatican and many Catholics on the question of ordination to priesthood. There is also a great divide within the U.S. laity on this question. To cite sociologist William V. D'Antonio and his colleagues, on the whole American "Catholics have greatly increased their support for having women priests since the earliest survey in 1974." Their 2005 survey found that 54 percent of American Catholics "thought it would be a good thing" if "married women were allowed to be ordained as priests," and 61 percent "thought it would be a good thing" if "celibate women were allowed to be ordained as priests." On the other hand, the same study found that 29 percent of American Catholics would strongly oppose such a change, for they regard "a celibate male clergy" as "essential" to the Church.[69]

In 2005 there were about 64 million U.S. Catholics, and while more than half were open to change on this question, some 19 million vehemently opposed it. That is a good number of Catholics, and the stakes are high. Moreover, the entire U.S. Catholic population is only about 6 percent of the global membership of the church, and although there are supporters of women's ordination on every continent, this is not such a priority issue in the developing world. Finally, papal authority, both in its teaching and its appointments of bishops, opposes even discussion of women priests. Thus it is highly unlikely that there will be a change in church policy soon.

John Allen may go too far when he predicts in *Future Church* that there will be no change on the question of women's ordination in this century, but I doubt we will see change in the next twenty years.[70] And David Gibson, another journalist, may be right in thinking that the "unparalleled import" of this momentous change "is such that the church should be of one mind, or as close to an accord as possible, before making such a transformation."[71] Meanwhile, where justice for women is concerned, members of the world church can act on matters where there is much greater agreement against sexism—matters such as female infanticide, genital mutilation, human trafficking, and the privileging of boys when it comes to food, medicine, and schooling.

Where sacramental sexism is concerned, however, we seem to have reached an impasse, and this presents a great spiritual challenge to those who advocate change. When the road to progress seems so definitively blocked, this is when we are in need of an active faith and religious imagination, of the sort shown by Gerard Manley Hopkins in his well-known poem, "God's Grandeur." The poem exudes an amazing confidence that the world, with all its problems, is not left to its own devices, "Because the Holy Ghost over the bent/World broods with warm breast and with ah! bright wings."[72] This is the same Spirit that Jesus promised would transform his followers after his death, and which Christians have continued to experience to this day in the mystery we name Pentecost. The world and the church are not the same today as they were fifty, or even ten, years ago. But some things do not change, and one of these is God's faithfulness and care for all people, especially those who are poor and disadvantaged. All that Jesus said about the *basileia*, the word translated as "Kingdom" or "Reign" of God, still applies. God *is* acting in history to bring to full realization the values of Her realm, and much of that activity is hidden from sight.

Besides contemplating Jesus and his view of God's action in history, opponents of ecclesiastical sexism can take inspiration from others who have experienced injustice from the church and yet remained faithful to the spirit of the gospel, which paradoxically they learned about in this flawed institution. An outstanding example is the witness of African American Catholics, who have demonstrated an "uncommon faithfulness" during centuries of injustice far more damaging to body and spirit than the sexism that excludes twenty-first-century women from ordination. As theologian M. Shawn Copeland reminds us in the book *Uncommon Faithfulness,* the church has a "blemished" record on slavery, and very few Catholics were abolitionists.[73] Nor did an unequivocal condemnation of slavery come from Rome until Vatican II.[74] Moreover, the racism that had sustained slavery did not end with the Emancipation Proclamation or Civil Rights legislation, but has shown itself in countless ways down to the present. Although white Catholics no longer discourage minority religious vocations so flagrantly, or relegate persons of color to the back of the communion line, we have not yet examined in the depth necessary for real change the ways that white privilege makes our lives unfairly easier than those of our brothers and sisters of color. When I think about the patience and holiness that Black, Hispanic-Latino, and Asian Catholics have shown despite racism in church members, leaders, and structures, I find sources of inspiration and suggestions for strategies for all Catholic women who long for an end to institutionalized sexism. The lives of two saintly African Americans come to mind here, Henriette Delille and Augustus Tolton, Catholics who showed great faith and creativity in dealing with obstacles to what they felt God was asking of them.

In *The Subversive Power of Love: The Vision of Henriette Delille*, M. Shawn Copeland describes Delille as a free woman of color in nineteenth-century New Orleans, who had been destined to follow her mother into the system of sexual slavery known there as plaçage, and end up as the concubine of a wealthy white man. Instead, Delille's love for God and neighbor led her to found a society of black women that eventually became the Sisters of the Holy Family, a group of vowed religious dedicated to the works of mercy among their own people. By her choice of this "countercultural life," Delille confronted the "congealed evil" of her own society, and, in Copeland's words, "reconceived, redefined, and reconsecrated the colonized and abused bodies of black women."[75] Delille's example offers inspiration for women today who may be discouraged about the barriers to their own hopes and dreams.

Augustus Tolton was baptized as an infant slave in 1854, and later his parents escaped slavery though his father died in the Union Army during the Civil War. A priest befriended the family and encouraged Augustus to pursue a priestly calling, but no seminary in this country would accept this black man. So Tolton went to Rome and studied at the College of the Propagation of the Faith, and was ordained in 1886 for his home diocese of Quincy, Illinois. But a white priest made ministry there impossible, so Tolton moved to Chicago, and served eleven years in the black community before dying from heat stroke when he was 43.[76] Like Henriette Delille, he is now being considered for sainthood. Both Delille and Tolton dealt with impasse by making a way out of "no way," and their lives are instructive for Catholic women who seek to act in response to God's call to live as creatively responsible moral agents. Such agents will imitate the creative Jesus who found imaginative and effective ways to respond to challenges, and who knew when to observe rules and when to go beyond them for the sake of neighbors in need.[77]

In our complex circumstances, we need a plural strategy, one that respects different gifts and callings. There are many tasks requiring wisdom and improvisational skill. All who seek change, however, must dedicate time and energy to the experience of God's presence, power, and love—in other words, to prayer. Our efforts must be sustained by the reality of divine love, which, as Copeland's book on Delille demonstrates, has an amazingly subversive power. There have never been sexist barriers to mysticism in our tradition, and women such as Catherine of Siena have at times had great influence on church leaders.[78] Besides the famous mystics, there have always been women of deep prayer in our parishes and communities, and these visionaries help us to see not only our own situation but the suffering of a world that yearns for God's peace, justice, and reconciliation. I believe that a crucial task for North American women today, especially those privileged by race, class, and education, is to keep the injustice we suffer in perspective, by expanding our vision to encompass *all* those God loves. As Carmelite thinker Constance FitzGerald has observed, "privileged women's experience of social or ecclesial marginalization" pales in comparison with "women's experience of chattel slavery or sexual and physical abuse."[79] And, I would add, it pales in comparison with the agony of seeing one's child die for want of clean water or basic health care, or because of senseless violence.

In light of all this, today's Catholic women—especially those of us who are well-fed, educated, and white—can allow our dreams of full equality in canon law to be deferred for a time, and focus more attention on the injustices experienced by marginalized and materially poor persons in this country, and throughout the world. It takes an active religious imagination to trust that God is coming to us from the future, and with our help is bringing the divine values of justice, truth, and love to greater realization in history. It takes such an imagination to be patient while the wheat and tares grow up together until the harvest. Such an imagination is evident in some words of the late bishop of Saginaw, Kenneth Untener:

> It helps now and then to step back and take the long view. The reign of God is not only beyond our efforts. It is beyond our vision. We accomplish in our lifetime only a tiny fraction of the magnificent enterprise that is God's work. Nothing we do is complete, which is another way of saying the reign of God always lies beyond us . . . We cannot do everything but there is a sense of liberation in realizing that because this enables us to do something and to do it well. It may be incomplete but it is a beginning, a step along the way, an opportunity for God's grace to enter and do the rest.[80]

Notes

1   Kathleen Sprows Cummings, *New Women of the Old Faith: Gender and American Catholicism in the Progressive Era* (Chapel Hill: University of North Carolina Press, 2009), p. 3.

2   Zeni Fox, "Snapshots of Laity in Mission: Consciousness of Responsibility for Ministry and Identity," in *Catholic Identity and the Laity: College Theology Society Annual Volume 54, 2008*, ed. Tim Muldoon (Maryknoll, New York: Orbis, 2009), p. 203.

3   NCR Staff. "Report on sisters quietly sent to Rome," *National Catholic Reporter* (20 January–2 February 2012), p. 13.

4   Deborah Gyapong, Catholic News Service, "Bishop freed after sentencing on porn charges," *National Catholic Reporter* (20 January-2 February 2012), p. 13. Catholic News Service, "Bishop resigns after disclosing he is father of two children," *National Catholic Reporter* (20 January–2 February 2012), p. 12.

5   Joshua J. McElwee, "Defense argues bishop was not required to report," *National Catholic Reporter* (13–26 April 2012), p. 6. On 6 September 2012 Bishop Finn was found guilty of the misdemeanor crime of "failing to report suspected child abuse" and given a two-year suspended sentence of probation. See Joshua J. McElwee, "Will the charter be honored? Bishop's conviction raises questions about child protection procedures," *National Catholic Reporter* (28 September–10 October 2012), p. 1.

6   "American Nuns, Conscience and the Vatican," http://www.nytimes.com/2012/04/20/opinion/american-nuns-conscienc (accessed 27 April 2012).

7   "Rome & Women Religious," *Commonweal* (18 May 2012), p. 5.

8   George Weigel, "The Vatican and the Sisters," *National Review Online* (23 April 2012), http://nationalreview.com/blogs/print/298611 (accessed 16 July 2012).

9   Mother Mary Assumpta Long, OP, "Doctrinal Assessment of the LCWR: Safeguarding the Integrity of Conscrated Life," *National Catholic Register,* 24 April 2012, http://www.ncregister.com/site/print_article/33206/ (accessed 16 July 2012).

10 Bethell observed of LCWR on the *PBS Newshour* for 19 April 2012, that "it wasn't just their job to avoid contradicting the church. It's their job to present the fullness of the Catholic faith and to help their members to understand it and to live it. And that's where they had been found short." http://www.pbs.org/newshour/bb/religion/jan-june12/vatican_04-19.html (accessed 16 July 2012). Ann Carey critiqued

LCWR in *Sisters in Crisis: The Tragic Unraveling of Women's Religious Communities* (Huntington, IN: Our Sunday Visitor Publishing Division, 1997), and objected to unfavorable coverage of the CDF action by mainstream media in "Nun Too Accurate Reporting," a blog post for *National Review Online* (4 June 2012), http://www.nationalreview.com/corner/301714/nun-too-accurate-reporting-ann-carey (accessed 17 July 2012).

11 Sandra M. Schneiders, *Prophets in Their Own Country: Women Religious Bearing Witness to the Gospel in a Troubled Church* (Maryknoll, NY: Orbis Books, 2011), p. 23.

12 Ibid., pp. 31–2.

13 Ibid., p. 92.

14 Ibid., pp. 102–3.

15 Ibid., p. 104.

16 Ibid., p. 105.

17 Ibid., p. 97.

18 Ibid., p. 76.

19 John R. Quinn, *The Reform of the Papacy: The Costly Call to Christian Unity* (New York: Crossroad Publishing Company, 1999), p. 9. He quotes here from Pope John Paul II's *Ut Unum Sint* #95 (Encyclical Letter on Commitment to Ecumenism). Quinn is Archbishop Emeritus of San Francisco, where he served from 1977 to 1995. He was President of the National Conference of Catholic Bishops from 1977 to 1980. Cardinal William Leveda succeeded him as archbishop of San Francisco from 1995 to 2005, prior to his appointment to the CDF.

20 Ibid., p. 178.

21 Ibid., p. 180.

22 *Pastoral Constitution on the Church in the Modern World (Gaudium et Spes)* #29, in Walter M. Abbott, SJ, ed., *The Documents of Vatican II* (New York: America Press, 1966), pp. 227–8.

23 A recent example is found in Anthony Ruff, OSB, "Swiss Catholic Bishop Calls for Reform," who reported on 24 April 2011 that Bishop Markus Büchel of the diocese of St Gall "spoke out openly for women's ordination. 'We must search for steps that lead there,' he said. 'I could imagine that women's diaconate could be such a step.' . . . Regarding priesthood for women, Büchel said, 'We can pray that the Holy Spirit enables us to read the signs of the times.'" According to Ruff, a media spokesperson had confirmed that the bishop meant what he said in the St Gall parish paper, http://www.arcwp.org/swiss.html (accessed 21 August 2012). Also, Phyllis Zagano reports in "Australian church is alive and kicking—mostly kicking" (*National Catholic Reporter,*

20 July–2 August 2012, p. 11) that three Australian bishops have resigned, more involuntarily than not, because they "wanted to talk about the elephants in the episcopal palaces." These are Bishops Patrick Power (Canberra), William Morris (Toowoomba), and Geoffrey Robinson (Sydney). Robinson is the author of *Confronting Power and Sex in the Catholic Church: Reclaiming the Spirit of Jesus* (Collegeville, MN: Liturgical Press, 2008). Earlier instances of U.S. bishops wanting to keep open the discussion about women's ordination include a conversation with Bishop Raymond Lucker (New Ulm, MN), taped shortly before his death in 2001, which William McDonough quotes in, "Bishop lived teachings of *Lumen Gentium* for 37 years, *National Catholic Reporter*, 6–19 July 2012, p. 16, and Juneau Bishop Michael H. Kenny's, "Women's Ordination: Uneasy Questions," *America* 171 (30 July–6 August 1994), pp. 3–4.

24   "An American Nun Responds to Vatican Criticism," interview of Sister Pat Farrell, OSF, by Terry Gross for National Public Radio's "Fresh Air." Transcript found at http://www.npr.org/templates/transcript/transcript. php?storyId=156858223.

25   LCWR Press Release, "Leadership Conference of Women Religious Decides Next Steps in Responding to CDF Report." http://www.lcwr. org/sites/default/files/media/files/lcwr_2012_assembly-press_releases_-_8-10-12.pdf (accessed 13 August 2012)

26   The Center for Applied Research in the Apostolate (CARA) statistics for 1965 show 179, 954 religious sisters, 58, 632 diocesan and religious priests, and 12,271 religious brothers; statistics for 2012 show 54,018 sisters, 43,431 priests, and 4477 brothers http://cara. georgetown.edu/caraservices/requestedchurchstats.html (accessed 17 October 2012).

27   According to the Pew Forum on Religion & Public Life's U.S. Religious Landscape Survey (2008), "While nearly one-in-three Americans (31%) were raised in the Catholic faith, today fewer than one-in four (24%) describe themselves as Catholics. These losses would have been even more pronounced were it not for the offsetting impact of immigration . . . Approximately one-third of the survey respondents who say they were raised Catholic no longer describe themselves as Catholic. This means that roughly 10% of all Americans are former Catholics." http://religions.pewforum.org/reports?sid=ST2008022501236, accessed 27 February 2008. In an article commenting on this study, "The hidden exodus: Catholics becoming Protestants," Thomas J. Reese, SJ, noted that if these ex-Catholics "were a separate denomination, they would be the third largest denomination in the United States, after Catholics and Baptists." *National Catholic Reporter* (15 April 2011), p. 1.

28 Patricia Wittberg, SC, "A Lost Generation?" *America* (20 February 2012), p. 13.

29 Ibid., p. 14.

30 Maureen Fiedler, SL, "Dear Sister Clare (And Vatican Investigation Committee)," *Courage: Newsletter of the Loretto Women's Network* (December 2010), p. 2.

31 Wittberg, p. 16.

32 Anne E. Patrick, "Conservative Case for the Ordination of Women," *New Catholic World* (May–June 1975), pp. 108–11.

33 CARA, "Frequently Requested Church Statistics," http://www.7.georgetown.edu/centers/cara/CARAServices/requestedchurchstats.html (accessed 24 July 2012). In "Priest leader hopes new study ignites 'major powwow,'" Dan Morris-Young observes in the 8–21 June 2012 *National Catholic Reporter* (p. 13), that "CARA reports the median age of active diocesan priests in this country is now 59, compared to 45 in 1970. In 1970, fewer than 10 percent of priests were over the age of 65. Now it is more than 40 percent."

34 For a sociological analysis of this trend, see Ruth A. Wallace, *They Call Her Pastor: A New Role for Catholic Women* (Albany: State University of New York Press, 1992).

35 See Gretchen Kloten Minney, *Called: Women Hear the Voice of the Divine* (Broomfield, CO: Wonder Why Publications, 2010), for brief biographies of 16 women involved in Roman Catholic Womenpriests or the Ecumenical Catholic Communion, a group related to the Old Catholic Church, which rejected papal infallibility in 1870. See also Elsie Hainz McGrath, Bridget Mary Meehan, and Ida Raming, *Women Find a Way: The Movement and Stories of Roman Catholic Womenpriests* (College Station, TX: Virtual Bookworm.com Publishing, Inc., 2008).

36 Anne E. Carr, *Transforming Grace: Christian Tradition and Women's Experience* (San Francisco: Harper & Row, 1988), p. 48.

37 Ibid., p. 36.

38 Ibid., p. 38.

39 Kevin Madigan and Carolyn Osiek, *Ordained Women in the Early Church: A Documentary History* (Baltimore: Johns Hopkins University Press, 2005), p. 205.

40 Gary Macy, *The Hidden History of Women's Ordination: Female Clergy in the Medieval West* (New York: Oxford University Press, 2007), pp. 47–8.

41 Ibid., pp. 46–7.

42 Gary Macy, "Diversity as Tradition: Why the Future of Christianity is Looking More Like Its Past." Santa Clara Lecture, Santa Clara University, 14 (8 November 2007): 11–12.

43 "Laity Near the Top?" *America* (21 February 2011), p. 5.

44 See, for example, Phyllis Zagano, *Holy Saturday: An Argument for the Restoration of the Female Diaconate in the Catholic Church* (New York: Crossroad, 2000); "The Question of Governance and Ministry for Women," *Theological Studies* 68 (June 2007): 348–67; "Remembering Tradition: Women's Monastic Rituals and the Diaconate," *Theological Studies* 72 (December 2011): 787–811; *Women & Catholicism: Gender, Communion, Authority* (New York: Palgrave Macmillan, 2011); and "Women Deacons: Future," in Gary Macy, William T. Ditewig, and Phyllis Zagano, *Women Deacons: Past, Present, Future* (New York: Paulist, 2011), pp. 69–104.

45 Zagano, *Women & Catholicism*, p. 133.

46 Zagano, "Whatever happened to women deacons?" NCRonline.org (4 February 2011); available at http://www.thefreelibrary.com/ Whatever+happened+to+women+deacons%3F-a0249390440 (accessed 16 August 2012).

47 Zagano, *Women & Catholicism*, p. 129.

48 Zagano, "Whatever happened to women deacons?"

49 Zagano, "Women Deacons: Future," pp. 96–9.

50 See Mary Jeremy Daigler, *Incompatible with God's Design: A History of the Women's Ordination Movement in the U.S. Roman Catholic Church* (Lanham, MD: Scarecrow Press, 2012).

51 For current information on these movements, see the websites, www. womensordination.org, www.womensordinationworldwide.org, www. arcwp.org, and www.romancatholicwomenpriests.org. The last site provides the fullest description of RCWP, including under "History," a list of ordinations from 2002 to 2012. Below the list are links to important documents about the movement: "Original Draft Constitution," states the principles and plans of the European founding group; and "Current Constitution RCWP-USA" provides a document approved in 2012 describing the group's vision, mission, principles, structures, and code of ethics. The Association of Roman Catholic Women Priests (ARCWP) (www.arcwp.org) uses a somewhat different governance structure, but maintains a close relationship with RCWP-USA, and their ordinations are listed together by year (accessed 21 August 2012). See also Ida Raming and Iris Müller. *"Contra Legem" – a Matter of Conscience: Our Lifelong Struggle for Human Rights in the Roman-Catholic Church* (Münster: Lit Verlag, 2011), for autobiographies and documentation, including correspondence with Professors Karl Rahner and Joseph Ratzinger.

52 In "Ordained Ministry as Envisioned by RCWP and by the Dutch Dominicans," Dr Patricia Fresen declares: "[w]hen we report that we have been ordained by bishops in communion with Rome, in full apostolic succession, we are taken very seriously, as is evidenced by the decrees of excommunication that have been issued against some of us . . ." The text of this 8 June 2008 paper is found at http://www. rk-kerkplein.org/home/themas/r-k_kerk/ambten/roman-catholic-women-priests-en-de-nederlandse-dominicanen-in-hun-visie-op-het-gewijde-ambt/?language=en, accessed 15 July 2010. The ARCWP website claims, "Our women priests are ordained in Apostolic Succession. The first women bishops were ordained by a male Roman Catholic bishop in apostolic succession and in communion with the pope." http://www. arcwp.org/about.html, accessed 21 August 2012.

53 Earlier decrees of excommunication were followed by an announcement from the Vatican on 15 July 2010 declaring that "the attempted ordination of a woman" is among the grave crimes against the sacraments, and thus subject to expedited penalties from the Congregation for the Doctrine of the Faith. John Allen reported this in "Vatican revises church law on sex abuse," 15 July 2010, http://ncronline.org/news/vatican/vatican-revises-church-law-sex-abuse, accessed 23 August, 2012; the site provides links to official documents. Also of interest are essays by Marian Ronan, "Ethical Challenges Confronting the Roman Catholic Women's Ordination Movement in the Twenty-first Century," *Journal of Feminist Studies in Religion* 23, 2 (2007): 149–69, which objects to the ordination of white European and American women in light of the emerging "Global South," as well as to some of the rhetoric and "individualism" she sees in the movement; and Hellena Moon, "Womenpriests: Radical Change or More of the Same?" *Journal of Feminist Studies in Religion* 24, 2 (2008): 115–34, which questions whether the RCWP model will lead to structural change within Catholicism, and objects to the "essentialism" regarding ideas of women held by some in the movement. Also, Phyllis Zagano offers a detailed description and assessment of the movement in *Women & Catholicism,* pp. 98–104, and discusses parallels with other cases of bishops acting to ordain candidates without Vatican authorization, particularly Marcel-François Lefebvre (France), Emmanuel Milingo (Zambia), and Felix Maria Davídek (Czechoslovakia). The last had ordained women priests and deacons for the Czech underground church, *Koinótés,* including Ludmila Javorová, whose story is recounted in Miriam Therese Winter, *Out of the Depths: The Story of Ludmila Javorova, Ordained Roman Catholic Priest* (New York: Crossroad, 2001). Zagano concludes that "the actions of the Roman Catholic Womenpriests movement have left its membership in a canonical and theological quagmire" (103), and declares that "[i]ndependent of Church penalties and restrictions, ordained members of the movement and those who profess to belong to it are considered as having left the Catholic Church" (104). Nevertheless she observes, "The question, if not of legitimacy at least of validity, remains regarding those originally ordained in the Roman Catholic Womenpriests movement, particularly regarding who may have been ordained by a recognized Roman Catholic bishop" (131).

54 "Roman Catholic Women Priests' Worship Communities: A Renewed Tradition in the United States and Canada: 10th Anniversary 29 June 2002-29 June 2012," www.arcwp.org/docs/nacommunity.pdf, accessed 21 August 2012.

55 "Original Draft Constitution," http://www.romancatholicwomenpriests. org/NEWhistory.htm, accessed 24 August 2012.

56 "Current Constitution RCWP-USA," http://www.romancatholicwomen priests.org/NEWhistory.htm, accessed 24 August 2012.

57 I discuss this movement further in Anne E. Patrick, *Women, Conscience, and the Creative Process* (New York: Paulist, 2011), pp. 21–4.

58 See note (1) above.

59 See note (2) above.

60 United States Conference of Catholic Bishops [USCCB], *Co-Workers in the Vineyard of the Lord: A Resource for Guiding the Development of Lay Ecclesial Ministry* (Washington, DC: USCCB, 2005), p. 10.

61 Edward P. Hahnenberg, "Serving in the Name of the Church: The Call to Lay Ecclesial Ministry," in *In the Name of the Church: Vocation and Authorization of Lay Ecclesial Ministry,* ed. William J. Cahoy (Collegeville, MN: Liturgical Press, 2012), p. 47.

62 Drawing on the work of leadership scholar Ron Heifetz and theologian Susan K. Wood, theologian William J. Cahoy characterizes the emergence of lay ecclesial ministry as an "adaptive response" to the Second Vatican Council's "empowering call of the baptized to full participation in the work of the church" and to the challenge of the "dramatic decline in the number of priests." See Cahoy, "Introduction: Collegeville Ministry Seminar II," in ibid., p. x. See also Bishop Matthew H. Clark, *Forward in Hope: Saying Amen to Lay Ecclesial Ministry* (Notre Dame, IN: Ave Maria Press, 2009); Zeni Fox, ed., *Lay Ecclesial Ministry: Pathways Toward the Future* (Lanham, MD: Rowman & Littlefield, 2010); and Paul J. Philibert, *The Priesthood of the Faithful: Key to a Living Church* (Collegeville, MN: Liturgical Press, 2005).

63 Susan K. Wood, "A Theology of Authorization of Lay Ecclesial Ministers," in Cahoy, op. cit., pp. 111–13.

64 USCCB, *Co-Workers*, p. 13. Statistics are from David DeLambo, *Lay Parish Ministry: A Study of Emerging Leadership* (New York: National Pastoral Life Center [NPLC], 2005), p. 45.

65 Tom Roberts, *The Emerging Catholic Church: A Community's Search for Itself* (Maryknoll, NY: Orbis Books, 2011), p. 29.

66 Lynda Robitaille, "A Canonical Wish List for the Authorization of Lay Ecclesial Ministers," in Cahoy, op. cit., p. 119.

67 See Heidi Schlumpf, "Femme fidèle: How women who work for the church keep the faith," *U.S. Catholic* (January 2011), pp. 12–17. In this issue the editors also interview Zeni Fox ("Follow the Laity," pp. 18–22), who voices her hope for a "national office for lay ministry and an office in every diocese" in the U.S. church, p. 22.

68 Although lay preaching is permitted by Canon 766 of the 1983 Code of Canon Law, Patricia A. Parachini observes the following in "Preaching in Many Voices," *Ministry and Liturgy* (August 2008), p. 4: "Despite the strong mandate during the past 40 years for laity to participate in the preaching of the Gospel, preaching by laypersons is sporadic and too often dependent on the leanings of a particular pastor or bishop for its implementation (or not)."

69 William V. D'Antonio, James D. Davidson, Dean R. Hoge, and Mary L. Gautier, *American Catholics Today: New Realities of Their Faith and Their Church* (Lanham, MD: Rowman & Littlefield, 2007), pp. 77, 26.

70 John L. Allen, Jr., *The Future Church: How Ten Trends Are Revolutionizing the Catholic Church* (New York: Doubleday, 2009), pp. 197–8. He takes an international perspective, and believes that "women will continue to move into other ministerial roles in the Church, often at rates that surpass those of comparable institutions in the secular world," with the result that "[a]side from the priesthood and episcopacy, ministry in the Catholic Church will progressively become 'women's work'", p. 198.

71 David Gibson, *The Coming Catholic Church: How the Faithful Are Shaping a New American Catholicism* (New York: HarperSanFrancisco, 2004), p. 71.

72 Quoted here from Laurence Perrine, *Sound and Sense: An Introduction to Poetry*, third edition (New York: Harcourt, Brace, & World, 1969), p. 187.

73 M. Shawn Copeland, "Introduction," in a volume she co-edited with LaReine-Marie Mosely and Albert J. Raboteau, *Uncommon Faithfulness: The Black Catholic Experience* (Maryknoll, NY: Orbis Books, 2009), p. 1. See also Bryan N. Massingale, *Racial Justice and the Catholic Church* (Maryknoll, NY: Orbis Books, 2010).

74 John T. Noonan, Jr., *A Church That Can and Cannot Change: The Development of Catholic Moral Teaching* (Notre Dame, IN: University of Notre Dame Press, 2005), p. 120.

75 M. Shawn Copeland, *The Subversive Power of Love: The Vision of Henriette Delille* (New York: Paulist, 2009), pp. 61, 52.

76 Tom Gallagher, "Against all odds: from slavery to priesthood to sainthood," *National Catholic Reporter* (3 December 2010), http://ncronline.org/print/21561 (accessed 28 February 2011).

77 I discuss this more fully in Anne E. Patrick, *Women, Conscience, and the Creative Process* (New York: Paulist, 2011), pp. 13–31.

78 See Mary Catherine Hilkert, *Speaking with Authority: Catherine of Siena and the Voices of Women Today* (New York: Paulist, 2001). This saint has inspired the founding in 2004 of Saint Catherine of Siena Virtual College "by a group of academics who were concerned about the plight of women in the world," http://www.catherineofsiena.net/about/history.asp (accessed 1 September 2011).

79 Constance FitzGerald, "From Impasse to Prophetic Hope: Crisis of Memory," *Proceedings of the Catholic Theological Society of America* 64 (2009): 28.

80 According to Bishop Thomas J. Gumbleton, who quotes these words in his homily for 28 March 2004, Untener had drafted them for John Cardinal Dearden to use at a Mass for deceased clergy in 1979. I thank Sara Moore Kerai, a chaplain at Georgetown University Hospital, for calling these words to my attention. They are cited here from, "The Peace Pulpit: Homilies by Bishop Thomas J. Gumbleton," *National Catholic Reporter* http://www.nationalcatholicreporter.org/peace/pfg032804.htm (accessed 29 March 2011).

SELECTED BIBLIOGRAPHY

Allen, John L., Jr. *The Future Church: How Ten Trends Are Revolutionizing the Catholic Church.* New York: Doubleday, 2009.

Bartunek, Jean M., Mary Ann Hinsdale, and James F. Keenan, eds. *Church Ethics and Its Organizational Context: Learning from the Sex Abuse Scandal in the Catholic Church.* Lanham, MD: Rowman & Littlefield, 2006.

Bourgeois, Roy. *My Journey from Silence to Solidarity.* Ed. Margaret Knapke. Yellow Springs, OH: fxBear, 2012.

Butler, Sara. *The Catholic Priesthood and Women: A Guide to the Teaching of the Church.* Chicago: Hillenbrand Books, 2006.

Cahoy, William J., ed. *In the Name of the Church: Vocation and Authorization of Lay Ecclesial Ministry.* Collegeville, MN: Liturgical Press, 2012.

Carey, Ann. *Sisters in Crisis: The Tragic Unraveling of Women's Religious Communities.* Huntington, IN: Our Sunday Visitor Publishing Division, 1997.

Carr, Anne E. *Transforming Grace: Christian Tradition and Women's Experience.* San Francisco: Harper & Row, 1988.

Caspary, Anita M. *Witness to Integrity: The Crisis of the Immaculate Heart Community of California.* Collegeville, MN: Liturgical Press, 2003.

Catholic Theological Society of America Task Force. "Tradition and the Ordination of Women." *CTSA Proceedings* 52 (1997): 197–204.

Clark, Matthew H. *Forward in Hope: Saying Amen to Lay Ecclesial Ministry.* Notre Dame, IN: Ave Maria Press, 2009.

Copeland, M. Shawn. *The Subversive Power of Love: The Vision of Henriette Delille.* New York: Paulist Press, 2009.

—, ed., with LaReine-Marie Mosely, and Albert J. Raboteau. *Uncommon Faithfulness: The Black Catholic Experience.* Maryknoll, NY: Orbis Books, 2009.

Cummings, Kathleen S. *New Women of the Old Faith: Gender and American Catholicism in the Progressive Era.* Chapel Hill: University of North Carolina Press, 2009.

Daigler, Mary Jeremy. *Incompatible with God's Design: A History of the Women's Ordination Movement in the U.S. Roman Catholic Church.* Lanham, MD: Scarecrow Press, 2012.

Daly, Mary. *The Church and the Second Sex.* Rev. ed. Boston: Beacon Press, 1975.

D'Antonio, William V., James D. Davidson, Dean R. Hoge, and Mary L. Gautier. *American Catholics Today: New Realities of Their Faith and Their Church.* Lanham, MD: Rowman & Littlefield, 2007.

Douglas, Mary. "A Modest Proposal: A place for women in the hierarchy." *Commonweal* (14 June 1996): 12–15.

—. "Sacraments, Society, and Women." In *Explorations in Anthropology and Theology,* ed. Frank A. Salamone and Walter Randolph Adams. Lanham, MD: University Press of America, pp. 231–44, 1997.

Ebest, Sally B., and Ron Ebest, eds. *Reconciling Catholicism and Feminism? Personal Reflections on Tradition and Change.* Notre Dame, IN: University of Notre Dame Press, 2003.

Farley, Margaret A. "The Church in the Public Forum: Scandal or Prophetic Witness?" *CTSA Proceedings* 55 (2000): 87–101.

—. *Compassionate Respect: A Feminist Approach to Medical Ethics and Other Questions.* New York: Paulist Press, 2002.

—. *Just Love: A Framework for Christian Sexual Ethics.* New York: Continuum, 2006.

—. "New Patterns of Relationship: Beginnings of a Moral Revolution." *Theological Studies* 36 (1975): 627–46.

—. *Personal Commitments: Beginning, Keeping, Changing.* San Francisco: Harper & Row, 1986.

—. "Power and Powerlessness: A Case in Point." *CTSA Proceedings* 37 (1982): 116–19.

Ferraro, Barbara, and Patricia Hussey, with Jane O'Reilly. *No Turning Back: Two Nuns Battle with the Vatican over Women's Right to Choose.* New York: Poseidon Press, 1990.

FitzGerald, Constance. "From Impasse to Prophetic Hope: Crisis of Memory." *CTSA Proceedings* 64 (2009): 21–42.

Foley, Nadine, OP, ed. *Journey in Faith and Fidelity: Women Religious Shaping Life for a Renewed Church.* New York: Continuum, 1999.

Fox, Zeni, ed. *Lay Ecclesial Ministry: Pathways Toward the Future.* Lanham, MD: Rowman & Littlefield, 2010.

Gaillardetz, Richard R., ed. *When the Magisterium Intervenes: The Magisterium and Theologians in Today's Church.* Collegeville: Liturgical Press, 2012.

Gardiner, Anne M., SSND, ed. *Women and Catholic Priesthood: An Expanded Vision: Proceedings of the Detroit Ordination Conference.* New York: Paulist, 1976.

Gibson, David. *The Coming Catholic Church: How the Faithful Are Shaping a New American Catholicism.* New York: HarperCollins, 2004.

Greeley, Andrew M., and Mary G. Durkin. *Angry Catholic Women*. Chicago: Thomas More Press, 1984.

Hahnenberg, Edward P. *Awakening Vocation: A Theology of Christian Call*. Collegeville, MN: Liturgical Press, 2010.

Halter, Deborah. *The Papal "No": A Comprehensive Guide to the Vatican's Rejection of Women's Ordination*. New York: Crossroad, 2004.

Helman, Ivy A. *Women and the Vatican: An Exploration of Official Documents*. Maryknoll, NY: Orbis Books, 2012.

Henold, Mary. *Catholic and Feminist: The Surprising History of the American Catholic Feminist Movement*. Chapel Hill, NC: University of North Carolina Press, 2008.

Hilkert, Mary C. *Speaking with Authority: Catherine of Siena and the Voices of Women Today*. New York: Paulist Press, 2001.

Hunt, Mary E., and Diann L. Neu, eds. *Women-Church Sourcebook*. Silver Spring, MD: WATERworks Press, 1993.

Johnson, Elizabeth A., ed. *The Church Women Want: Catholic Women in Dialogue*. New York: Crossroad, 2002.

Kennedy, Ethne, SH, ed. *Gospel Dimensions of Ministry*. Chicago: NAWR, 1973.

—, ed. *Women in Ministry: A Sisters' View*. Chicago: NAWR Publications, 1972.

Kineke, Genevieve. *The Authentic Catholic Woman*. Cincinnati: St. Anthony Messenger Press, 2006.

Kolbenschlag, Madonna, ed. *Authority, Community, and Conflict*. Kansas City, MO: Sheed & Ward, 1986.

Lewis, Helen M., and Monica Appleby. *Mountain Sisters: From Convent to Community*. Lexington, KY: The University Press of Kentucky, 2003.

Macy, Gary. "Diversity as Tradition: Why the Future of Christianity is Looking More Like Its Past." Santa Clara Lecture, Santa Clara University, vol. 14 (8 November 2007).

—. *The Hidden History of Women's Ordination: Female Clergy in the Medieval West*. New York: Oxford University Press, 2007.

Macy, Gary, William T. Ditewig, and Phyllis Zagano. *Women Deacons: Past, Present, Future*. New York: Paulist Press, 2011.

Madigan, Kevin, and Carolyn Osiek. *Ordained Women in the Early Church: A Documentary History*. Baltimore: Johns Hopkins University Press, 2005.

McGrath, Elsie Hainz, Bridget M. Meehan, and Ida Raming, eds. *Women Find a Way: The Movement and Stories of Roman Catholic Womenpriests*. College Station, TX: Virtual Bookworm.com Publishing, Inc., 2008.

Milhaven, Annie L., ed. *The Inside Stories: 13 Valiant Women Challenging the Church*. Mystic, CT: Twenty-Third Publications, 1987.

Minney, Gretchen Kloten. *Called: Women Hear the Voice of the Divine*. Broomfield, CO: Wonder Why Publications, 2010.

Niebuhr, H. Richard. *Christ and Culture*. New York: Harper & Row, 1951.

Noonan, John T., Jr. *A Church That Can and Cannot Change: The Development of Catholic Moral Teaching.* Notre Dame, IN: University of Notre Dame Press, 2005.

Oakley, Francis, and Bruce Russett, eds. *Governance, Accountability, and the Future of the Catholic Church.* New York: Continuum, 2004.

Patrick, Anne E. "Conservative Case for the Ordination of Women." *New Catholic World* (May–June, 1975): 108–11.

—. *Liberating Conscience: Feminist Explorations in Catholic Moral Theology.* New York: Continuum, 1996.

—. "'Toward Renewing the Life and Culture of Fallen Man': 'Gaudium et Spes' as Catalyst for Catholic Feminist Theology." In *Questions of Special Urgency,* ed. Judith A. Dwyer. Washington, DC: Georgetown University Press, pp. 55–78, 1986.

—. *Women, Conscience, and the Creative Process: 2009 Madeleva Lecture in Spirituality.* New York: Paulist Press, 2011.

Philibert, Paul J. *The Priesthood of the Faithful: Key to a Living Church.* Collegeville, MN: Liturgical Press, 2005.

Quinn, John R. *The Reform of the Papacy: The Costly Call to Christian Unity.* New York: Crossroad Publishing Company, 1999.

Quiñonez, Laura A., and Mary D. Turner. *The Transformation of American Catholic Sisters.* Philadelphia: Temple University Press, 1992.

Raming, Ida, and Iris Müller. *"Contra Legem" – a Matter of Conscience: Our Lifelong Struggle for Human Rights in the Roman-Catholic Church.* Münster: Lit Verlag, 2011.

Roberts, Tom. *The Emerging Catholic Church: A Community's Search for Itself.* Maryknoll, NY: Orbis Books, 2011.

Robinson, Geoffrey. *Confronting Power and Sex in the Catholic Church: Reclaiming the Spirit of Jesus.* Collegeville, MN: Liturgical Press, 2008.

Rogers, Carole G. *Habits of Change: An Oral History of American Nuns.* Rev. ed. New York: Oxford University Press, 2011.

Ross, Susan A. "Can God Be a Bride? Some Problems with an Ancient Metaphor." *America* (November 1, 2004): 14–15.

—. *Extravagant Affections: A Feminist Sacramental Theology.* New York: Continuum: 1998.

Ruether, Rosemary R. *Women-Church: Theology and Practice of Feminist Liturgical Communities.* San Francisco: Harper & Row, 1986.

Schneiders, Sandra M. *Beyond Patching: Faith and Feminism in the Catholic Church.* Rev. ed. New York: Paulist Press, 2004.

—. *Buying the Field: Religious Life in Mission to the World,* vol. 3 of *Religious Life in a New Millennium.* New York: Paulist Press, 2013.

—. *Finding the Treasure: Locating Catholic Religious Life in a New Ecclesial and Cultural Context,* vol. 1 of *Religious Life in a New Millennium.* New York: Paulist Press, 2000.

—. *Prophets in Their Own Country: Women Religious Bearing Witness to the Gospel in a Troubled Church.* Maryknoll, NY: Orbis Books, 2011.

—. *Selling All: Commitment, Consecrated Celibacy, and Community in Catholic Religious Life,* vol. 2 of *Religious Life in a New Millennium.* New York: Paulist Press, 2001.

Schumacher, Michele M., ed. *Women in Christ: Toward a New Feminism.* Grand Rapids, MI: Eerdmans, 2004.

Schuurman, Douglas J. *Vocation: Discerning Our Callings in Life.* Grand Rapids, MI: William B. Eerdmans, 2004.

Steinfels, Peter. *A People Adrift: The Crisis of the Roman Catholic Church in America.* New York: Simon & Schuster, 2003.

Taylor, Sarah M. *Green Sisters: A Spiritual Ecology.* Cambridge: Harvard University Press, 2007.

United States Conference of Catholic Bishops. *Co-Workers in the Vineyard of the Lord: A Resource for Guiding the Development of Lay Ecclesial Ministry.* Washington, DC: USCCB, 2005.

Wallace, Ruth A. *They Call Her Pastor: A New Role for Catholic Women.* Albany: State University of New York Press, 1992.

Ware, Ann P., SL., ed. *Midwives of the Future: American Sisters Tell Their Story.* Kansas City, MO: Leaven Press, 1985.

Weaver, Mary J. *New Catholic Women: A Contemporary Challenge to Traditional Religious Authority.* Rev. ed. Bloomington: Indiana University Press, 1995.

—, ed. *What's Left: Liberal American Catholics.* Bloomington: Indiana University Press, 1999.

Winter, Miriam T. *Out of the Depths: The Story of Ludmila Javorova, Ordained Roman Catholic Priest.* New York: Crossroad, 2001.

Winter, Miriam T., Adair Lummis, and Allison Stokes. *Defecting in Place: Women Claiming Responsibility for Their Oown Spiritual Lives.* New York: Crossroad, 1994.

Wittberg, Patricia, SC. "A Lost Generation?" *America* (February 20, 1012): 13–16.

—. *The Rise and Fall of Catholic Religious Orders: A Social Movement Perspective.* Albany: State University of New York Press, 1994.

Zagano, Phyllis. *Holy Saturday: An Argument for the Restoration of the Female Diaconate in the Catholic Church.* New York: Crossroad, 2000.

—. "The Question of Governance and Ministry for Women." *Theological Studies* 68 (June 2007): 348–67.

—. "Remembering Tradition: Women's Monastic Rituals and the Diaconate." *Theological Studies* 72 (December 2011): 787–811.

—. *Women & Catholicism: Gender, Communion, Authority.* New York: Palgrave Macmillan, 2011.

INDEX